Webster's
Vocabulary
Builder

Webster's Vocabulary Builder

Created in Cooperation with the Editors of
MERRIAM-WEBSTER

FEDERAL
STREET
PRESS

A Division of Merriam-Webster, Incorporated
Springfield, Massachusetts

This 2006 edition published by
Federal Street Press
A Division of Merriam-Webster, Incorporated
P.O. Box 281
Springfield, MA 01102

Federal Street Press books are available for bulk purchase
for sales promotion and premium use.
For details write the manager of special sales,
Federal Street Press, P.O. Box 281, Springfield, MA 01102

ISBN 13   978-1-59695-009-2
ISBN 10   1-59695-009-9

Printed in the United States of America

06   07   08   09   10   5   4   3   2   1

Introduction

This book is designed to achieve two goals: to add a large number of words to your permanent working vocabulary, and to teach the most useful of the classical word-building roots to help you continue expanding your vocabulary in the future.

In order to achieve these goals, this volume employs an original approach that takes into account how people learn and remember. Many vocabulary builders simply present their words in alphabetical order, many provide little or no discussion of the words and how to use them, and a few even fail to show the kinds of sentences in which the words usually appear. But memorizing a series of random and unrelated things, especially for more than a few hours, can be difficult and time-consuming. The fact is that we tend to remember words easily and naturally when they appear in some meaningful text, when they have been shown to be useful and therefore worth remembering, and when they have been properly explained to us. Knowing precisely how to use a word is just as important as knowing what it means, and this book provides that needed additional information.

Greek and Latin have been the sources of most of the words in the English language. (The third principal source is the family of Germanic languages.) Almost all of these words were added to the language long after the fall of the Roman Empire, and they continue to be added to this day. New words are constantly being invented, and most of them, especially those in the sciences, are still making use of Greek and Latin roots. Many words contain more than one root, as you'll see in the following pages, and some mix Greek and Latin (and even Germanic) roots.

The roots in this book are only a fraction of those that exist, but they include the roots that have produced the largest number of common English words. These roots (sometimes called *stems*) all formed part of Greek and Latin words. Some are shown in more than one form (for example, FLECT/FLEX), which means that they changed form in the original language, just as *buy* and *bought* are forms of the same English word. A knowledge of Greek and Latin roots will help you remember the meanings of the words in this book, but it will also enable you to guess at the meanings of new words that you run into elsewhere. Remember what a root means and you will have at least a fighting chance of understanding a word in which it appears.

Each of the roots in this book is followed by four words based on the root. Each group of eight words (two roots) is followed by two quizzes. Every fifth group is a special eight-word section that may contain words based on classical mythology or history, words borrowed directly from Greek or Latin, or other special categories of terms. Each set of 40 words makes up a unit. In addition, the brief paragraphs discussing each word include in *italics* many words closely related to the main words, in order to at least suggest how those related words may be used as well. Mastering a single word—for example, *phenomenon*—can thus increase your vocabulary by several words—for example, *phenomenal, phenomenally,* and the plural form *phenomena.*

The words presented here are not all on the same level of difficulty—some are quite simple and some are truly challenging—but the great majority are words that could be encountered on the Scholastic Aptitude Test (SAT) and similar standardized tests. Most of them are in the vocabularies of well-educated Americans, including professionals such as scientists, lawyers, professors, doctors, and editors. Even those words you feel familiar with may only have a place in your *recognition* vocabulary—that is, the words that you recognize when you see or hear them but that you are not sure enough about to use in your own speech and writing.

Each main word is followed by its most common pronunciation. A few of the pronunciation symbols may be unfamiliar to you, but they can be learned very easily by referring to the pronunciation key on page ix.

The definition comes next. We have tried to provide only the most common senses or meanings of the word, in simple and straightforward language, and no more than two definitions of any word are given. A more complete range of definitions can be found in a college dictionary such as *Webster's New Explorer College Dictionary.*

An example sentence marked with a bullet (•) follows the definition. This sentence by itself can indicate a great deal about the word, including the kind of sentence in which it often appears. It can also serve as a memory aid, since when you meet the word in the future, you may recall the example sentence more easily than the definition.

An explanatory paragraph rounds out your introduction to each word. The paragraph may do a number of things. It may tell you what else you need to know in order to use the word intelligently and correctly, since the example sentence can't do this all by itself. It may tell you more about the word's roots and its history. It may discuss additional meanings. It will often give you additional example sentences that demonstrate various ways to use the word and to expect to see it used. It may demonstrate the use of closely related words. The paragraph may even offer an informative or entertaining glimpse into a subject not strictly related to the word. The intention is to make you as comfortable as possible with each word in turn and to enable you to start using it immediately, without fear of embarrassment.

The quizzes immediately following each eight-word group, along with the review quizzes at the end of each unit, will test your memory. Many of these quizzes are similar to those used on standardized tests such as the SAT. Some of them ask you to identify *synonyms,* words with the same or very similar meaning, or *antonyms,* words with the opposite meaning. Perhaps more difficult are the *analogies,* which ask that you choose the word that will make the relationship between the last two words the same as the relationship between the first two. Thus, you may be asked to complete the analogy "calculate : count :: expend :——" (which can be read as "*Calculate* is to *count* as *expend* is to——") by choosing one of four words: *stretch, speculate, pay,* and *explode.* Since *calculate* and *count* are nearly synonyms, you will choose a near synonym for *expend,* so the correct answer is *pay.*

Studies have shown that the only way a new word will remain alive in your vocabulary is if it is regularly reinforced through use and through reading. Learn the word here and look and listen for it elsewhere—you'll probably find yourself running into it frequently, just as when you have bought a new car you soon realize how many other people own the same model.

Start using the words immediately. As soon as you feel confident with a word, start trying to work it into your writing wherever appropriate—your papers and reports, your diary and your poetry. An old saying goes, "Use it three times and it's yours." That may be, but don't stop there. Make the words part of your *working* vocabulary, the words that you can not only recognize when you see or hear them, but that you can comfortably call on whenever you need them. Astonish your friends, amaze your relatives, astound *yourself*, and have fun.

Acknowledgments: This book has benefited from the contributions of numerous members of the Merriam-Webster staff. Michael G. Belanger, John M. Morse, Brett P. Palmer, Stephen J. Perrault, and Mark A. Stevens edited the manuscript. Brian M. Sietsema and Eileen M. Haraty entered the pronunciations. James G. Lowe prepared the answer key. Florence A. Fowler undertook the immense task of preparing the manuscript for typesetting. The text was proofread by Susan L. Brady, Rebecca R. Bryer, Paul F. Cappellano, Jennifer N. Cislo, Jill J. Cooney, Jennifer S. Goss, Donna L. Rickerby, Michael D. Roundy, Katherine C. Sietsema, Amy West, and Karen L. Wilkinson, under the direction of Maria A. Sansalone and Madeline L. Novak.

Pronunciation Symbols

ə . . . . abut, collect, suppose

'ə, ˌə . humdrum

ər . . . . operation, further

a . . . . map, patch

ā . . . . day, fate

ä . . . . bother, cot, father

à . . . . a sound between \a\ and \ä\, as in an Eastern New England pronunciation of aunt, ask

aú . . . now, out

b . . . . baby, rib

ch . . . chin, catch

d . . . . did, adder

e . . . . set, red

ē . . . . beat, easy

f . . . . . fifty, cuff

g . . . . go, big

h . . . . hat, ahead

hw . . . whale

i . . . . . tip, banish

ī . . . . . site, buy

j . . . . . job, edge

k . . . . kin, cook

l . . . . lily, cool

m . . . . murmur, dim

n . . . . nine, own

ⁿ . . . . indicates that a preceding vowel is pronounced through both nose and mouth, as in French bon \bōⁿ\

ŋ . . . . sing, singer, finger, ink

ō . . . . bone, hollow

ȯ . . . . saw

ȯi . . . . toy

p . . . . pepper, lip

r . . . . . rarity

s . . . . source, less

sh . . . shy, mission

t . . . . tie, attack

th . . . thin, ether

th . . . then, either

ü . . . . boot, few \'fyü\

 u̇ . . . . put, pure \'pyu̇r\

v . . . . vivid, give

w . . . . we, away

y . . . . yard, cue \'kyü\

z . . . . zone, raise

zh . . . vision, pleasure

\ . . . . . slant line used in pairs to mark the beginning and end of a transcription: \'pen\

' . . . . . mark at the beginning of a syllable that has primary (strongest) stress: \'shəf-əl-ˌbōrd\

ˌ . . . . . mark at the beginning of a syllable that has second-ary (next-strongest) stress: \'shəf-əl-ˌbōrd\

- . . . . . mark of a syllable division in pronunciations

Unit 1

BELL comes from the Latin word meaning "war." *Bellona* was the little-known Roman goddess of war; her husband, Mars, was the god of war.

antebellum \ˌan-ti-'be-ləm\ Existing before a war, especially before the American Civil War (1861–65).

• When World War I was over, the French nobility found it impossible to return to their extravagant antebellum way of life.

Often the word *antebellum* summons up images of ease, elegance, and entertainment on a grand scale that disappeared in the postwar years. That way of life in the American South depended on a social structure that collapsed after the war. The years after the Civil War—and many other wars—were colored for some people by nostalgia and bitterness (Margaret Mitchell's *Gone with the Wind* shows this through the eyes of the Southern gentry), and for others by relief and anticipation.

bellicose \'be-li-ˌkōs\ Warlike, aggressive, quarrelsome.

• The country often elected the more bellicose party after a period of tension along the border, hoping that military action would result.

The international relations of a nation with a bellicose foreign policy tend to be stormy and difficult, since such a nation looks for opportunities to fight rather than to negotiate. Combative by nature, it is happiest when quarreling or, better yet, actively engaged in battle.

belligerence \bə-'li-jə-rəns\ Aggressiveness, combativeness.

● The belligerence in Turner's voice told them that the warning was a serious threat.

The belligerence of Marlon Brando's performance as the violent Stanley Kowalski in *A Streetcar Named Desire* electrified the country. *Belligerent* speeches by leaders of the Soviet Union and the United States throughout the Cold War kept the world on edge for years. Iraq's shocking belligerence toward Kuwait and its own Kurdish people resulted in hundreds of thousands of deaths.

rebellion \ri-'bel-yən\ Open defiance and opposition, sometimes armed, to a person or thing in authority.

● The substitute teacher attempted to end the student rebellion by insisting on absolute quiet.

These days, some degree of rebellion against parents and other authority figures is viewed as a normal part of growing up, as long as it is not destructive and does not go on too long. Rebellion, armed or otherwise, has often served to alert those in power to the discontent of those they control. The American War of Independence was first viewed by the British as a minor rebellion that would soon run its course.

PAC/PEAS is related to the Latin words for "agree" and "peace." The *Pacific Ocean*—that is, the "Peaceful Ocean"—was named by Magellan because it seemed so calm after the storms near Cape Horn. (He obviously never witnessed a Pacific hurricane.)

---

pacify \'pa-sə-ˌfī\ (1) To soothe anger or agitation. (2) To subdue by armed action.

● It took the police hours to pacify the angry demonstrators.

Unhappy babies are often given a rubber device for sucking called a *pacifier* to make them stop crying. In the same way, someone stirred up by anger or some other strong emotion can usually be pacified by resolving or removing its causes. In a usage that became popular during the Vietnam War, *pacification* of an area meant using armed force to neutralize the enemy there and to quiet the local people who may have been supporting them.

pacifist \'pa-sə-fist\ A person opposed to war or violence, especially someone who refuses to bear arms or to fight, on moral or religious grounds.

● Always a strong pacifist, in later life he took to promoting actively the cause of peace and nonviolence.

Pacifists have not always met with sympathy or understanding. Refusing to fight ever for any reason, or even just in a particular situation when the reasons for fighting seem clear to many others, calls for strong faith in one's own moral or religious convictions, since it has often resulted in persecution by those who disagree. The Quakers and the Jehovah's Witnesses are *pacifist* religious groups; Henry D. Thoreau and Martin Luther King are probably the most famous American pacifists.

pact \'pakt\ An agreement between two or more people or groups; a treaty or formal agreement between nations to deal with a problem or to resolve a dispute.

● The girls made a pact never to reveal what had happened on that terrifying night in the abandoned house.

Since a pact often ends a period of unfriendly relations, the word has "peace" at its root. *Pact* is generally used in the field of international relations, where we often speak of an "arms pact" or a "fishing-rights pact." But it may also be used for a solemn agreement or promise between two people.

appease \ə-'pēz\ To make peaceful and quiet; to calm, satisfy.

● The Aztecs offered mass human sacrifices—of 80,000 prisoners on one occasion!—in order to appease their gods.

When the European nations agreed to let Adolf Hitler take over part of Czechoslovakia in 1938, in a vain attempt to prevent a larger war, their opponents shouted that they were practicing a foolish *appeasement* that was doomed to fail. (They were right—within months Hitler had violated the *pact*.) A child's anger may be appeased with a little effort; an angry god or goddess may demand something extreme. We may speak of hunger being appeased by food. Appeasing usually involves giving something, whereas *pacifying* can refer to anything from stroking a baby to using armed force to stop an uprising.

Quizzes

A. Match the word on the left to the correct definition on the right:

1.	antebellum	a.	quarrelsome
2.	appease	b.	solemn agreement
3.	rebellion	c.	to make peaceful
4.	pacify	d.	before the war
5.	pacifist	e.	aggressiveness
6.	belligerence	f.	opposition to authority
7.	pact	g.	to calm by satisfying
8.	bellicose	h.	one who opposes war

B. Fill in each blank with the correct letter:

a.	antebellum	e.	rebellion
b.	pacifist	f.	bellicose
c.	pact	g.	pacify
d.	appease	h.	belligerence

1. The native _____ began at midnight, when a gang of youths massacred the Newton family and set the house afire.

2. The grand _____ mansion has hardly been altered since it was built in 1841.

3. The Senate Republicans, outraged by their treatment, were in a _____ mood.

4. To _____ the younger managers, the company will double their bonuses this year.

5. The cease-fire _____ that had been reached with such effort was shattered by the news of the slaughter.

6. Their relations during the divorce proceedings had been mostly friendly, so his _____ in the judge's chambers surprised her.

7. The world watched in amazement as the gentle _____ Gandhi won India its independence with almost no bloodshed.

8. Her soft lullabies could always _____ the unhappy infant.

HOSP/HOST comes from the Latin word *hospes* and its stem *hospit-* meaning both "host" and "guest." Many words based on it came to English through French, which often dropped the *-pi-*, leaving *host-*. *Hospitality* is what a good *host* or *hostess* offers to a guest. A *hospital* was once a house for religious pilgrims and other travelers, or a home for the aged.

hostage \\'häs-tij\\ A person given or held to ensure that an agreement, demand, or treaty is kept or fulfilled.

● The kidnappers released their hostage unharmed once all their demands were met.

Opponents in war sometimes exchange hostages to ensure that a truce or treaty remains unbroken. Hostages may also be taken by kidnappers or terrorists or rebels to use in bargaining for money or concessions. It may seem strange that the word *hostage* is connected with *host* and in fact with *guest* as well, since hostages are now unwilling guests, at the mercy of their *hostile* hosts.

hospice \\'häs-pəs\\ A place or program to help care for the terminally ill.

● Uncle Harold was moved to the hospice only after my aunt had almost collapsed with exhaustion while caring for him.

In the Middle Ages, hospices run by monks and nuns gave shelter and food to travelers and the poor. Now, hospices are institutions that take care of people who are too ill to be at home but whose lives cannot be saved by hospital care—often those with incurable cancer or AIDS, for example. More and more Americans are relying on "home hospice care"—care by visiting nurses and volunteers for terminally ill patients who have decided to live their last months at home.

hostel \\'häs-təl\\ An inexpensive, supervised place for young travelers to stay overnight.

● Generations of American college students have traveled through Europe cheaply by staying at hostels instead of hotels.

Throughout Europe and in some other parts of the world, a network of youth hostels provides cheap, safe (although not always quiet) overnight shelter for younger bicyclists, hikers, and canoeists. The United States has over 200 youth hostels, many of them in New England. Worldwide, there are more than 5,000.

inhospitable \,in-hä-'spi-tə-bəl\ (1) Not welcoming or generous; unfriendly. (2) Providing no shelter or food (such as a desert).

● Shot down by government agents, the smuggler struggled for survival on the rocky, inhospitable island.

An inhospitable host fails to make his guests comfortable, in order to show them they are unwelcome. An inhospitable territory, such as Death Valley or Antarctica, may be barren and harsh in its climate. In a similar way, a country may be called inhospitable to democracy, just as a company may be called inhospitable to new ideas.

AM/IM comes from the Latin word *amare*, "to love." *Amiable* means "friendly or good-natured," and *amigo* is Spanish for "friend."

---

amicable \'a-mi-kə-bəl\ Friendly, peaceful.

● Their relations with their in-laws were generally amicable, despite some bickering during the holidays.

Amicable often describes relations between two groups or especially two nations—for example, the United States and Canada, which are proud of sharing the longest unguarded border in the world. When *amicable* describes personal relations, it tends to indicate a rather formal friendliness.

enamored \i-'na-mərd\ Charmed or fascinated; inflamed with love.

● Rebecca quickly became enamored of the town's rustic surroundings, its slow pace, and its eccentric characters.

Computer hackers are always enamored of their new programs and games. Millions of readers have found themselves enamored with Jane Austen's novels. And Romeo and Juliet were utterly enamored of each other. (Note that both *of* and *with* are commonly used after *enamored.*)

inimical \i-'ni-mi-kəl\ Hostile, unfriendly, or harmful.

• This latest report, like so many earlier ones, found that too great a concern with test scores was inimical to a broad education.

The *in-* with which *inimical* begins negates the meaning of the root. This word rarely describes a person; instead, it is generally used to describe forces, concepts, or situations. For example, high inflation may be called inimical to economic growth; tolerance of racist comments in an office may be seen as inimical to minorities; and rapid population growth may be inimical to a country's standard of living.

paramour \\'par-ə-ˌmur\\ A lover, often secret, not allowed by law or custom.

• He was her paramour for many years before she finally divorced her husband.

Paramour includes the prefix *par -,* "by or through." This implies a relationship based solely on love, often physical love, rather than on a social custom or ceremony. Today it usually refers to the lover of a married man or woman.

Quizzes

A. Choose the odd word:

1. hostel   a. shelter b. hotel c. prison d. dormitory
2. inimical   a. unfriendly b. sympathetic c. antagonistic
      d. harmful
3. hospice   a. nursing b. travel c. hospital d. illness
4. amicable   a. difficult b. friendly c. pleasant
      d. peaceful
5. enamored   a. strengthened b. charmed c. fond
      d. fascinated
6. inhospitable   a. inimical b. barren c. unfriendly
      d. inviting
7. paramour   a. lover b. husband c. mistress
      d. significant other
8. hostage   a. exchange b. guarantee c. pledge d. hotel

B. Complete the analogy:

1. charming : enchanting :: inimical : _____
      a. sublime b. harmful c. direct d. cautious

2. lush : barren :: inhospitable : _____
    a. deserted b. sunny c. rocky d. welcoming
3. house : mortgage :: hostage : _____
    a. treaty b. gunman c. terrorist d. prisoner
4. gentle : tender :: enamored : _____
    a. lively b. charmed c. cozy d. enraged
5. picnic : dinner :: hostel : _____
    a. restaurant b. supper c. bar d. inn
6. frozen : boiling :: amicable : _____
    a. calm b. comfortable c. shy d. unfriendly
7. auditorium : arena :: hospice : _____
    a. spa b. nursing home c. club d. motel
8. friend : companion :: paramour : _____
    a. lover b. theater c. mother d. wife

CRIM comes from the Latin for "fault or crime" or "accusation," and produces such English words as *crime* and *criminal.*

criminology \ˌkri-mə-'nä-lə-jē\ The study of crime, criminals, law enforcement, and punishment.

• His growing interest in criminology led him to become a probation officer.

Criminology includes the study of all aspects of crime and law enforcement—criminal psychology, the social setting of crime, prohibition and prevention, investigation and detection, apprehension and punishment. Thus, many of the people involved—legislators, social workers, probation officers, judges, etc.—could possibly be considered *criminologists,* though the word usually refers to scholars and researchers only.

decriminalize \dē-'kri-mə-nə-ˌlīz\ To remove or reduce the criminal status of.

• An angry debate over decriminalizing doctor-assisted suicide raged all day at the statehouse.

Decriminalization of various "victimless crimes"—crimes that do not directly harm others, such as private gambling and drug-taking—has been recommended by conservatives as well as liberals, who claim that it would ease the burden on the legal system and decrease the amount of money flowing to criminals. Decriminalization is sometimes distinguished from legalization, since it may still call for a small fine like a traffic ticket, or it may apply only to use or possession, leaving the actual sale of goods or services illegal.

incriminate \in-'kri-mə-ˌnāt\ To show evidence of involvement in a crime or a fault.

• The muddy tracks leading to and from the cookie jar were enough to incriminate them.

We often hear of *incriminating* evidence, the kind that strongly links a suspect to a crime. Verbal testimony may incriminate by placing the suspect at the scene of the crime or describe behavior that involves him or her in it. We can also say that a virus has been incriminated as the cause of a type of cancer, and that television has been incriminated in the decline in study skills among young people.

recrimination \rē-ˌkri-mə-'nā-shən\ An accusation in retaliation for an accusation made against oneself; the making of such an accusation.

• Their failure to find help led to endless and pointless recriminations over the responsibility for the accident.

Defending oneself from a verbal attack by means of a counterattack is almost as natural as physical self-defense. So a disaster often brings recriminations among those connected with it, and divorces and battles over child custody usually involve recriminations between husband and wife.

PROB/PROV comes from the Latin words for "prove or proof" and "honesty or integrity." To *prove* a statement is to "make it honest," and *probate* court is where the genuineness of the wills of deceased people must be *proved*.

---

approbation \ˌa-prə-'bā-shən\ A formal or official act of approving; praise, usually given with pleasure or enthusiasm.

● The senate signaled its approbation of the new plan by voting for it unanimously.

Approbation indicates both formal recognition of an accomplishment and happy acceptance of it. An official commendation for bravery is an example of approbation. Getting reelected to office usually indicates public approbation. The social approbation that comes from being a star quarterback in high school makes all the pain worthwhile.

disprove \dis-'prüv\ To show that something is not what it has been claimed to be; refute.

● A week before the election he was still struggling to disprove his opponent's lies about his connections to organized crime.

Disprove, which includes the negative prefix *dis-*, is clearly the opposite of *prove*. One may have to disprove something for which the evidence has already been accepted, so the *disprover* often encounters violent objections to the new evidence that weakens the old. Galileo was forced to deny the new findings with which he and Copernicus had disproved the old conception of the earth's being at the center of the planetary system.

probity \'prō-bə-tē\ Absolute honesty and uprightness.

● Her unquestioned probity helped win her the respect of her fellow judges.

Probity is a quality the American public generally hopes for in its elected officials but doesn't always get. Bankers, for example, have traditionally been careful to project an air of probity; the savings-and-loan scandal of the 1980s has made it even more necessary. An aura of probity surrounds such public figures as Walter Cronkite and Bill Moyers, men to whom many Americans would entrust their children and their finances.

reprobate \'re-prə-,bāt\ A person of thoroughly bad character.

● Finally, on the verge of physical and financial ruin, the reprobate dropped his lowlife friends, joined AA, and begged his wife to come back.

Reprobate (which includes the prefix *re-*, "back or backward") is often said in a tone of joshing affection. The related verb is *reprove* or "scold," since the reprobate deserves a constant scolding. Shakespeare's great character Falstaff—a lazy, lying, boastful, sponging drunkard—is the model of an old reprobate.

Quizzes

A. Indicate whether the following pairs of words have the same or different meanings:

1. decriminalize / tolerate   same __ / different __
2. probity / fraud   same __ / different __
3. criminology / murder   same __ / different __
4. incriminate / acquit   same __ / different __
5. disprove / distinguish   same __ / different __
6. recrimination / approbation   same __ / different __
7. reprobate / scoundrel   same __ / different __
8. approbation / criticism   same __ / different __

B. Match the definition on the left to the correct word on the right:

1. utter honesty   a. approbation
2. approval   b. reprobate
3. rascal   c. recrimination
4. demonstrate as false   d. criminology
5. study of illegal behavior   e. probity
6. accuse   f. disprove
7. reduce penalty for   g. decriminalize
8. counterattack   h. incriminate

GRAV comes from the Latin word meaning "heavy, weighty, serious." Thus, a *grave* matter is serious and important.

gravid \'gra-vəd\ Pregnant or enlarged with something.

• The gravid sow moved heavily from trough to tree, where she settled into the shaded dust and lay unmoving for the rest of the afternoon.

Gravid implies weight and bulk, but actually describes a pregnant female even at an early stage of her pregnancy. It has the related senses of inflation that results from any cause and that will lead to a change of some kind. Thus, a writer may be gravid with ideas as she sits down to write; a speaker may make a gravid pause before announcing his remarkable findings; and a cloud may be gravid with rain.

gravitas \'gra-və-,täs\ Great or very dignified seriousness.

● The head of the committee never failed to carry herself with the gravitas she felt was appropriate to her office.

This word comes to us straight from Latin. Among the Romans, gravitas was thought to be essential to the character and functions of any adult (male) in authority. Even the head of a household or a low-level official would strive for this important quality. We use *gravitas* today to identify the same solemn dignity in men and women.

gravitate \'gra-və-,tāt\ To move or be drawn toward something, especially by natural tendency or as if by an invisible force.

● During hot weather, the town's social life gravitated toward the lake.

To gravitate implies a natural, perhaps irresistible, response to a force that works like *gravity*, drawing things steadily to it as if by their own weight. Thus, moths gravitate to a flame, children gravitate to an ice-cream truck, gawkers gravitate to an accident, and everyone at a party gravitates to the bar.

gravity \'gra-və-tē\ Weighty importance, seriousness, or dignity.

● Laughing and splashing each other, they failed to realize the gravity of their situation until the canoe was within twenty feet of the falls.

Although closely related to *gravitas*, *gravity* can apply to situations and problems as well as to people. Gravity in the physical sense is, of course, what gives us weight and holds us on the earth. But weight can also mean seriousness. Thus, gravity in the nonphysical sense can mean seriousness in a person's manner but also the seriousness or danger in a situation.

LEV comes from the Latin adjective *levis,* meaning "light," and the verb *levare,* meaning "to raise or lighten." *Levitation* is the magician's trick in which a body seems to rise into the air by itself. And a *lever* is a bar used to lift something by means of *leverage*.

alleviate \ə-'lē-vē-,āt\ To lighten, lessen, or relieve, especially physical or mental suffering.

• Cold compresses alleviated the pain of the physical injury, but only time could alleviate the effect of the insult.

Physical pain or emotional anguish, or a water shortage or traffic congestion, can all be alleviated by providing the appropriate remedy. However, some pain or anguish or shortage or congestion will remain: to alleviate is not to cure.

elevate \'e-lə-,vāt\ (1) To lift up or raise. (2) To raise in rank or status.

• Last year's juniors have been elevated to the privileged status of seniors.

An *elevator* lifts things up. You may elevate a sprained ankle to reduce the swelling. When a Boy Scout reaches the rank of Eagle Scout, his rank is as *elevated* as it can get. *Elevated* language is language that, as in many poems and speeches, sounds formal or intellectual or in some way "higher" than common speech.

leavening \'le-və-niŋ\ Something that lightens and raises; something that modifies, eases, or animates.

• The speech was on a dull subject—"Microeconomic Theory in the 1970s"—but its leavening of humor made the time pass quickly.

The word *leavening,* when used in the kitchen, usually refers to yeast or baking powder. (*Unleavened* bread is often hard and dense; when it is used in religious ceremonies, it may be intended as a reminder of past hardship.) Young children may provide the leavening at a family reunion, and a cheerful receptionist may be the leavening in an otherwise dull office.

levity \'le-və-tē\ Frivolity, lack of appropriate seriousness.

● The Puritan elders tried to ban levity of all sorts from the community's meetings.

Levity originally was thought to be a physical force exactly like gravity but pulling in the opposite direction. Even as late as the last century, scientists were arguing about its existence. But today *levity* refers to lightness in manner. This was once regarded as almost sinful, so the word has an old-fashioned ring to it and is usually used in a half-serious tone of disapproval.

Quizzes

A. Fill in each blank with the correct letter:

a.	gravid	e.	alleviate
b.	gravitate	f.	leavening
c.	gravitas	g.	levity
d.	gravity	h.	elevate

1. As the ____ of the situation slowly became apparent, the crowd's mood changed from anxiety to hysteria.
2. With no ____, the muffins came out dense, chewy, and inedible.
3. At their father's funeral they showed the same solemn ____ at which they had often laughed during his lifetime.
4. Uncomfortable with their mean jokes, he tried to ____ the tone of the conversation.
5. Attracted magically by the music, all animals and natural objects would ____ toward the sound of Orpheus's lyre.
6. The lightning hung in the air for a ____ moment before the explosion of thunder.
7. The neighboring nations organized an airlift of supplies to ____ the suffering caused by the drought.
8. The board meeting ended in an unusual mood of ____ when a man in a gorilla suit burst in.

B. Match the word on the left to the correct definition on the right:

1. levity   a. solemn dignity
2. gravitas   b. relieve
3. gravid   c. lift, raise

4.	alleviate	d.	something that lightens
5.	elevate	e.	move toward as if drawn
6.	gravity	f.	lack of seriousness
7.	leavening	g.	pregnant
8.	gravitate	h.	seriousness

Words from Mythology and History

cicerone \‚si-sə-'rō-nē\ A guide, especially one who takes tourists to museums, monuments, or architectural sites and explains what is being seen.

• While in Paris, they placed themselves in the care of a highly recommended cicerone to ensure that they saw and learned what was most noteworthy.

Cicerones (or *ciceroni*) take their name from the Roman statesman and orator Cicero, who was renowned for his long-windedness as well as for his elegant style, though they rarely match his scholarship or eloquence.

hector \'hek-tər\ To bully; to intimidate or harass by bluster or personal pressure.

• He would swagger around the apartment entrance with his friends and hector the terrified inhabitants going in and out.

In the *Iliad,* Hector was the leader of the Trojan forces, and the very model of nobility and honor. In the war against the Greeks he killed several great warriors before being slain by Achilles. His name began to take on its current meaning only after it was adopted by a crowd of bullying young rowdies in late-17th-century London.

hedonism \'hē-də-‚ni-zəm\ An attitude or way of life based on the idea that pleasure or happiness should be the chief goal.

• In her new spirit of hedonism she went for a massage, picked up champagne and chocolate truffles, and made a date with an old boyfriend for that evening.

Derived from the Greek word for "pleasure," hedonism over the ages has provided the basis for several philosophies. The ancient Epicureans and the more modern Utilitarians both taught and pursued *hedonistic* principles. Hedonism is often said to be more typical of those living in southern and tropical climates than of northerners, but it varies greatly from person to person everywhere.

nestor \\'nes-ˌtȯr\ A senior figure or leader in one's field.

● After dinner the guest of honor, a nestor among journalists, shared some of his wisdom with the other guests.

Nestor was another character from the *Iliad,* the eldest of the Greek leaders at Troy. He was noted for his wisdom and his talkativeness, both of which increased as he aged. These days a nestor need not go on at such length; he may share his knowledge or give advice with few words.

spartan \\'spär-tən\ Marked by simplicity and often strict self-discipline or self-denial.

● His spartan life bore no relation to the lush language of his poetry.

In ancient times, the Greek city of Sparta had a reputation for enforcing a highly disciplined, severe way of life among its citizens so as to keep them ready for war at any time. The city required physical training for men and women and maintained a common dining hall and communal child care, but provided few physical comforts. The term *spartan* today may sometimes suggest communal life (for example, in the army) but always signifies strictness and frugality.

stentorian \\sten-'tȯr-ē-ən\ Extremely loud, often with especially deep richness of sound.

● Even without a microphone, his stentorian voice broadcast the message of peace to the farthest reaches of the auditorium.

Stentor, like Hector, was a warrior in the *Iliad,* but on the Greek side. His unusually powerful voice made him the natural choice for delivering announcements and proclamations to the assembled Greek army. One who speaks in a stentorian voice thus can be heard clearly at a considerable distance.

stoic \'stō-ik\ Seemingly indifferent to pleasure or pain.

● She bore the pain of her broken leg with stoic patience.

The *Stoics* were members of a philosophical movement that first appeared in ancient Greece and lasted through the Roman era. They taught that humans should seek to free themselves from joy, grief, and passions of all kinds in order to attain wisdom. They have given their name to a personal attitude that some cultures and individuals still proudly cultivate.

sybaritic \si-bə-'ri-tik\ Marked by a luxurious or sensual way of life.

● Eventually their sybaritic excesses consumed all their savings and forced them to lead a more restrained life.

The ancient city of Sybaris, founded by the Greeks in Italy, was famous for the wealth and hedonistic self-indulgence of its citizens, whose love of extravagance and sensuality made *sybaritic* a term for such leanings in any era.

Quiz

Choose the closest definition:

1. hedonism   a. preference for males b. habit of gift-giving c. tendency to conceal feelings d. love of pleasure
2. hector   a. encourage b. harass c. deceive d. swear
3. cicerone   a. guide b. cartoon character c. orator d. lawyer
4. spartan   a. cheap b. militaristic c. severe d. luxurious
5. nestor   a. journalist b. long-winded elder c. domestic hen d. judge
6. stoic   a. pleasure-seeking b. bullying c. repressed d. unaffected by pain
7. sybaritic   a. pleasure-seeking b. free of luxury c. sisterly d. ice-cold
8. stentorian   a. obnoxious b. muffled c. loud d. dictated

Review Quizzes

A. Fill in each blank with the correct letter:

a. belligerence
b. stentorian
c. appease
d. sybaritic
e. gravid
f. alleviate
g. inimical

h. inhospitable
i. incriminate
j. gravitate
k. hector
l. enamored
m. stoic
n. pacify

1. Councillor Hawkins had a folksy drawl, but his simplest statements were _____ with meaning.
2. The mood at the resort was _____, and the drinking and dancing continued long into the night.
3. To rattle the other team, they usually _____ them constantly.
4. The judge was known for issuing all his rulings in a _____ voice.
5. With its thin soil and long winters, the area is _____ to farming.
6. Thoroughly _____ of the splendid Victorian house, they began to plan their move.
7. She attempted to _____ his anxiety by convincing him he wasn't to blame.
8. Whenever she entered a bar alone, the lonely men would always _____ toward her.
9. Their refusal to cease work on nuclear weapons was seen as an _____ act by the neighboring countries.
10. There was nowhere for miles where he could _____ his intense nicotine craving.
11. Unable to calm the growing crowd, he finally ordered the police to _____ the area by force.
12. Whenever her boyfriend saw anyone looking at her, his _____ was alarming.
13. He bore all his financial losses with the same _____ calm.
14. Who would have guessed that it would take the killer's own daughter to _____ him.

B. Choose the closest definition:

1. hedonism   a. fear of heights b. hatred of crowds
   c. liking for children d. love of pleasure
2. levity   a. lightness b. policy c. leverage d. literacy
3. gravity   a. disturbance b. danger c. engraving
   d. seriousness
4. reprobate   a. researcher b. commissioner
   c. scoundrel d. reformer
5. bellicose   a. fun-loving b. warlike c. impatient d. jolly
6. decriminalize   a. discriminate b. legalize c. legislate
   d. decree
7. antebellum   a. preventive b. unlikely c. impossible
   d. prewar
8. hostage   a. prisoner b. hostess c. criminal d. hotel
9. pact   a. bundle b. form c. agreement d. presentation
10. amicable   a. technical b. sensitive c. friendly d. scenic
11. criminology   a. crime history b. crime book c. crime
    study d. crime story
12. approbation   a. approval b. resolution c. reputation
    d. substitution

**C. Match the definition on the left to the correct word
on the right:**

1. secret lover   a.   elevate
2. show as false   b.   gravitas
3. accusation   c.   disprove
4. integrity   d.   probity
5. shelter   e.   recrimination
6. nursing service   f.   paramour
7. peace lover   g.   hospice
8. raise   h.   hostel
9. dignity   i.   rebellion
10. revolt   j.   pacifist

Unit 2

AG comes from the Latin word for "do, go, lead, drive." An *agenda* is a list of things to be done. An *agent* is usually someone who does things on behalf of another, just as an *agency* is an office that does business for others.

---

agitate \'a-jə-,tāt\ (1) To move something with an irregular, rapid, violent action. (2) To stir up or excite.

● Philip found Louisa highly agitated at the news of her son's disappearance.

Agitate can mean to shake or stir something physically, but more often its meaning is emotional or political. *Agitation* for a cause—a new union, civil rights, a change of government—involves talking it up, passing out information, and holding meetings, though sometimes as secretly as possible. An *agitated* person or animal usually feels severely anxious and upset, not pleasantly excited.

litigate \'li-tə-,gāt\ To carry on a lawsuit by judicial process.

● If the company chooses to litigate, it may give the protesters the chance to make their points even more effectively in the courts and newspapers.

Litigation has become almost a way of life in America, where there are many more lawyers than in any other country on earth. In this increasingly *litigious* society, the courts have been overwhelmed with petty disputes. Television has responded to the trend by producing heroes like Judge Wapner of *People's Court*, a man who can show *litigants* the absurdity of their case while rendering a just verdict. (The Latin *litigare* includes the root *lit*, "lawsuit," and thus means basically "to drive a lawsuit.")

prodigal \'prä-də-gəl\ Recklessly or wastefully extravagant; spendthrift.

● Rodney had been the most prodigal with his expected inheritance and had the most to gain from a redistribution of the estate.

The Latin *prodigere* means "to squander"—that is, to "drive away" money and goods. In the biblical story of the prodigal son, the father welcomes home the spendthrift and now-penniless young man, despite his *prodigality*, just as the Church stands ready to welcome back the repenting sinner. *Prodigal* can apply to more than money. Farmers may make prodigal use of their soil, or may give their animals prodigal amounts of antibiotics. Rich countries are almost always prodigal with their resources. In a bloody and pointless war, lives are lost on a prodigal scale.

synagogue \'si-nə-ˌgȯg\ The center of worship and communal life of a Jewish congregation; temple.

● Though the neighborhood was now dangerous at night, the older members refused to move and abandon the beloved synagogue they had attended since the 1940s.

Synagogue begins with the prefix *syn-*, "together," so the word refers basically to "coming together." Synagogues have existed for more than 2,500 years. The oldest synagogue in America, dating from 1763, was built in Rhode Island, the most religiously tolerant of the original thirteen colonies.

VEN/VENT comes from *venire*, the Latin verb meaning "come." To *intervene* in a case or an argument is to "come between" the two opponents. An *avenue* is a street, or originally an access road by which to "come toward" something. Groups "come together" at a *convention*.

---

advent \'ad-ˌvent\ A coming or arrival; a coming into use.

● The advent of spring was always marked by the blue crocuses pushing up through the snow.

Advent includes the prefix *ad-*, "to or toward," and thus means basically a "coming toward." The Advent season in the Christian religion consists of the weeks leading up to Christmas, when the coming of Christ is anticipated. The advent of mass printing with Gutenberg's printing press in the mid-15th century had an enormous effect on European society and politics; the advent of the computer in the mid-20th century has promised to change ours even more profoundly.

provenance \'präv-nəns\ Origin or source.

● The wedding guests wondered about the provenance of this mysterious woman, about whom Seth had never breathed a word.

Provenance refers to any source or origin in general, but is used particularly to refer to the history of ownership of a piece of art, which may be necessary to prove that a work is authentic. The provenance of Rubens's paintings is varied; some have been in a single family or in a single museum for centuries, while some have been lost without a trace, leaving their provenance a mystery. Tracing the provenance of an idea or invention such as television may be a complicated task.

venturesome \'ven-chər-ˌsəm\ Inclined to seek out risk or danger; bold, daring, adventurous.

● Kate, with her bungee jumping, free-falling, and rock climbing, had always been the most venturesome of the four.

America, perhaps with a touch of arrogance, likes to think of itself as a land of venturesome people who push fearlessly forward in all ages and in all fields, and it clearly took a venturesome spirit to mount the successful flight to the moon that ended in July 1969. In past centuries, however, the most venturesome explorers were to be found in Greece, Italy, Spain, Portugal, and Britain—that is, the rich countries on the sea or ocean.

venue \'ven-ˌyü\ (1) The place where a trial is held. (2) The locale of an event.

● To Dr. Slaughter the important thing was to get a change of venue; hoping to conceal his past, he wanted a judge who knew him neither by sight nor by reputation.

The importance of venue in jury makeup and the subsequent outcome of a trial was vividly shown in the famous Rodney King case.

A suburban jury acquitted the men accused of beating King; after a change of venue, an urban jury convicted two of the men. The venues of championship boxing matches, on the other hand, are chosen with maximum profits in mind.

Quizzes

A. Choose the correct synonym:

1. synagogue   a. courthouse b. arena c. temple d. cinema
2. provenance   a. part of France b. origin c. Italian cheese d. invitation
3. prodigal   a. brilliant b. poor c. missing d. lavish
4. venturesome   a. daring b. western c. forthright d. timid
5. agitate   a. soothe b. vibrate c. consume d. shake up
6. advent   a. propaganda b. arrival c. commerce d. departure
7. litigate   a. select a jury b. judge c. argue in court d. negotiate
8. venue   a. jury b. place c. menu d. decision

B. Complete the analogy:

1. venturesome : timid :: ＿＿＿ : ＿＿＿
   a. stiff : flexible b. antique : artificial c. attractive : shapely d. bellicose : belligerent
2. litigate : argue :: ＿＿＿ : ＿＿＿
   a. border : enclose b. negotiate : discuss c. demonstrate : describe d. scold : praise
3. synagogue : worship :: ＿＿＿ : ＿＿＿
   a. theater : ticket b. church : mosque c. stadium : match d. hymn : song
4. provenance : destination :: ＿＿＿ : ＿＿＿
   a. travel : itinerary b. menu : meal c. recording : transcript d. birthplace : hometown
5. agitate : placate :: ＿＿＿ : ＿＿＿
   a. alternate : switch b. hesitate : rush c. blame : scold d. modify : alter

6. venue : locale :: _____ : _____
    a. arrival : departure b. country : nation c. court :
    jury d. prosecutor : judge
7. advent : departure :: _____ : _____
    a. Christmas : New Year's b. poverty : wealth
    c. rainfall : precipitation d. journey : expedition
8. prodigal : spendthrift :: _____ : _____
    a. stingy : miserly b. cautious : reckless c. artificial :
    natural d. opposite : similar

CAP/CEP/CIP comes from *capere,* the Latin verb meaning "take, seize." *Capture,* which is what a *captor* does to a *captive,* has the same meaning. *Captivate* once meant literally "capture," but now means only to capture mentally through charm or appeal. In some other English words this root produces, its meaning is harder to find.

---

reception \ri-'sep-shən\ (1) The act of receiving. (2) A social gathering where guests are formally welcomed.

● Although the reception of her plan was enthusiastic, it was months before anything was done about it.

Reception is the noun form of *receive.* So at a formal reception guests are received or welcomed or "taken in." If your idea for a great practical joke gets a lukewarm reception, it has not been well-received or *accepted.* Bad TV reception means the signal isn't being received well. And when a new novel receives good reviews we say it has met with a good critical reception.

incipient \in-'si-pē-ənt\ Starting to come into being or to become evident.

● He felt the stirrings of incipient panic as he riffled through the file and realized that the letter had been removed.

An incipient career as an actor in New York tends to involve a lot of waiting on tables while waiting for auditions. Identifying a cancer at its incipient stage may allow its development to be slowed or reversed. An environmental pessimist may speak of the incipient extinction of whales or bald eagles.

perceptible \pər-'sep-tə-bəl\ Noticeable or able to be felt by the senses.

● Her change in attitude toward him was barely perceptible, and he couldn't be sure that he wasn't imagining it.

Perceptible includes the prefix *per-*, meaning "through," so the word refers to whatever can be taken in through the senses. A *perceptive* person picks up hints and shades of meaning that others can't *perceive*. Such people rely on their sharp *perceptions*, their observations of whatever kind. So very often what is perceptible to one person—a tiny sound, a slight change in the weather, a different tone of voice—will not be to another.

susceptible \sə-'sep-tə-bəl\ (1) Open to some influence; responsive. (2) Able to be submitted to an action or process.

● Impressed with her intelligence and self-confidence, he was highly susceptible to her influence.

With its prefix *sus-*, "up," *susceptible* refers to what "takes up" or absorbs like a sponge. When negotiating the settlement of World War II at Yalta with Churchill and Roosevelt, Stalin may have found the other two susceptible to his threats and bullying and thus managed to hold on to much of Eastern Europe. Students are usually susceptible to the teaching of a strong and imaginative professor. In a similar way, a sickly child will be susceptible to colds, and an unlucky adult will be susceptible to back problems.

FIN comes from the Latin word for "end" or "boundary." *Final* describes last things, and a *finale* or a *finish* is an ending. But its meaning is harder to trace in some of the other English words derived from it.

---

affinity \ə-'fi-nə-tē\ (1) Sympathy; attraction. (2) Relationship.

● He knew of Carl's affinity to both wine and violence, and intended to take advantage of them.

Affinity gives a sense of things touching along their boundaries and therefore being of interest to each other. Felix Mendelssohn showed an affinity for music at a very early age and composed several fully developed symphonies while still in his teens; Stevie Wonder revealed his own musical affinity long before he made his debut at the age of 10. A strong affinity for another person may deepen into love. A critic may notice affinities between the works of two writers. A naturalist may speak of the affinity between two bird species—that is, their close physical relation to each other.

definitive \di-'fi-nə-tiv\ (1) Authoritative and final. (2) Specifying perfectly or precisely.

● The team's brilliant research provided a definitive description of the virus and its strange mutation patterns.

Something definitive is complete and final. A definitive example is the perfect example. A definitive biography contains everything we'll ever need to know about someone. Ella Fitzgerald's 1950s recordings of American popular songs have even been called definitive, though no one has ever wanted them to be the last.

infinitesimal \ˌin-ˌfi-nə-'te-sə-məl\ Extremely or immeasurably small.

● Looking more closely at the research data, he now saw an odd pattern of changes so infinitesimal that they hadn't been noticed before.

Infinitesimal includes the negative prefix *in-*, "not"; the resulting word describes something endlessly small. When Antonie van Leeuwenhoek invented the microscope in the 17th century, he was able to see organisms that had been thought too *infinitesimally* small to exist. But today's electron microscope allows us to see infinitesimal aspects of matter even he could not have imagined.

finite \'fī-ˌnīt\ Having definite limits.

● Her ambitions were infinite, but her wealth was finite.

It came as a shock to America in the early 1970s to realize that world and national resources were finite rather than unlimited. The debate continues as to whether the universe is finite or *infinite* and, if it is finite, how to think about what lies beyond it. Religion has always concerned itself with the question of the finite (that is, human life on earth) versus the infinite (God, eternity, and infinity).

But *finite* is mostly used in scientific writing, often with the meaning "definitely measurable."

Quizzes

A. Fill in each blank with the correct letter:

a. affinity   e. finite
b. susceptible   f. incipient
c. definitive   g. infinitesimal
d. reception   h. perceptible

1. By the fall there had been a _____ change in the mood of the students.
2. An _____ speck of dust on the lens can keep a CD player from functioning.
3. They waited weeks to hear about the board's _____ of their proposal.
4. She feels an _____ to her imaginary friend that she has never felt to her parents.
5. Small children are often _____ to nightmares after hearing ghost stories in the dark.
6. When the power failed as the wind began to reach gale force, she sensed _____ disaster.
7. We have a _____ number of choices, in fact maybe only three or four.
8. This may be the best book on the subject so far, but I wouldn't call it _____.

B. Match the word on the left to the correct definition on the right:

1. affinity   a. noticeable
2. susceptible   b. ultimate
3. definitive   c. beginning
4. reception   d. easily influenced
5. finite   e. tiny
6. incipient   f. attraction
7. infinitesimal   g. receiving
8. perceptible   h. limited

JAC/JEC comes from *jacere,* the Latin verb meaning "throw" or "hurl." To *reject* something is to throw (or push) it back. To *eject* something is to throw (or drive) it out. To *object* is to throw something in the way of something else.

adjacent \ə-'jā-sənt\ (1) Near, neighboring. (2) Sharing a common boundary or border.

● The warehouse was adjacent to the junction of the two raging rivers, so the body could have been quickly disposed of.

Adjacent contains the prefix *ad-,* "near or toward," so what is adjacent lies near its neighbor. In the former Yugoslavia, the Serbs and Croats have seized adjacent land from the Bosnians. Anyone buying a house is naturally curious about who lives on the adjacent lots. In geometry we speak of adjacent sides and angles. Though in each of these cases *adjacent* means "touching," it may also mean simply "neighboring" or "nearby."

conjecture \kən-'jek-chər\ To guess.

● They could conjecture that he had met his end in the Andes at the hands of the guerrillas.

Formed with the prefix *con-, conjecture* means literally "to throw together"—that is, to produce a theory by putting together a number of facts. From his calculations, Columbus conjectured that he would reach Asia if he sailed westward. His later *conjecture* of a Northwest Passage from the Atlantic to the Pacific over the North American continent was eventually proved correct, but only after hundreds of years had passed.

dejected \di-'jek-təd\ Downcast, depressed.

● Despite the glorious weather, they walked home from the hospital dejected.

Dejected, which includes the prefix *de-,* meaning "down," literally means "thrown down" or "cast down." It usually refers to a temporary state of mind—for example, the mood of a losing football team or a *rejected* lover—rather than ongoing depression.

trajectory \trə-'jek-tə-rē\ The curved path that an object makes in space, or that a thrown object follows as it rises and falls to earth.

● Considering the likely range, trajectory, and accuracy of a bullet fired from a cheap handgun at 150 yards, the murder seemed incredible.

Formed with part of the prefix *trans-*, "across," *trajectory* means a "hurling across." By calculating the effect of gravitational and other forces, the trajectory of an object launched into space at a known speed can be computed precisely. Missiles stand a chance of hitting their target only if their trajectory has been plotted accurately. Though the word is most used in physics and engineering, we can also say, for example, that the trajectory of a whole life may be set in a person's youth, or that a historian has described the long trajectory of the French empire in a new book.

TRACT comes from *trahere*, the Latin verb meaning "drag or draw." Something *attractive* draws us toward it. A *tractor* drags other vehicles behind it, with the help of the *traction* of its wheels.

---

detract \di-'trakt\ To decrease the importance, value, or effectiveness of something.

● None of the gossip in the new biography detracts in the least from her greatness as a writer.

With the prefix *de-*, meaning "away," *detract* means "draw away from." A fact that doesn't match up with the rest of the prosecution's case detracts from it. Richard Nixon's involvement in the Watergate coverup was felt to detract so seriously from his ability to carry out his presidential duties that he had to resign, especially after his *detractors* had impeached him. (Don't confuse *detract* with *distract*, which means "take attention away from.")

protracted \prō-'trak-təd\ Drawn out, continued, or extended.

● No one was looking forward to a protracted struggle for custody of the baby.

Protracted usually applies to something drawn out in time. A protracted strike may cripple a company; a protracted rainy spell may rot the roots of vegetables. Before Jonas Salk and Albert Sabin discovered vaccines to prevent polio, the many victims of the disease had no choice but to suffer a protracted illness and its permanent aftereffects.

retraction \ri-'trak-shən\ A taking back or withdrawal; a denial of what one has previously said.

● The following week, the newspaper reluctantly printed a retraction of the errors in the article, but the damage had been done.

The prefix *re-* ("back") gives *retraction* the meaning of "drawing back." Someone who has been wrongly accused may demand a retraction from his accuser—though today it seems more likely that he'll just go ahead and sue. Thousands of citizens were forced to publicly *retract* their "wrong" ideas by the Soviet government in the 1930s and the Chinese government in the 1960s. Retractions tend to be rather formal and rarely private.

intractable \in-'trak-tə-bəl\ Not easily handled, led, taught, or controlled.

● The army's corruption was known to be the country's intractable problem, and all foreign aid ended up in the colonels' pockets.

Intractable simply means "untreatable," and even comes from the same root. It may describe both people and conditions. An intractable alcoholic goes back to the bottle immediately after "drying out." A cancer patient may suffer intractable pain that doctors are unable to treat. Homelessness is now regarded by many as an intractable problem—though it hardly existed twenty years ago.

Quizzes

A. Choose the odd word:

1. conjecture   a. suppose b. conclude c. guess d. know
2. protracted   a. lengthened b. continued c. circular
      d. extended
3. dejected   a. excited b. downcast c. depressed d. forlorn
4. retraction   a. withdrawal b. regret c. disavowal
      d. denial

5. trajectory   a. curve b. path c. line d. target
6. detract   a. decrease b. diminish c. defy d. minimize
7. adjacent   a. near b. adjourned c. touching d. bordering
8. intractable   a. impossible b. uncontrollable
     c. stubborn d. unteachable

B. **Match each definition on the left to the correct word
    on the right:**

1.	denial	a.	protracted
2.	assume	b.	adjacent
3.	depressed	c.	trajectory
4.	difficult	d.	retraction
5.	take away	e.	conjecturé
6.	drawn out	f.	intractable
7.	curved path	g.	detract
8.	nearby	h.	dejected

DUC, from the Latin verb *ducere*, "to lead," shows up constantly in English. *Duke* means basically "leader." The Italian dictator Mussolini was known simply as "Il Duce." But such words as *produce* and *reduce* also contain the root, even though their meanings show it less clearly.

---

conducive \kən-'dü-siv\ Tending to promote, encourage, or assist; helpful.

● She found the atmosphere there conducive to study and even to creative thinking.

Something conducive "leads to" a desirable result. A cozy living room may be conducive to relaxed conversation, just as a boardroom may be conducive to more intense discussions. Particular tax policies are often conducive to savings and investment, whereas others are conducive to consumer spending. Notice that *conducive* is almost always followed by *to*.

deduction \dē-'dək-shən\ (1) Subtraction. (2) The reaching of a conclusion by reasoning.

● Foretelling the future by deduction based on a political or economic theory has proved to be extremely difficult.

A tax deduction is a subtraction from your gross income allowed by the government for certain expenses, which will result in your paying lower taxes. To *deduct* is simply to subtract. But *deduction* also means "reasoning," and particularly reasoning based on general principles to produce specific findings. Mathematical reasoning is almost always deduction, for instance, since it is based on general rules. But when Dr. Watson exclaims "Brilliant deduction, my dear Holmes!" he simply means "brilliant reasoning," since Sherlock Holmes's solutions are based on specific details he has noticed rather than on general principles.

induce \in-'düs\ (1) Persuade, influence. (2) Bring about.

● To induce him to make the call we had to promise we wouldn't do it again.

Inducing often refers to gentle persuasion—inducing a friend to go to a concert, or inducing a child to stop crying, for instance. But an *inducement* may occasionally be a bit menacing, such as the Godfather's "Make him an offer he can't refuse." *Induce* also sometimes means "produce"; thus, doctors must at times induce labor in a pregnant woman. *Induction* often means the opposite of *deduction,* and is in fact closer to what Sherlock Holmes was actually doing.

seduction \si-'dək-shən\ (1) Temptation to wrong, especially temptation to sexual intercourse. (2) Attraction or charm.

● The company began its campaign of seduction of the smaller firm by inviting its top management to a series of weekends at expensive resorts.

Seduction, with its prefix *se-,* "aside," means basically "led aside or astray." In Nathaniel Hawthorne's novel *The Scarlet Letter,* Hester Prynne has to wear a scarlet A, for "adulteress," for all to see after it is revealed that she has been *seduced* by the Reverend Dimmesdale. Seduction also takes less physical forms. Advertisements constantly try to seduce us (often using sex as a temptation) into buying products we hadn't even known existed.

SEC/SEQU comes from the Latin verb *sequi,* meaning "to follow." A *sequel* follows the original novel, film, or television show. The *second* follows the first. But a *non sequitur* is a conclusion that does "not follow" from what was said before.

consequential \ˌkän-sə-ˈkwen-shəl\ (1) Resulting. (2) Important.

• None of our discussions thus far has been very consequential; next week's meeting will be the important one.

Something that is consequential follows or comes along with something else. The "resulting" meaning of *consequential* is usually seen in legal writing. For example, "consequential losses" are losses that are claimed to have resulted from some improper behavior, about which the lawyer's client is suing. But normally *consequential* means "significant" or "important," and is especially used for events that will produce large *consequences* or results.

execute \ˈek-si-ˌkyüt\ (1) To carry out or perform. (2) To put to death legally or formally.

• He was aware that he hadn't been hired to think independently but rather simply to execute the governor's policies.

Execute joins *ex-,* "out," and *sec* to produce the meaning "follow through" or "carry out." An artist executes (or produces) a painting or sculpture only after having planned it first. A policy or regulation must have been prepared before it can be executed (or put into practice). And a person may be executed (or put to death) by the state only after a death sentence has been issued.

obsequious \äb-ˈsē-kwē-əs\ Excessively submissive, obedient, or flattering.

• Since he loves flattery, he surrounds himself with obsequious people, none of whom he ever really trusts.

A man may be obsequious toward his overbearing wife, or vice versa. Obsequious assistants are often called "yes-men" or "toadies" or even less complimentary things behind their backs. (Uriah Heep, in *David Copperfield,* is probably the most famous example in literature.) *Obsequiousness* has never been admired, but it has often been adopted as a good strategy.

sequential \si-'kwen-chəl\ (1) Arranged in order or in a series. (2) Following in a series.

● In writing the history of the revolution, he found it hard to put some of the events in sequential order.

Things in *sequence,* or regular order, are arranged *sequentially.* Most novels and films move sequentially, but some use techniques such as flashbacks that interrupt the movement forward in time. Sequential courses in college must be taken in the proper order, just as sequential tasks or steps must be done in order.

Quizzes

A. Match the definition on the left to the correct word on the right:

1.	flattering	a.	deduction
2.	persuade	b.	obsequious
3.	temptation	c.	induce
4.	subtraction	d.	execute
5.	helpful	e.	seduction
6.	ordered	f.	consequential
7.	produce	g.	conducive
8.	significant	h.	sequential

B. Fill in each blank with the correct letter:

a.	conducive	e.	consequential
b.	deduction	f.	execute
c.	induce	g.	obsequious
d.	seduction	h.	sequential

1. The detectives insisted on a detailed and _____ account of the evening's events.
2. She fended off all his clumsy attempts at _____.
3. Conditions on the noisy hallway were not at all _____ to sleep.
4. She was barely able to _____ the task in the time allotted.
5. He sometimes thought that missing that plane had been the most _____ event of his life.
6. They arrived at the correct conclusion by simple _____.

---

7. The assistant's _____ manner drove the other employees wild.
8. He had tried to _____ sleep by all his usual methods, with no success.

Words from Mythology

apollonian \a-pə-'lō-nē-ən\ Harmonious, ordered, rational, calm.

● After years of Romantic emotionality, many artists began to adopt a more apollonian style, producing carefully detailed patterns and avoiding extremes of all kinds.

The god Apollo governed the sun, light, and music. Due partly to the work of Nietzsche and other German scholars, we now associate Apollo with the forces of calm rationality and may call anything that has these qualities *apollonian*. This is not the whole story, however. Apollo was also the god of prophecy, so he was not entirely a force of reason; he had a terrible temper and an appetite for young girls as well.

bacchanalian \ba-kə-'nāl-yən\ Frenzied, orgiastic.

● The bacchanalian partying on graduation night resulted in three wrecked cars, two lawsuits by unamused parents, and more new experiences than most of the participants could remember the next day.

The Roman god of drama, wine, and ecstasy, Bacchus was the focus of a widespread celebration, the *Bacchanalia,* at which there was wine in abundance and celebrants were expected to cut loose from normal restraints and give in to all sorts of wild desires. The festivities got so out of hand that in 186 B.C. the Roman authorities had them banned. Much the same bacchanalian spirit fills New Orleans' Mardi Gras carnival each year.

delphic \'del-fik\ Unclear, ambiguous, or confusing.

● All she could get from the old woman were a few delphic comments that left her more confused than ever about the missing documents.

Delphi in Greece was the site of a temple to Apollo at which there was an oracle, a woman through whom Apollo would speak, foretelling the future. The Greeks consulted the oracle frequently on matters both private and public. The prophecies were given in obscure poetry that had to be interpreted by priests, and even then was subject to disastrous misinterpretation. Modern-day descendants of the oracle include some political commentators, who continue to utter words of delphic complexity each week.

Dionysian \dī-ə-'ni-zhē-ən\ Frenzied, orgiastic.

● Only in the tropics did such festivals become truly Dionysian, he said, which was why he was booking his flight to Rio.

Dionysus was the Greek forerunner of Bacchus. He was the inventor of wine, the first intoxicant, which he gave to the human race. For that gift and for all the uninhibited behavior that it led to, Dionysus became immensely popular, and he appears in a great many myths. He is often shown with a wine goblet, his hair is full of vine leaves, and he is frequently attended by a band of goat-footed satyrs and wild female spirits called maenads. The Greek Dionysian worship began as solemn rituals but eventually became great celebrations with much drunken lewdness.

jovial \'jō-vē-əl\ Jolly, expansively good-natured.

● Their grandfather was as jovial as their grandmother was quiet and withdrawn.

Jove, or Jupiter, was the Romans' chief god. He was generally a cheerful, sociable, fatherly figure, although his anger could destroy offenders in a flash. Every department-store Santa Claus strives to attain this appearance of generous *joviality*.

mercurial \mər-'kyūr-ē-əl\ Having rapid and unpredictable changes of mood.

● His mother's always mercurial temper became even more unpredictable, to the point where the slightest thing would trigger a violent fit.

The god Mercury and the planet named for him were thought to govern eloquence and cleverness. As the gods' messenger, with his winged cap and sandals, he was the very symbol of speed. The planet Mercury was named for him because it is the fastest of the planets. His name was also given to the liquid silver metal that skitters out of one's hand so quickly it is almost impossible to hold. A mercurial person isn't necessarily physically quick, but changes moods with bewildering speed.

olympian \ō-'lim-pē-ən\ Lofty, superior, and detached.

● The mafia don's manner grew increasingly olympian as he aged, but the old-timers could still remember when he was a hotheaded young thug.

The Greek gods lived high atop Mount Olympus, which allowed them to watch what went on in the human realm below and intervene as they saw fit. But they tended not to worry much about the affairs of these weak and short-lived creatures, although they did insist on being properly worshiped by them. We American voters sometimes feel that Congress treats us in an olympian manner as it determines how our money will be spent.

venereal \və-'nir-ē-əl\ Having to do with sexual intercourse or diseases transmitted by it.

● In the 19th century syphilis especially was often fatal, and venereal diseases killed some of the greatest figures of the time.

Venus was the Roman goddess of love, the equivalent of the Greek Aphrodite. Since she governed all aspects of human sensuality and sexuality, she has given her name to the diseases acquired through sexual contact. Most of these venereal diseases have been around for centuries, but only in this century have doctors devised tests to identify them or medicines to cure them. Today the official term is *sexually transmitted disease,* or STD; but even this name turns out to be ambiguous, since some of these diseases can be contracted in other ways as well.

Quiz

Choose the correct synonym and the correct antonym:

1. Dionysian   a. frenzied   b. angry   c. calm   d. fatal
2. apollonian   a. fruity   b. irrational   c. single
        d. harmonious

3. mercurial   a. stable   b. changeable   c. sociable
   d. depressed
4. jovial   a. youthful   b. mean-spirited   c. merry
   d. magical
5. olympian   a. involved   b. lame   c. detached   d. everyday
6. venereal   a. sensual   b. intellectual   c. diseased
   d. arthritic
7. bacchanalian   a. restrained   b. dynamic   c. orgiastic
   d. forthright
8. delphic   a. clear   b. dark   c. stormy   d. ambiguous

Review Quizzes

A. Choose the closest definition:

1. venue   a. prosecution   b. justice   c. location   d. street
2. incipient   a. sensitive   b. beginning   c. visible   d. final
3. affinity   a. eternity   b. attraction   c. intensity
   d. retraction
4. deduction   a. addition   b. flirtation   c. tax   d. reasoning
5. execute   a. dismiss   b. carry out   c. disturb   d. announce
6. sequential   a. important   b. noticeable   c. consecutive
   d. distant
7. obsequious   a. powerful   b. official   c. notorious
   d. obedient
8. agitate   a. excite   b. amaze   c. explain   d. exclaim
9. prodigal   a. poor   b. departed   c. wasteful   d. returning
10. synagogue   a. palace   b. temple   c. club   d. society

B. Match the definition on the left to the correct word on the right:

1. guess	a.	olympian
2. arrival	b.	perceptible
3. lengthy	c.	conjecture
4. godlike	d.	venturesome
5. ordered	e.	protracted
6. bold	f.	advent
7. noticeable	g.	susceptible

8. sensitive   h. dejected
9. significant   i. sequential
10. unhappy   j. consequential

C. Fill in each blank with the correct letter:

a. mercurial   f. litigate
b. obsequious   g. bacchanalian
c. intractable   h. detract
d. provenance   i. retraction
e. adjacent   j. trajectory

1. Before deciding to _____ the matter, they had tried to negotiate a solution out of court.
2. Nothing his enemies could say managed to _____ from his heroic public image.
3. The prison situation is _____, and likely to get worse.
4. The company issued a _____ the next day, apologizing to those who had been offended.
5. The new study of the painting's _____ proved it to be a genuine Monet.
6. Because they lived _____ to the paint factory, their garden suffered from the effects of pollution.
7. The disappointing _____ of his career often puzzled his friends.
8. The smilingly _____ sales clerk bustled off in search of more jackets.
9. By 2:00 a.m. the party was a scene of _____ frenzy.
10. Her only excuse for her behavior was her well-known _____ temper.

Unit 3

AMBI/AMPHI means "on both sides" or "around"; *ambi-* comes from Latin and *amphi-* from Greek. An *ambidextrous* person can use the right and the left hand equally well. An *amphibian*, such as a frog or salamander, is able to live and breathe both on land and in the water.

ambiguous \am-'bi-gyù-wəs\ (1) Doubtful or uncertain especially from being obscure or indistinct. (2) Unclear in meaning because of being understandable in more than one way.

● Successful politicians are good at giving ambiguous answers to questions on controversial issues.

Ambiguous comes from the Latin verb *ambigere*, "to be undecided," which in turn includes the verb *agere*, "to drive." Something that is ambiguous drives the observer in two directions. When we speak of eyes as being of an ambiguous color, we mean that we cannot decide which color they are—blue or green? The *ambiguity* of the smile of the Mona Lisa makes us wonder what she's thinking about. An ambiguous order is one that can be taken in at least two ways. An order to "shut up!," on the other hand, may be very rude, but at least it's *unambiguous*.

ambient \'am-bē-ənt\ Existing or present on all sides.

● The ambient lighting in the restaurant was low, but there was a bright candle at each table.

A scientist might measure how long it takes a heated substance to cool to the ambient temperature, the temperature of the surrounding air. Ambient light is the light that fills an area or surrounds something that is being viewed, like a television screen or a painting. A restaurant with low ambient light and candles at each table is probably trying for a romantic *ambience,* or atmosphere.

ambivalent \am-'bi-və-lənt\ (1) Holding opposite feelings and attitudes at the same time toward someone or something. (2) Continually wavering between opposites or alternate courses of action.

● He was extremely ambivalent about the trip: he badly wanted to travel but hated to miss the summer activities at home.

Ambivalent is a fairly new word, less than a hundred years old, but it is ultimately related to the Latin verb *valere,* which means "to be strong." An ambivalent person is someone who has strong feelings on more than one side of a question or issue. We might feel *ambivalence* about accepting a high-paying job that requires us to work long hours, or about lending money to someone we like but don't know well. Anyone who has ever been on a diet and been offered something like a Tutti-Frutti Chocolate Banana Sundae El Supremo probably knows what it's like to feel ambivalent.

amphitheater \'am-fə-ˌthē-ə-tər\ (1) An oval or circular building with an open area ringed by rising tiers of seats, used in ancient Rome for contests and spectacles. (2) A large modern theater or stadium.

● The Romans held popular contests between gladiators or between gladiators and wild beasts in their amphitheaters.

The basic design of an amphitheater reflects the forms of entertainment for which it was originally built: gladiatorial contests and other spectacles. The most famous of the ancient amphitheaters was Rome's Flavian Amphitheater, now more commonly known as the Colosseum. Built between 70 and 82 A.D., this structure could hold nearly 50,000 people. The ruins of more than 75 amphitheaters have been found in the ancient lands that were once part of the Roman Empire.

EP/EPI comes from Greek and means variously "upon," "besides," "attached to," "over," "outer," or "after." An *epiphenomenon* is a phenomenon that occurs as a result of the original phenomenon. An *epicenter* is the portion of the earth's surface directly over the focus of an earthquake. The *epidermis* is the outer layer of the skin, overlying the inner layer or "dermis."

ephemeral \i-'fe-mə-rəl\ (1) Lasting a day only. (2) Lasting a very short time.

● The benefits from the strategy will only be ephemeral, but we'll be paying for it for years to come.

Something that is literally ephemeral is "over" in a day, *hēmera* being the Greek word for "day." Ephemeral plants such as day-lilies have blooms that last only a day. More often, though, *ephemeral* is not to be taken quite so literally. In the world of show business, for example, fame is apt to be breathtakingly ephemeral, a year in the limelight followed by total obscurity.

epiphyte \'e-pi-,fīt\ A plant that obtains its nutrients from the air and the rain and usually grows on another plant for support.

● The strangler fig begins life as an epiphyte on a tree branch, drops its tendrils to take root in the ground around the trunk, and slowly covers and strangles the tree to death.

Epiphytic plants are sometimes also known as "air plants" because they seemingly survive on thin air. They rely on their host plants merely for physical support, not nourishment. Tropical epiphytes include orchids, ferns, and members of the pineapple family. To a newcomer in the tropical rainforest, the sight of a great tree with large epiphytes hanging from every level can be eerie and aston-ishing. The less interesting epiphytes of the temperate zone include lichens, mosses, and algae.

epitaph \'e-pi-,taf\ An inscription on a grave or tomb in memory of the one buried there.

● The great English architect Christopher Wren designed London's majestic St. Paul's Cathedral, the site of his tomb and epitaph: "Si monumentum requiris, circumspice" ("If you seek my monument, look around you").

Epitaph includes the root from the Greek word *taphos,* "tomb" or "funeral." Traditionally, *epitaph* refers to a tombstone inscription, but it can also refer to brief memorial statements that resemble such inscriptions. One of the most famous is Henry Lee's epitaph for George Washington: "First in war, first in peace, and first in the hearts of his countrymen."

epithet \'e-pi-,thet\ (1) A descriptive word or phrase occurring with or in place of the name of a person or thing. (2) An insulting or demeaning word or phrase.

● King Richard I was known by the epithet "Lionhearted."

Sometimes an epithet follows a given name, as in Erik the Red and Billy the Kid. Other times, the epithet precedes the personal name, as in Mahatma ("Great-souled") Gandhi. Still other times, the epithet is used in place of the actual name, as in the case of El Greco ("the Greek") and El Cid ("the Lord"). In its other commonly used sense, *epithet* refers to a name intended to insult or mock someone. When enemies are said to be "hurling epithets" at each other, it means they are exchanging angry insults.

Quizzes

A. Fill in each blank with the correct letter:

a.	ambiguous	e.	epithet
b.	epiphyte	f.	ambivalent
c.	ambient	g.	ephemeral
d.	epitaph	h.	amphitheater

1. An ____ seems to live on air and water alone.
2. When the ____ light is low, photographers use a flash.
3. She felt ____ about the invitation, and couldn't decide whether to accept or decline.
4. Is any ____ inscribed on Grant's Tomb?
5. Andrew Jackson's ____, describing his lean toughness, was "Old Hickory."
6. Lord Raglan's ____ order confused the commander of the Light Brigade and led to its disastrous charge.
7. Spring and all its blossoms are ____, here but a moment and then gone.
8. On New Year's Day, the ____ known as the Rose Bowl becomes the site of one of college football's great face-offs.

B. Match each word on the left with its correct definition on the right:

1. ambivalent   a. having more than one
2. epithet   meaning

3. amphitheater
4. epiphyte
5. ambiguous
6. epitaph
7. ambient
8. ephemeral

b. surrounding
c. wavering
d. grave inscription
e. stage surrounded with tiered seats
f. descriptive nickname
g. short-lived
h. non-parasitic plant growing on another

HYPO/HYP as a prefix can mean variously "under," "beneath," "down," or "below normal." Many *hypo-* words are medical. A *hypodermic* needle injects medication under the skin. *Hypotension*, or low blood pressure, can be just as unhealthy as *hypertension*, and *hypoglycemia*, low blood sugar, just as unhealthy as diabetes.

---

hypochondriac \,hī-pō-'kän-drē-,ak\ A person unduly concerned with health and often suffering from delusions of physical disease.

● Hercule Poirot, the dapper hero of Agatha Christie's mysteries, is a notorious hypochondriac, always trying to protect himself from drafts.

One disease a hypochondriac really does suffer from is *hypochondria*, which is the mental depression that comes from worrying too much about health and is often accompanied by delusions of physical ailments. Somewhat surprisingly, *hypochondria* derives from *hypo-* and *chondros*, the Greek word for "cartilage." The cartilage in question is that of the sternum, or breastbone. From ancient times medical authorities had believed that certain internal organs or regions were the seat of various diseases, both physical and mental. The region beneath the centrally located breastbone was thought to be the seat of hypochondria.

hypocrisy \hi-'pä-krə-sē\ A pretending to be what one is not or to feel what one does not really feel.

● The protesters were objecting to the hypocrisy of doing business with a government whose racist policies were condemned by everyone.

Hypocrisy comes from a Greek word that means "the act of playing a part on a stage." A *hypocrite* is a person who says or does one thing while thinking or feeling something entirely different underneath. Most of us are good at detecting *hypocritical* behavior in others, but we don't always see it so easily in ourselves.

hypothermia \hī-pō-'thər-mē-ə\ Subnormal temperature of the body.

● By the time rescuers were able to pull the skater from the pond's icy waters, hypothermia had reached a life-threatening stage.

Hypothermia may constitute a grave medical emergency. Typical causes include submersion in icy water and prolonged exposure to cold. Hypothermia begins to be a concern when body temperature dips below 95°F. Below 90°F, the point at which the normal reaction of shivering ceases, emergency treatment is called for.

hypothetical \hī-pə-'the-tə-kəl\ (1) Involving an assumption made for the sake of argument or for further study or investigation. (2) Imagined for purposes of example.

● The presidential candidate refused to say what she would do if faced with a hypothetical military crisis.

Hypothetical and its parent word *hypothesis* come from *hypo-* and the Greek verb *tithenai*, "to put." To *hypothesize* is to suppose, or to put (something) under consideration. *Hypothetical* applies to something that is assumed to be true so that it can serve as the basis for a line of reasoning. Thus, the theory that the dinosaurs became extinct because of a giant meteor striking the earth involves the hypothesis that such a collision would have certain effects on the earth's climate.

THERM/THERMO comes from the Greek word meaning "warm." A *thermometer* measures the amount of warmth in a body, the air, or an oven; a *thermostat* makes sure the temperature stays at the same level. In a *thermodynamic* process, heat affects the behavior of atoms, particles, or molecules. *Thermoelectricity* is produced by the direct action of heat on certain combinations of metals.

---

thermal \'thər-məl\ (1) Of, relating to, or caused by heat. (2) Designed to insulate in order to retain body heat.

● The glider circled slowly, seeking a thermal updraft from a plowed field that would take it spiraling upward.

Before polypropylene and thermal weave, union suits—that is, long thermal underwear that covered the entire body—were sometimes donned in October and not taken off until April. Worn by sodbusters, cowboys, and townsfolk alike, they kept America warm during its formative years. They undoubtedly also kept America itchy and a little on the smelly side through the cold months. But then, bathing even once a week was considered the height of cleanliness until very recently.

thermocline \'thər-mə-ˌklīn\ The region in a body of water that divides the warmer, oxygen-rich surface layer from the colder, oxygen-poor deep water.

● The warm water above the thermocline is relatively shallow: for most of the world's oceans the top layer is only about 150 to 300 feet deep.

The *-cline* of *thermocline* comes from a Greek word meaning "to slope" and refers to the gradual series of temperature changes that occur in this kind of zone. In a freshwater lake there is very little mixing between the layers of warm and cold water during the summer. During the autumn, however, a major turnover occurs. The oxygen-rich surface water cools and sinks to the bottom, and the nutrient-rich water near the bottom is displaced to the top. The cycle is reversed the following spring.

thermocouple \'thər-mō-ˌkə-pəl\ A device for measuring temperature that makes use of the way different metals respond to heat.

● Thermocouples can be used to measure temperatures as high as 2300°C or as low as -270°C, far beyond the range of ordinary thermometers.

Thermocouples use wires made of two different metals, such as copper and iron. The wires are joined at both ends; one end is placed against the object whose temperature is being measured, while the other end is kept at a known, constant temperature. The thermocouple generates a voltage that depends on the difference in temperature between the two joined ends of the wires and can be measured to obtain the temperature of the object.

thermonuclear \‚thər-mō-'nü-klē-ər\ Of or relating to the changes in the nucleus of atoms with low atomic weight, such as hydrogen, that require a very high temperature to begin.

• During the 1950s and 1960s American families built thousands of home underground shelters to protect themselves from thermonuclear blasts.

The sun's light comes from a sustained thermonuclear reaction deep within it. On earth, such thermonuclear reactions have been used to develop the hydrogen bomb, a bomb based on a fusion reaction that must be triggered by a fission bomb that uses uranium or plutonium. "Little Boy" and "Fatman," the bombs dropped on Hiroshima and Nagasaki to end World War II, were fission bombs. The thermonuclear era began only in 1952, and has produced bombs hundreds of times more powerful.

Quizzes

A. Choose the closest definition:

1. hypothermia   a. excitability b. subnormal temperature c. external temperature d. warmth

2. thermocline   a. area of warm water b. area of cold water c. area between warm and cold water d. deep ocean water

3. hypocrisy   a. dislike b. low energy c. insincerity d. nickname

4. thermal   a. keeping out b. keeping warm c. keeping safe d. keeping cold

5. hypothetical   a. typical b. substandard c. sympathetic d. assumed

6. hypochondriac   a. person with imaginary visions b. person with heart congestion c. person with imaginary ailments d. person with imaginary relatives

7. thermocouple   a. temperature gauge b. nuclear reaction trigger c. ocean current gauge d. altitude gauge

8. thermonuclear   a. nuclear reaction requiring high
   heat b. chemical reaction requiring a vacuum
   c. biological reaction producing bright light
   d. nuclear reaction based on distance from the sun

**B. Indicate whether the following pairs of words have
the same or different meanings:**

1. thermocouple / hot bodies   same ___ / different ___
2. hypochondriac / invalid   same ___ / different ___
3. thermal / insulating   same ___ / different ___
4. thermonuclear / destructive   same ___ / different ___
5. hypocrisy / truthfulness   same ___ / different ___
6. hypothetical / supposed   same ___ / different ___
7. thermocline / warm hillside   same ___ / different ___
8. hypothermia / low blood sugar   same ___ / different ___

POLY comes from *polys,* the Greek word for "many." *Polysyllabic* words, of which there are a few in this book, are words of many syllables. *Polygamy* is marriage in which one has many spouses, or at least more than the legal limit of one. A *polygraph* is an instrument for recording variations in many different bodily pulsations simultaneously to reveal whether someone is lying.

---

polychromatic \pä-lē-krō-'ma-tik\ Showing a variety or a change of colors; multicolored.

● *The Wizard of Oz* begins in black and white but suddenly becomes gloriously polychromatic once Dorothy and Toto land in Oz.

Male peacocks are almost miraculously polychromatic, with their feathers of gleaming blue, green, white, and brown. The polychromatic content of light becomes apparent when it passes through a prism like mist or a faceted piece of glass; the prism organizes it into its distinct wavelengths, each creating a band of color in the rainbow. *Polychromatic* takes its meaning straight from its roots: *poly-,* "many," and *chrom-,* "color."

polyglot \'pä-lē-ˌglät\ (1) One who can speak or write several languages. (2) Having or using several languages.

● As trade between countries increases, there is more need for polyglots who can act as negotiators.

Polyglot contains the root *glot*, meaning "language." It is used both as a noun and as an adjective. An international airport is bound to be polyglot, with people from all over the world speaking their native languages. One of history's more intriguing polyglots was the Holy Roman Emperor Charles V. He claimed that he addressed his horse only in German, he conversed with women in Italian and with men in French, but he reserved Spanish for his talks with God.

polymer \'pä-lə-mər\ A chemical compound formed by a reaction in which two or more molecules combine to form larger molecules with repeating structural units.

● Nylon, a polymer commercially introduced in 1938, can be spun and woven into fabrics or cast as tough, elastic blocks.

There are natural polymers, such as shellac and rubber, but synthetic polymers came into being in 1870 with Celluloid, which, although a synthetic compound, is made from natural cotton and camphor. After many decades of development, the *polymeric* compounds now include *polypropylene*, used in milk crates, luggage, and hinges; *polyurethane*, used in paints, adhesives, molded items, rubbers, and foams; and *polyvinyl chloride*, used to make pipes that won't rust.

polyphony \pə-'li-fə-nē\ Music consisting of two or more independent but harmonious melodies.

● At concerts she preferred Mahler and Beethoven, but when she was working she listened only to Renaissance polyphony.

Polyphony is usually avoided in American folk and popular music, which almost always employs a strong melody with a much less important accompaniment. But it is typical of Dixieland, bluegrass, and almost any kind of music where more than one musician improvises at once. *Polyphony* is used primarily for music of the Renaissance and Baroque eras from about 1400 to 1750; J. S. Bach is the most famous master of polyphony.

PRIM comes from *primus*, the Latin word for "first." Something that is *primary* is first in time, development, rank, or importance. A *primer* is a book of first instructions on a subject. A *primate* is a bishop or archbishop of the first rank—but also a monkey or ape. Something *primitive* is in its first stage of development. Something *primeval* had its origin in the first period of world or human history.

primal \ˈprī-məl\ (1) Original or primitive. (2) First in importance.

● She argued that to restore the economy, the primal necessity was to reform the health care system.

We might speak of the primal innocence of youth, or of the primal intensity of someone's devotion to a cause. Certain psychologists employ "primal scream" therapy, in which patients relive painful experiences from their past and express their frustration and anger through screaming and even violence.

primiparous \prī-ˈmi-pə-rəs\ (1) Bearing a first offspring. (2) Having borne only one previous offspring.

● The purpose of the study was to compare the average duration of labor for primiparous women with that of multiparous women.

Primiparous is used of animals as well as humans. It is typically used with *multiparous*, "having had one or more previous pregnancies." The terms are common in laboratory research, veterinary science, and human obstetrics. An individual who is a *primipara* may exhibit certain characteristics, or be subject to certain circumstances, that are peculiar to first pregnancies.

primogeniture \prī-mō-ˈje-nə-ˌchu̇r\ An exclusive right of inheritance belonging to the eldest son of a single set of parents.

● Many of the world's monarchies descend by the principle of primogeniture.

Primogeniture arose in England following the Norman Conquest of 1066. The practice began as a means of ensuring that fiefs (that is, estates) would not be broken up among the sons of a vassal. Eventually the right of the eldest son to inherit all of his father's estate was written into law. Primogeniture was one of the English practices that Americans were eager to abolish once independence had been attained. Leading the campaign against it was Thomas Jefferson.

primordial \prī-'mȯr-dē-əl\ (1) First created or developed. (2) Existing in or from the very beginning.

• Many astronomers think the universe is continuing to evolve from a primordial cloud of gas.

Primordial can be traced back to the Latin word *primordium*, or "origin." It applies to something that is only the starting point in a course of development or progression. The substance out of which the earth was formed and all life on it evolved is commonly spoken of as "the primordial ooze." A primordial cell is the first formed and least specialized in a line of cells. A primordial land-scape is one that bears no sign of human use.

Quizzes

A. Fill in each blank with the correct letter:

a.	primiparous	e.	polychromatic
b.	polyglot	f.	primordial
c.	primogeniture	g.	polymer
d.	polyphony	h.	primal

1. In the 1980s many women chose to remain ____, content with just one child.
2. Rubber is a natural ____ that remains the preferred material for many applications.
3. The asteroids in our solar system may be remnants of a ____ cloud of dust.
4. The Beatles occasionally experimented with ____, sometimes imitating the music of Bach.
5. Royal titles are still passed from one generation to the next on the basis of ____.
6. Having gone to school in four countries as a child, she was already a fluent ____
7. They were charmed by the ____ innocence of the little village.
8. The house, once white, was now dazzlingly ____.

B. Indicate whether the following pairs of words have the same or different meanings:

1. polychromatic / overly dramatic   same ___ / different ___
2. primogeniture / first generation   same ___ / different ___
3. polymer / molecule with
   repeating units   same ___ / different ___
4. primiparous / firstborn   same ___ / different ___
5. polyglot / speaking many
   languages   same ___ / different ___
6. primal / most important   same ___ / different ___
7. polyphonic / many-colored   same ___ / different ___
8. primordial / primitive   same ___ / different ___

HOM/HOMO comes from *homos*, the Greek word for "same." In an English word it can mean "one and the same" or "similar" or "alike." A *homograph* is one of two or more words spelled alike but different in meaning or derivation or pronunciation. A *homosexual* is a person who exhibits sexual desire toward others of the same sex.

---

homonym \'hä-mə-ˌnim\ One of two or more words pronounced and/or spelled alike but different in meaning.

● The *pool* of "a pool of water" and the *pool* of "a game of pool" are homonyms.

Homonym is a troublesome word because it can refer to three distinct classes of words. Homonyms can be words that merely sound alike—such as *to, too,* and *two*—but are different in spelling and meaning. Homonyms can also be words that are spelled alike—such as *bow* (of a ship) and *bow* (and arrow)—but are different in pronunciation and meaning. Finally, homonyms can be words with identical spellings and pronunciations but different meanings—such as *quail* (the bird) and *quail* (to cringe). Some writers and speakers prefer to limit *homonym* to this last sense.

homogeneous \ˌhō-mə-'jē-nē-əs\ (1) Of the same or a similar kind. (2) Of uniform structure or composition throughout.

• Though she was raised in a small town, she liked living in the city because the population there wasn't so homogeneous.

A slab of rock is homogeneous if it consists of the same material throughout, like granite or marble. A neighborhood might be called homogeneous if all the people in it are similar, having pretty much the same background, education, and outlook. *Homogeneity* is fine in a rock, but some people find it a little boring in a neighborhood. Foods can be homogeneous too. Milk, for example, is *homogenized* so that its fatty part, the cream, is spread evenly throughout, giving the milk a consistent, homogeneous texture.

homologous \hō-'mä-lə-gəs\ Developing from the same or a similar part of a remote ancestor.

• Arms and wings are homologous structures that reveal our ancient relationship to the birds.

In his discussion of the panda's thumb, Stephen Jay Gould carefully explains how this thumb is not homologous to the human thumb. Although in function the two digits are similar, the panda's thumb developed from a bone in its wrist and is an addition to the five "fingers" of its paw. The panda's thumb is indispensable for stripping bamboo of its tasty leaves, the staple of the panda's diet; but it did not develop *homologously* with our thumb. The tiny stirrup and anvil bones of our inner ear, however, do seem to be homologous with the bones that allow a garter snake to swallow a frog whole.

homophone \'hä-mə-ˌfōn\ One of two or more words pronounced alike but different in meaning or derivation or spelling.

• The words *wood* and *would* are familiar homophones.

Since *phon-* means "sound," homophones basically sound the same. *Tide* and *tied, made* and *maid, horse* and *hoarse* are pronounced identically, but differ in meaning, derivation, and spelling. This occasionally leads to confusion. If Groucho Marx had said "I'm a little hoarse," we might well have expected him to give a little whinny. Puns depend on *homophonic* pairs for their effect; while many find that homophonic humor grates, others think it is just great.

DIS comes from Latin, where it means "apart." In English, its meanings have increased to include "do the opposite of" (as in *disestablish*), "deprive of" (as in *disfranchise*), "exclude or expel from" (*disbar*), "the opposite or absence of" (*disunion, disaffection*), "not" (*disagreeable*), and "completely" (*disannul*). The original meaning can still be seen in a word like *dissipate*, which means "to break up and scatter."

diffraction \di-'frak-shən\ (1) The bending or spreading of a beam of light especially when it passes through a narrow opening or is reflected from a ruled surface. (2) Similar changes in other waves, such as sound waves.

• Through the occurrence of diffraction, the thin bands of light passing through venetian blinds become a sea of soft light on the opposite wall.

Diffraction contains the root *fract-*, "broken" (*dis-* here has changed to *dif-*), so *diffracted* light is light that is broken up. Diffracted sound is also broken up. The diffraction of the sound waves bends them around the corner, so a conversation carried on in one room can be overheard in another.

dissension \di-'sen-shən\ Disagreement in opinion.

• There was so much dissension at the meeting that nothing got done, and everyone went home angry.

Dissension is a common feature of our political system. One party suggests a new law or policy, and then the other party often *dissents*, arguing that the new law or policy will have a terrible effect on the country, and proposing a different new law or policy of its own. This leads the first party to dissent in turn, and so on. Things usually get worked out in the end. Since *dissentious* behavior of this kind keeps everyone on their toes, most people feel that it's a good thing overall. But not everyone agrees.

disseminate \di-'se-mə-ˌnāt\ To spread widely as if by sowing seeds.

• Television and computer networks now make it possible to disseminate information throughout the world very quickly.

In *disseminate,* the prefix *dis-* keeps its original Latin sense
"apart." This prefix was attached in Latin to the verb *seminare,*
"to sow," which itself was derived from the noun *semen,* "seed."
The image lying behind *disseminate* is that of a farmer sowing
seeds over a wide area by throwing them with a sweep of the arm,
the same image that has given us *broadcast* (which has the basic
sense "to cast broadly"). It's appropriate, then, that one of the best
ways to bring about the *dissemination* of news is by broadcasting
it over television and radio.

dissipate \'di-sə-,pāt\ (1)To cause to spread out to the point of
vanishing; disperse. (2) To spend wastefully or foolishly; squander.

● The moderator's good humor slowly dissipated the tension that
had filled the meeting room.

Dissipate suggests a gradual disintegration or vanishing, as if by
crumbling, scattering, or evaporation. A police force dissipates an
unruly mob. The sun dissipates the morning mist. In its second
sense, *dissipate* implies frittering away something until it is
exhausted. A foolish lottery winner might dissipate his or her
money in extravagant spending sprees, buying 18 Ferraris, say, or
a lifetime supply of expensive imported underwear.

Quizzes

A. Choose the closest definition:

1. dissipate   a. drink slowly b. scatter c. make pale
   d. undo
2. homonym   a. word meaning the same as another
   b. word spelled and sounded the same as another
   c. one with same name as another d. one who loves
   another of the same sex
3. disseminate   a. spread widely b. plant in rows
   c. dissolve d. make longer
4. homogeneous   a. self-loving b. unusually brilliant
   c. having many parts d. consistent throughout
5. diffraction   a. breaking up of friendships b. breaking up
   of light waves c. breaking up of meetings d. breaking
   up of atoms

6. homologous   a. of different length   b. of similar size
   c. of different stages   d. of similar origin
7. dissension   a. confusion   b. disagreement
   c. satisfaction   d. curiosity
8. homophone   a. word that sounds like another   b. word
   that means the same thing as another   c. word that
   looks like another   d. word relating to sexual desire

**B. Match the definition on the left to the correct word
on the right:**

1. word spelled like another   a.   dissension
2. spend foolishly   b.   homophone
3. having a consistent   c.   diffraction
   texture   d.   homonym
4. conflict   e.   disseminate
5. evolutionarily related   f.   homologous
6. spread over a wide area   g.   dissipate
7. word sounding like   h.   homogeneous
   another
8. breaking up of light or
   sound waves

Latin Borrowings

ad hoc \'ad-'häk\ Formed or used for a particular purpose or for
immediate needs.

● The faculty formed an ad hoc committee to deal with the question
of first-amendment rights on campus.

Ad hoc literally means ''for this'' in Latin, a meaning clearly
reflected in its uses in English. An ad hoc investigating committee
is authorized to look into a matter of limited scope and not to go
on a fishing expedition for other wrongdoing. An ad hoc ruling by
an athletic council is intended to settle a particular case, and is not
meant to serve as a model for later rulings. Problems that come up
in the course of a project often require immediate, ad hoc solutions.

ad hominem \'ad-'hä-mə-nem\ Marked by an attack on an opponent's character rather than by an answer to the arguments made or the issues raised.

● The presidential debates often consist of ad hominem attacks rather than serious discussion of important issues.

Ad hominem in Latin means "to the man." It comes from the field of rhetoric (that is, speaking and writing), where it was first used to describe arguments that appeal to the listener's emotions and not to the intellect. The easiest way to do this is to engage in personal attacks against one's opponent. When debaters cannot justify their own positions or prove their opponents wrong, they may resort to ad hominem charges. Ad hominem arguments require neither truth nor logic to be effective. Consequently, the popularity of such arguments has never waned.

alter ego \'ȯl-tər-'ē-gō\ (1) A trusted friend or personal representative. (2) The opposite side of a personality.

● The White House chief of staff is a political alter ego: he knows, or should know, who and what the President considers important.

In Latin, *alter ego* literally means "second I." An alter ego can be thought of as a person's clone or second self. A professional alter ego might be a trusted aide who knows exactly what the boss wants done. A personal alter ego might be a close friend who is almost like a twin. *Alter ego* can also refer to the second, hidden side of one's own self. In Robert Louis Stevenson's classic *The Strange Case of Doctor Jekyll and Mr. Hyde,* Dr. Jekyll is a good-hearted, honorable man. But after taking a potion, his alter ego, the loathsome and diabolical Mr. Hyde, takes control over his personality.

de facto \dē-'fak-tō\ Being such in practice or effect, although not formally recognized; actual.

● Although there was never a general declaration of war, the two countries were in a de facto state of war for almost a decade.

Literally meaning "from the fact," *de facto* in English is applied to whatever has the substance of something but not the formal name. A de facto government is one that operates with all of the power of a regular government, but without the official recognition. De facto segregation does not stem from any legislative order, but it is just as real and deep-rooted as segregation that has been authorized by law.

de jure \dē-'jùr-ē\ By right of law.

● With the completion of the adoption proceedings, the Millers became the de jure as well as the de facto parents of the child.

Literally meaning "by right" in Latin, *de jure* is typically used in sentences where it is set in opposition to *de facto*. It is used with reference to things that have the force of law or operate under a right recognized by law. A de jure president is one duly elected under a nation's laws. A de facto ruler, on the other hand, may be exercising power that has been acquired through illegal means.

ex post facto \eks-,pōst-'fak-tō\ Done, made, or formulated after the fact.

● Most of Carl's so-called reasons are merely ex post facto excuses for impulsive behavior.

Ex post facto is Latin for "from a thing done afterward." Approval for a project that is given ex post facto—after the project already has been begun or completed—is mainly given to save face. An ex post facto law is one that criminalizes an action after it was committed, even though the action was not a crime at the time that it was committed.

modus operandi \'mō-dəs-,ä-pə-'ran-,dī\ A usual way of doing something.

● A criminal who commits repeated crimes can often be identified by his modus operandi.

Modus operandi is Latin for "method of operating." Although often associated with police work and a favorite word of mystery writers, *modus operandi* is used in other contexts as well. For example, a frequent gambler who likes to play the horses may have a particular modus operandi for picking winners. The modus operandi of a cutthroat retailer may be to undersell competitors, drive them out of business, and then raise prices afterwards.

modus vivendi \'mō-dəs-vi-'ven-dē\ (1) A practical compromise or arrangement that is acceptable to all concerned. (2) A way of life.

● During the budget crisis, the Democratic governor and the Republican legislature established a modus vivend† that let them put aside their differences and tackle the problem at hand.

Modus vivendi literally means "manner of living" in Latin, and it sometimes has that meaning in English as well. Usually, though, a modus vivendi is a working arrangement that disputing parties can live with, at least until a more permanent solution can be found. Typically, a modus vivendi is an arrangement that ignores differences and difficulties. Two people going through a bitter divorce may be able to arrive at a modus vivendi that allows them to at least maintain an appearance of civility and dignity.

Quiz

Choose the closest definition:

1. alter ego   a. church structure b. bad conscience
     c. intimate friend d. self-love
2. modus vivendi   a. pie with ice cream b. compromise
     c. stalemate d. immoral conduct
3. ad hoc   a. for this purpose b. permanent c. long-
     range d. for many reasons
4. ex post facto   a. in anticipation b. sooner or later
     c. coming after d. someday
5. ad hominem   a. based on personalities b. based on
     logic c. based on issues d. based on sexual preference
6. modus operandi   a. procedure b. way of moving
     c. crime d. arrest
7. de facto   a. in transit b. in effect c. in debt d. in theory
8. de jure   a. by might b. by claim c. by right d. by word

Review Quizzes

A. Complete the analogy:

1. monochromatic : dull :: polychromatic : _____
     a. neutral b. bland c. sharp d. vivid
2. peace : tranquility :: dissension : _____
     a. cooperation b. disagreement c. unity
     d. communication

3. brief : lengthy :: ex post facto : _____
   a. beforehand b. afterward c. during d. actually
4. local : here :: ambient : _____
   a. there b. somewhere c. nowhere d. everywhere
5. marriage : dowry :: primogeniture : _____
   a. favoritism b. flattery c. inheritance d. divorce
6. antonym : up / down :: homophone : _____
   a. pause / paws b. three / tree c. imagine / dream
   d. retreat / advance
7. seek : flee :: ad hominem : _____
   a. to the time b. to the issue c. to the end d. to the
   maximum
8. desirable : despised :: thermal : _____
   a. cool b. soft c. warm d. springy

B. Fill in each blank with the correct letter:

a.	ad hoc	i.	diffraction
b.	ambivalent	j.	modus vivendi
c.	modus operandi	k.	primiparous
d.	epithet	l.	alter ego
e.	thermonuclear	m.	polyglot
f.	de jure	n.	hypochondriac
g.	polymer	o.	amphitheater
h.	homogeneous		

1. A real _____, she could speak four languages and read
   three others.
2. The independent-minded teenager and her overprotective
   parents struggled to arrive at a _____ that both sides
   could accept.
3. The usual _____ for the songwriters was for one to write
   the lyrics first and then for the other to compose the
   music.
4. She is such a close friend that she seems like my _____.
5. The de facto segregation in the North closely resembled
   the _____ segregation of the South.
6. _____ explains why sound can be heard around a corner,
   even though no straight path between source and hearer
   exists.

7. Much thought has gone into the designing of _____ power plants that run on nuclear fusion.

8. The development of the first synthetic _____ for use as fabric revolutionized the garment industry.

9. "Gray-eyed" is the standard _____ used to describe the goddess Athena.

10. The _____ mothers were shown to have on average more complications during pregnancy.

11. Jessica was _____ about going to the party: it sounded exciting, but she wouldn't know any of the other guests.

12. In her middle age she became a thorough _____, always convinced she was suffering from some new disease.

13. You should blend all ingredients thoroughly to produce a _____ mixture.

14. An _____ committee should be named to come up with ideas for redecorating the waiting room.

15. The play was presented in the open-air _____ under the stars.

C. Indicate whether the following pairs have the same or different meanings:

1. de facto / actually   same ___ / different ___
2. hypothermia / heat prostration   same ___ / different ___
3. primordial / existing from the beginning   same ___ / different ___
4. thermocline / cold ocean depths   same ___ / different ___
5. polyphonic / religious   same ___ / different ___
6. primal / first   same ___ / different ___
7. ambiguous / unclear   same ___ / different ___
8. modus operandi / way of life   same ___ / different ___
9. homologous / blended   same ___ / different ___
10. disseminate / broadcast   same ___ / different ___
11. thermocouple / lovebirds   same ___ / different ___
12. epiphyte / parasite   same ___ / different ___
13. de jure / legally   same ___ / different ___
14. epitaph / grave inscription   same ___ / different ___
15. dissipate / dispel   same ___ / different ___

Unit 4

VOR, from the Latin verb *vorare*, means "to eat." The ending *-ivorous* shows up in words that refer to eaters of certain kinds of food. *Frugivorous* (for "fruit-eating"), *granivorous* (for "grain-eating"), and *graminivorous* (for "grass-eating") are somewhat common. Some *-ivorous* words such as *insectivorous* and *nectarivorous,* are easy to understand at a glance. Others can get pretty complex; insects that feed on the sap of plants, for instance, are *phytosuccivorous.*

---

carnivorous \kär-'ni-və-rəs\ Meat-eating or flesh-eating.

• The dragonfly lives up to its name by being a carnivorous terror that can pluck its prey out of midair at speeds up to 30 miles per hour.

Usually when we think of carnivorous beings we think of large animals such as lions, tigers, or cheetahs. However, many smaller animals, including some kinds of mice and the tiny creatures that make up coral reefs, are also *carnivores*. And there are even a few carnivorous plants, such as the Venus's-flytrap, the pitcher plant, and the sundew, all of which *devour* their insect prey after trapping them by ingenious means.

herbivorous \hər-'bi-və-rəs\ Plant-eating.

• In spite of their frightening appearance, marine iguanas are peaceable herbivorous animals that feed mostly on seaweed.

While many herbivorous animals (such as rabbits and cows) are noted for their passive ways, such behavior is not universal among *herbivores*. A rhinoceros is herbivorous but capable of inflicting serious damage if threatened. Among dinosaurs, the herbivorous

Diplodocus had a thick tail that could be used as a lethal weapon against attacking carnivorous enemies.

omnivorous \äm-'ni-və-rəs\ (1) Feeding on both animals and plants. (2) Intensely interested in everything.

● Good writers are often also omnivorous readers who enjoy equally fiction and nonfiction, prose and poetry, philosophy and science.

We tend to think of human beings as omnivorous, but in fact there are many kinds of plants that we simply cannot digest. Bears are truer *omnivores*. Their diet can include bulbs, berries, nuts, young plant shoots, insects, grubs, and dead animals, including fish, deer, and beaver. Humans do seem to possess an omnivorous curiosity. And it probably took that kind of curiosity—plus a good deal of courage—to be the first human to eat an oyster.

voracious \və-'rā-shəs\ (1) Having a huge appetite. (2) Very eager.

● One of the hardest parts of dieting is watching skinny people with voracious appetites consume large amounts of food without gaining weight.

Voracious can be applied to both people and their appetites. Teenagers are voracious eaters because they have voracious appetites. Some vacationers become voracious readers; others are voracious for other kinds of pleasure. *Voracious* often suggests an appetite in excess of what is good for us. We are sometimes told that we are a nation of voracious borrowers because of our voracious demand for consumer goods and voracious government spending, and none of this is good news.

CARN comes from the Latin *carn-*, the stem of *caro*, "flesh," and words including this root usually refer to flesh in some form. The word *carnivore*, for example, which we met in the preceding section, means "an eater of meat."

---

carnage \'kär-nij\ Great destruction of life (as in a battle); slaughter.

● People from around the world made appeals to parties on all sides of the conflict to stop the carnage of the war in Bosnia.

Carnage does not refer only to slaughter on the battlefield. As long as tens of thousands of people die each year in automobile accidents, it is appropriate to speak of carnage on the nation's highways. And in some contexts *carnage* can simply mean violence or its results. Those concerned about the effect of all of the violence we are exposed to each day point in particular to the carnage on television and in the movies.

carnal \'kär-nəl\ Having to do with bodily pleasures.

● The news stories about students going on Spring Break focused as usual on the carnal pleasures associated with the annual ritual.

Carnal is sometimes used to mean "having to do with the human body," but more often it refers solely to the pleasures and appetites of the body. Most religions stress the superiority of spiritual enlightenment over carnal pleasures. Very frequently, *carnal* simply means "sexual," especially when the sexual activity is mostly physical in nature. Novels about Hollywood often rely heavily on detailed descriptions of the carnal adventures of their main characters.

carnival \'kär-nə-vəl\ (1) A season of merrymaking just before Lent; an occasion for festivities and excess. (2) A traveling group that presents a variety of amusements.

● Whether in Argentina, Brazil, or Trinidad, carnival is one of the most exciting events of the year, involving parades, parties, and dressing up in costume.

Just before Lent many cities hold a time of merrymaking called a carnival. The roots that apparently make up *carnival* mean "flesh" and "remove," and a common result of carnival was the eating up of meat that wouldn't keep through the 40-day season of Lent, a time of fasting and self-discipline when meat was indeed removed from the table. In the Americas, carnival is most famous in Rio de Janeiro and New Orleans (whose version of carnival is called Mardi Gras), but carnival takes place in most parts of the world where Lent is observed.

incarnation \ˌin-kär-'nā-shən\ (1) A particular physical form or version of something. (2) A person showing a trait to a marked degree.

● During the Gulf War, press reports depicted Saddam Hussein as the incarnation of evil.

Incarnation originally referred to gods and deities taking on fleshly form, but now it more commonly refers to anything in the physical world that clearly illustrates some principle. The crowded streets of Hong Kong are said to be the incarnation of business and commerce. Sometimes *incarnation* can simply mean "a version" or "a form or state." An old building, for instance, can pass through several incarnations—as first an inn, then a private home, and then a store—before being returned to its original purpose.

Quizzes

A. Indicate whether the following pairs have the same or different meanings:

1. carnage / slaughter   same ___ / different ___
2. omnivorous / grazing   same ___ / different ___
3. incarnation / burial   same ___ / different ___
4. voracious / extremely hungry   same ___ / different ___
5. carnal / spiritual   same ___ / different ___
6. herbivorous / vegetarian   same ___ / different ___
7. carnival / Lent   same ___ / different ___
8. carnivorous / meat-eating   same ___ / different ___

B. Fill in each blank with the correct letter:

a. incarnation   e. voracious
b. omnivorous   f. herbivorous
c. carnage   g. carnal
d. carnivorous   h. carnival

1. Sheep, cattle, and antelope are ___; unlike dogs and cats, they show no interest in meat.
2. The school tried to shield students from ___ temptations.
3. It took an hour and several full picnic baskets to satisfy the bear's ___ appetite.

4. My sister and I rode the Ferris wheel every night the _____ was in town.
5. From the variety of books on his shelves, we could tell he was an _____ reader.
6. Even the ambulance drivers were horrified by the _____ of the accident.
7. As a child she loved to watch them throw meat to the _____ ones, especially the lions and tigers.
8. In Greek mythology the _____ of Zeus could be in the form of a bull or a swan or golden rain as well as a human.

CRED comes from *credere,* the Latin verb meaning "to believe." If something is *credible* it is believable, and if it is *incredible* it is almost unbelievable. We have a good *credit* rating when institutions believe in our ability to repay a loan, and we carry *credentials* so that others will believe we are who we say we are.

credence \'krē-dəns\ Mental acceptance of something as true or real; belief.

• He scoffed and said that no one still gives any credence to the story of the Loch Ness monster.

Credence is close in meaning to *belief,* but there are differences. Unlike *belief, credence* is seldom used in connection with faith in a religion or philosophy. Instead *credence* is often used in reference to reports, rumors, and opinions. Claims that a political candidate can become the next President gain credence only after the candidate wins a few primaries. Stories about Elvis sightings persist, but they lack credence for most people.

creditable \'kre-di-tə-bəl\ Worthy of praise.

• Even though the young team did not win the tournament, they turned in a creditable performance in the playoffs.

A creditable performance is one that makes us believe in the worth or value of the performer. A creditable effort, a creditable first novel, or a creditable new restaurant are all worthy of praise. Don't let the similarity in spelling fool you: *creditable* does not mean the same thing as *credible*.

credulity \kri-'dü-lə-tē\ Readiness and willingness to believe on the basis of little evidence.

• Thrillers and action movies only succeed if they don't strain our credulity too much.

Credulity most often appears in the phrase "to strain credulity," but a particularly far-fetched story may also be said to stretch credulity or to put demands on or make claims on our credulity. Credulity is not always a bad thing. There is no limit to the credulity of Boston and Chicago baseball fans, for example, and that probably makes life bearable for them. The related adjective is *credulous*. F. Scott Fitzgerald once defined advertising as "making dubious promises to a credulous public"—that is, a naive or gullible public.

creed \'krēd\ (1) A statement of the basic beliefs of a religious faith. (2) A set of guiding principles or beliefs.

• She had made her money on Wall Street by following the simple creed: Buy low, sell high.

We get the word *creed* from the Latin *credo*, "I believe," which is the first word of many religious creeds, such as the Apostles' Creed and the Nicene Creed. *Creed* can refer both to the statement of beliefs of a religion and to the religion itself; hence our common phrase "regardless of race, creed, or color." It can also be applied to any guiding principles. Reducing the size of company workforces—making companies "lean and mean"—has become the central creed for many corporate executives.

FID comes from *fides*, the Latin word for faith. *Fidelity* is another word for "faithfulness." *Confidence* is having faith in someone or something. And an *infidel* is someone who lacks a particular kind of religious faith.

---

affidavit \ˌa-fə-'dā-vət\ A sworn statement made in writing.

• Each member of the family had signed an affidavit stating that he or she believed the will to be valid.

In Latin *affidavit* means "he or she has sworn an oath," and affidavits are always sworn written documents. During the McCarthy era in the 1950s, many people were forced to make affidavits in which they swore that they were not members of the Communist party. Affidavits are usually made without an opposing lawyer being present. When police officers file an affidavit to get a search warrant, they don't inform anyone except the judge of their intent. In this respect, affidavits are different from depositions, which are made with attorneys for both parties present and able to ask questions.

diffident \'di-fə-dənt\ (1) Lacking confidence; timid. (2) Cautious or unassertive.

• The teacher tried to encourage even the most diffident students to make a try at public speaking.

Diffident means lacking faith in oneself. It often refers to a distrust in one's abilities or opinions that leads to hesitation in acting or speaking. For example, many patients feel diffident around their doctors and don't dare ask them many questions. A helpful friend tries to instill confidence in place of *diffidence*.

fiduciary \fi-'dü-shē-ˌer-ē\ (1) Having to do with a confidence or trust. (2) Held in trust for another.

• Managers of pension funds have a fiduciary responsibility to invest funds for the sole and exclusive benefit of those who will receive the pensions.

A fiduciary relationship is one in which one person places faith in another. Stockbrokers and real-estate agents have fiduciary duties to their clients, which means that they must act in the clients' best financial interests. Similarly, members of a company's board of directors have a fiduciary responsibility to protect the financial interests of shareholders. There are legal requirements for those with fiduciary responsibility, and they can be sued for breach of fiduciary duty if they fail in their responsibilities.

perfidy \'pər-fə-dē\ Faithlessness, disloyalty, or treachery.

• While working for the CIA he became a double agent for another country, and it seems he paid a high price for his perfidy.

The Latin phrase *per fidem decipere,* meaning "to betray the trust of," may have been the original source of *perfidus,* from which *perfidy* comes. The most famously *perfidious* figure in U.S. history is probably Benedict Arnold, the American army officer in the Revolutionary War who plotted with the British to surrender West Point to them—an act that made his name an epithet for traitor.

Quizzes

A. Fill in each blank with the correct letter:

a.	perfidy	e.	creed
b.	creditable	f.	affidavit
c.	diffident	g.	fiduciary
d.	credulity	h.	credence

1. She gave little _____ to his story about his deranged girlfriend and the kitchen knife.
2. This is a _____ piece of work, one of the best reports I've received this year.
3. For her own best friend to take up with her former husband was _____ that could never be forgiven.
4. He's so _____ that you'd never believe he gives talks in front of international organizations.
5. The family trust had been so badly mismanaged that it appeared there had been a violation of _____ responsibility.
6. Their longtime _____ had been one of respect for the environment and all animal life.
7. The _____ stated that no oral agreement had ever been made.
8. Her _____ is enormous; no story in the supermarket tabloids is too far-fetched for her.

B. Match the definition on the left to the correct word on the right:

1. bad faith   a. perfidy
2. timid   b. creditable
3. acceptance   c. diffident

4.	trust-based	d.	credulity
5.	sworn document	e.	creed
6.	well-done	f.	affidavit
7.	principles	g.	fiduciary
8.	trustfulness	h.	credence

CURR/CURS comes from *currere*, the Latin verb meaning "to run." Although the sense of speed may be lacking from words based on this root, the sense of movement remains. *Current*, for instance, refers to running water in a stream or river. And an *excursion* is a trip from one place to another.

concurrent \kən-'kər-ənt\ Happening or operating at the same time.

● The convicted killer was sentenced to serve three concurrent life terms in prison.

Things that are concurrent usually not only happen at the same time but also are similar to each other. So, for example, multitasking computers are capable of performing concurrent tasks. When we take more than one medication at a time, we run the risks involved with concurrent drug use. And most movie theaters today run several movies concurrently.

cursory \'kər-sə-rē\ Hastily and often carelessly done.

● Having spent the weekend going to parties, she was only able to give the chapter a cursory reading before class on Monday.

Unlike the other words in this section, *cursory* always implies speed but also stresses a lack of attention to detail. When citizens complain about a cursory police investigation of a crime, they are distressed by its lack of thoroughness, not its speed. Cursory observations are made quickly, but more importantly they are probably shallow or superficial.

discursive \dis-'kər-siv\ Passing from one topic to another.

● Some days he allowed himself to write long discursive essays in his diary instead of his usual simple reporting of the day's events.

The Latin verb *discurrere* meant "to run about," and from this word we get our word *discursive*, which often means rambling about over a wide range of topics. A discursive writing style is generally not encouraged by writing teachers. But some of the great writers of the 19th century, such as Charles Lamb and Thomas de Quincey, have shown that the discursive essay, especially when gracefully written and somewhat personal in tone, can be a pleasure to read.

precursor \\'prē-ˌkər-sər\\ One that goes before and indicates the coming of another.

• Scientists are trying to identify special geological activity that may be a precursor to an earthquake, which will help them predict the quake's size, time, and location.

A precursor is literally a "forerunner," but the two words function a little differently. A forerunner may simply come before another thing, but a precursor generally paves the way for something. The Office of Strategic Services in World War II was the precursor of today's Central Intelligence Agency. The blues music of the 1930s and 1940s was a precursor to the rock and roll of today. The war in Bosnia could be a precursor to more armed conflict in Eastern Europe and the former Soviet Union.

PED comes from the Latin *ped-*, the stem of *pes*, meaning "foot," which is related to the Greek *pod-* and *pous*, with the same meaning. From *ped-* we get *pedicure*, "care of the feet, toes, and toenails." From *pod-* we get *podiatrist*, "a foot doctor."

---

expedient \\ik-'spē-dē-ənt\\ Suitable for bringing about a desired result, often without regard for what is fair or right.

• Reporters suggested that it would be politically expedient to nominate a vice-presidential candidate from a state with a large number of electoral votes.

Expedient comes from the Latin verb *expedire*, meaning "to prepare" or "to be useful"—perhaps because the best way to prepare for something is to get your feet moving. *Expedient* can simply mean "desirable" or "advantageous." For instance, it is often more expedient to take the train to New York than to drive and try to find a parking place. However, *expedient* often indicates placing self-interest ahead of moral concerns. As a company faces more and more lawsuits over its defective products, for example, it may realize that the expedient solution is to declare bankruptcy.

expedite \'ek-spə-ˌdīt\ To speed up the process or progress of.

● The sales department was looking for ways to expedite the shipping and billing of incoming orders.

Expedite comes from the same Latin verb as *expedient*, but *expedite* usually indicates only speed or efficiency and doesn't involve moral issues at all. Many people concerned about health-care issues, for example, have campaigned to get the FDA to expedite its approval of new drugs. And new kinds of educational software are expected to expedite the learning process.

impediment \im-'pe-də-mənt\ Something that interferes with movement or progress.

● Her poorly developed verbal ability was the most serious impediment to her advancement.

Impediment comes from a Latin verb that meant "to interfere with" or "to get in the way of progress"—perhaps by catching one's feet. In English, *impediment* still suggests an obstruction or obstacle along a path; for example, a lack of adequate roads and bridges is an impediment to economic development. Impediments usually get in the way of something we want. We speak of an impediment to communication, marriage, or progress, but something that slows the progress of aging, disease, or decay isn't usually called an impediment.

pedestrian \pə-'des-trē-ən\ Commonplace, ordinary, or un-imaginative.

● While politicians endlessly discussed the great issues facing Russia, the Russians worried about such pedestrian concerns as finding enough food, shelter, and clothing.

A *pedestrian* is, of course, someone who travels on foot. But the sense of this word as defined above is actually its original meaning. To be pedestrian was to be drab or dull, as if plodding along on foot rather than speeding on horseback or by coach. *Pedestrian* is often used to describe a writing style that is colorless or lifeless, but it can also describe politicians, public tastes, and personal qualities and possessions. In comparison with the elaborate stage shows put on by today's rock artists, for instance, most of the stage antics of the rock stars of the 1960s seem pedestrian.

Quizzes

A. Fill in each blank with the correct letter:

a. concurrent   e. cursory
b. expedite   f. impediment
c. precursor   g. discursive
d. pedestrian   h. expedient

1. The warm days in March were a ＿＿ to spring floods that were sure to come.
2. They hoped the new computer system would ＿＿ the delivery of supplies.
3. After only a ＿＿ look at the new car, he knew he had to have it.
4. The presence of her little sister was a definite ＿＿ to her romantic plans for the evening.
5. She came to enjoy the ＿＿ style of the older, rambling essays.
6. Putting the blame on others for her mistakes was the ＿＿ solution, but it enraged her coworkers.
7. Convention-goers had to decide which of the ＿＿ meetings to attend.
8. His sister's trips to Borneo made his vacations at the seashore seem ＿＿.

B. Match the definition on the left to the correct word on the right:

1. simultaneous   a. impediment
2. obstacle   b. precursor
3. hasty   c. expedient
4. forerunner   d. discursive
5. convenient   e. pedestrian

6.	speed up	f.	expedite
7.	rambling	g.	cursory
8.	ordinary	h.	concurrent

FLECT/FLEX comes from *flectere,* the Latin verb meaning "to bend." Things that are *flexible* can be bent. When light is *reflected,* it is bent and bounces back to us.

---

deflect \di-'flekt\ To turn aside, especially from a straight or fixed course.

• The stealth technology used on some of our bombers and fighter planes works by deflecting radar energy.

The physical meaning of *deflect* is frequently used. Thus, residents along rivers will build levees to deflect flood waters away from their homes, and workers wear eye shields to deflect tiny particles flying out of machines. But the nonphysical meaning is also common. Politicians make highly publicized trips to deflect attention from scandals or a terrible economy. Celebrities make a show of giving to charity to deflect resentment over the amount of money they make. And we all have tried to change the subject to deflect questions we really didn't want to answer.

flexor \'flek-ˌsȯr\ A muscle that bends a part of the body, such as an arm or a leg.

• Her fitness instructor told her she could improve her posture by strengthening her hip flexors.

Flexors are any muscles that act to bend a part of the body, from neck to baby toe and all the *flexible* parts in between. Each flexor is paired with an *extensor* that acts to straighten the part after it is bent. Though you'll encounter *flexor* in reading about health and fitness, it is mostly a technical term. For instance, the names for the flexors that move the little toe (it takes three) are *flexor digiti minimi brevis, flexor digitorum brevis,* and *flexor digitorum longus.*

genuflect \'jen-yu̇-ˌflekt\ To kneel on one knee and then rise as an act of respect.

● Pilgrims in China not only genuflect before religious shrines but also may lay themselves flat on the ground and light incense as well.

Genuflection, which contains the root *genu-,* "knee," has long been a mark of respect and obedience. King Arthur's Knights of the Round Table genuflected not only when he knighted them but whenever they greeted him formally. This custom remains in countries today that are still ruled by royalty, and in some churches each worshiper is expected to genuflect whenever entering or leaving a pew on the central aisle. By genuflecting you show loyalty to a human or god and admit your duty to obey his or her orders.

inflection \in-'flek-shən\ A change in the pitch, tone, or loudness of the voice.

● She couldn't understand her grandfather's words, but she knew from his inflection that he was asking a question.

Changing the pitch, tone, or loudness of our words are ways we communicate meaning in speech, though not on the printed page. A rising inflection on the last syllable of a sentence generally indicates a question and a falling inflection indicates a statement, for example. Another way of *inflecting* words is by adding endings. We add *-s* to make nouns plural and *-ed* to put verbs in the past tense, and these changes are also referred to as inflections.

POST comes from a Latin word meaning "after" or "behind." A *postscript* is a note that comes after an otherwise completed letter, usually as an afterthought. *Postpartum* refers to the period following childbirth and all of its related events and complications. To *postdate* a check is to give it a date after the day when it was written.

---

posterior \pō-'stir-ē-ər\ Situated toward or on the back; rear.

● One of the goals of his fitness program was to reduce the dimensions of the posterior parts of his anatomy.

Posterior comes from the Latin word *posterus,* meaning "coming after." *Posterior* is often used as a technical term in biology and medicine to refer to the back side of things. It is the opposite of

anterior, which refers to the front side. For example, as more people took up running as a sport, doctors began to see an increase in
stress fractures along the posterior as well as the anterior surface
of the lower leg bones. When used as a noun, *posterior* simply
means "buttocks."

posthumous \'päs-chə-məs\ (1) Published after the death of the
author. (2) Following or happening after one's death.

● Vincent Van Gogh's rise to posthumous fame as one of the
world's great artists came despite the fact that he scarcely sold a
single painting during his lifetime.

Posthumous fame is fame that comes a little late, since the meaning
of *posthumous* in Latin is "late born." In fact, its original meaning
in English is "born after the death of the father." Bill Clinton is
the posthumous son of a father who died in an automobile accident.
The word is now mostly used of artistic works that appear after the
death of the artist. From the poetry of Emily Dickinson to the diary
of Anne Frank, posthumous works have often become legendary.

postmodern \ˌpōst-'mä-dərn\ Having to do with a movement in
art, architecture, or literature that is a reaction against modernism
and that calls for the reintroduction of traditional elements and
techniques as well as elements from popular culture.

● The postmodern AT&T building in New York, with its
"Chippendale" top that makes it look a little like an antique
dresser, aroused a storm of criticism.

Although *postmodern* literally translates as "after modern" and
would therefore seem likely to mean "ultramodern," it usually
really means "antimodern." In the 1970s architects began to be
dissatisfied with the stark simplicity of most modern architecture
and began to include in their designs traditional elements such as
columns, arches, and keystones, and also startling color contrasts
such as might have come from advertising and pop culture. Similar
developments took place in literature, and there too the movement
has been greeted with a mixture of approval, disapproval, and
sometimes amusement.

postmortem \ˌpōst-'mȯr-təm\ (1) Occurring after death. (2) Following the event.

● In their postmortem discussion of the election, the reporters tried to explain how the polls and predictions could have been so completely wrong.

Post mortem is Latin for "after death." In English, *postmortem* refers to an examination, investigation, or process that takes place after death. Postmortem examinations of bodies are often needed to determine the time and cause of death; rigor mortis, the temporary stiffening of muscles after death, is one postmortem change that doctors look at to determine time of death. We have come to use *postmortem* to refer to any examination or discussion that takes place after an event.

Quizzes

A. Choose the closest definition:

1. posthumous   a. before the event b. born prematurely
       c. occurring after death d. early in development
2. flexor   a. radar detector b. muscle c. sunscreen d. bone
3. posterior   a. on the front b. on the back
       c. underneath d. on top
4. deflect   a. fold over b. kneel c. turn aside d. protect
5. postmodern   a. ultramodern b. traditional
       c. contemporary d. using past styles
6. inflection   a. style in art b. change in pitch
       c. muscle d. part to the rear
7. genuflect   a. kneel b. flex a muscle c. fold back
       d. change one's tone of voice
8. postmortem   a. after the event b. before the event
       c. caused by the event d. causing the event

B. Complete the analogy:

1. postscript : letter :: postmortem : _____
       a. examination b. death c. body d. morgue
2. flexor : extensor :: bend : _____
       a. fold b. twist c. straighten d. break
3. prenatal : before birth :: posthumous : _____
       a. after birth b. before life c. after death d. famous
4. deflect : shield :: reflect : _____
       a. shield b. laser c. metal d. mirror

5. inflection : tone of voice :: hue : _____
    a. cry b. color c. tone d. rainbow
6. genuflect : obedience :: wave : _____
    a. friendship b. respect c. awe d. power
7. inferior : better :: posterior : _____
    a. in front b. behind c. beside d. above
8. abstract : painting :: postmodern : _____
    a. tradition b. design c. style d. architecture

Words from Mythology

calypso \kə-'lip-sō\ A folk song or style of singing of West Indian origin that has a lively rhythm and words that are often made up by the singer.

● If you take a Caribbean vacation in December you end up listening to a lot of Christmas carols played to a calypso beat.

In Homer's *Odyssey*, the nymph Calypso detains Odysseus for seven years on his way home from the Trojan War. She uses all her wiles to hold him on her lush, hidden island, but he still longs for home. The calypso music of the West Indian islands has the same captivating, bewitching power as the nymph. The lyrics that are often improvised to the melodies, however, often make fun of local people and happenings. Calypso may not have been the original name for this music; it may instead have simply replaced a similar-sounding native Caribbean word.

odyssey \'ä-də-sē\ (1) A long, wandering journey full of trials and adventures. (2) A spiritual journey or quest.

● Their six-month camping trip around the country was an odyssey they would always remember.

Odysseus, the hero of Homer's *Odyssey*, spends 20 years traveling home from the Trojan War. He has astonishing adventures and learns a great deal about himself and the world; he even descends to the underworld to talk to the dead. Thus, an odyssey is any long, complicated journey, often a quest for a goal, and may be a spiritual or psychological journey as well as an actual voyage.

palladium \pə-'lä-dē-əm\ A precious, silver-white metal related to platinum that is used in electrical contacts and as an alloy with gold to form white gold.

● Most wedding rings today are simple bands of gold, platinum, or palladium.

Pallas Athena was one of the poetical names given to the Greek goddess Athena, although it is no longer clear what *Pallas* was supposed to mean. When an asteroid belt was discovered between Mars and Jupiter, most of the asteroids were named after figures in Greek mythology, and one of the first to be discovered was named Pallas, in 1803. In the same year, scientists first isolated the element palladium, and they named the new element in honor of the recently discovered asteroid.

Penelope \pə-'ne-lə-pē\ A modest domestic wife.

● Critics of Hillary Rodham Clinton would perhaps have preferred her to be a Penelope, quietly keeping house and staying out of politics.

In the *Odyssey,* Penelope waits 20 long years for her husband Odysseus to return from Troy. During that time, she must raise their son and fend off the attentions of numerous rough suitors. She preserves herself for a long time by saying that she cannot remarry until she has finished weaving a funeral shroud for her aging father-in-law; however, what she weaves each day she secretly unravels each night. A Penelope, thus, appears to be the perfect, patient, faithful wife, and she uses her clever intelligence to keep herself that way.

procrustean \prō-'krəs-tē-ən\ Ruthlessly disregarding individual differences or special circumstances.

● The school's procrustean approach to education seemed to assume that all children learned in the same way and at the same rate.

Procrustes was a bandit in the Greek tale of the hero Theseus. He ambushed travelers and, after robbing them, made them lie on an iron bed. He would make sure they fit this procrustean bed by cutting off the parts that hung off the ends or stretching those that were too short. Either way, they died. Something procrustean, therefore, takes no account of individual differences but cruelly and mercilessly makes everything the same.

protean \'prō-tē-ən\ (1) Displaying great versatility or variety. (2) Able to take on many different forms or natures.

● He was attempting to become the protean athlete, with contracts to play professional baseball, football, and basketball.

Proteus was the figure in the *Odyssey* who revealed to Menelaus how to get home to Sparta with the notorious Helen of Troy. Before he would give up the information, though, Menelaus had to capture him—no mean feat, since he had the ability to change into any natural shape he chose. The word *protean* came to describe this ability to change into many different shapes or to play many different roles in quick succession.

sibyl \'si-bəl\ A female prophet or fortune-teller.

● Her mother treated her as if she were the family sibyl, able to predict what fate was about to befall her sisters.

The sibyls were ancient prophetesses who lived in Babylonia, Greece, Italy, and Egypt. The most famous was the Sibyl of Cumae in Italy, a withered crone who lived in a cave. Her prophecies were collected into twelve books, three of which survived to be consulted by the Romans in times of national emergencies. Whether or not she was the first sibyl, her name or title became the term for all such prophets.

siren \'sī-rən\ A woman who tempts men with bewitching sweetness.

● Reporters treated her like a sex symbol, but she lacked the graceful presence and air of mystery of a real siren.

The sirens were a group of partly human female creatures in Greek mythology that lured sailors onto destructive rocks with their singing. Odysseus and his men encountered the sirens after leaving Troy. The only way to sail by them safely was to make oneself deaf to their enchanting song, so Odysseus packed the men's ears with wax. But he himself, ever curious, wanted to hear, so he had himself tied to the mast to keep from flinging himself into the water or steering his ship toward sure destruction. A siren today is almost always a woman, though she need not sing or cause shipwrecks. But a *siren song* may be any appeal that lures a person to act against his or her better judgment.

Quiz

Fill in each blank with the correct letter:

a. odyssey
e. sibyl
b. calypso
f. procrustean
c. Penelope
g. siren
d. palladium
h. protean

1. They danced and sang to the rhythm of the ____ music long into the night.
2. While he was away on maneuvers, his wife stayed loyally at home like a true ____.
3. He took a ____ attitude toward the needs of his employees, enforcing a single set of work rules for everyone.
4. On their four-month ____ they visited most of the major cities of Asia.
5. The wedding rings were white gold, a mixture of gold and ____.
6. She won her reputation as the office ____ after her third successful prediction of who would get married next.
7. Actors like Robin Williams seem ____ in their ability to assume different characters.
8. In her fatigued state, sleep's ____ song lured her from her duties.

Review Quizzes

A. Choose the closest definition:

1. carnival   a. festival b. feast c. funeral d. frenzy
2. precursor   a. shadow b. forerunner c. follower d. oath
3. diffident   a. angry b. different c. aggressive d. shy
4. pedestrian   a. useless b. footlike c. unusual d. boring
5. credence   a. creation b. belief c. doubt d. destruction
6. creditable   a. believable b. acceptable
      c. praiseworthy d. incredible
7. expedite   a. speed up b. bounce off c. slow down
      d. absorb

8. impediment   a. help b. obstacle c. footpath
   d. obligation
9. voracious   a. vast b. hungry c. fierce
   d. unsatisfied
10. protean   a. meaty b. powerful c. changeable
    d. professional

**B. Indicate whether the following pairs of words have
     the same or different meanings:**

1. procrustean / merciful   same ___ / different ___
2. credulity / distrust   same ___ / different ___
3. concurrent / simultaneous   same ___ / different ___
4. flexor / straightener   same ___ / different ___
5. odyssey / journey   same ___ / different ___
6. deflect / absorb   same ___ / different ___
7. perfidy / betrayal   same ___ / different ___
8. posterior / front   same ___ / different ___
9. siren / temptress   same ___ / different ___
10. herbivorous / plant-eating   same ___ / different ___

C. Complete the analogy:

1. fiduciary : trustworthy :: carnivorous : _____
   a. vegetarian b. meat-eating c. greedy d. hungry
2. cursory : brief :: carnal : _____
   a. musical b. festive c. deadly d. sexual
3. genuflect : kneel :: affidavit : _____
   a. financial affairs b. courtroom testimony c. legal
   advice d. sworn statement
4. sibyl : future :: creed : _____
   a. belief b. music c. attraction d. qualification
5. carnage : death :: Penelope : _____
   a. wife b. mother c. daughter d. siren
6. palladium : metal :: surgeon : _____
   a. farmer b. veterinarian c. doctor d. lawyer
7. expedient : effective :: discursive : _____
   a. fast b. slow-moving c. wide-ranging d. all-knowing
8. procrustean : inflexible :: inflection : _____
   a. way of life b. tone of voice c. financial affairs
   d. part of speech

Unit 5

MAL as a combining form means "bad." *Malpractice* is bad medical practice. A *malady* is a bad condition—a disease or illness—of the body or mind. *Malodorous* things smell bad. And a *malefactor* is someone guilty of bad deeds.

malevolent \mə-'le-və-lənt\ Having or showing intense ill will or hatred.

● Captain Ahab sees Moby Dick not simply as a whale but as a malevolent, evil foe.

Malevolence runs deep. Malevolent enemies have bitter and lasting feelings of ill will. Malevolent racism and bigotry can erupt in acts of violence against innocent people. Malevolence can also show itself in hurtful words, and sometimes it can be seen in something as small as an angry look or gesture.

malicious \mə-'li-shəs\ Desiring to cause pain, injury, or distress to another.

● The boys didn't take the apples with any malicious intent; they were just hungry and didn't know any better.

Malicious and *malevolent* are closely related. Both refer to ill will that shows itself in a desire to see someone else suffer. While *malevolent* suggests deep and lasting dislike, however, *malicious* usually means petty and spiteful. Malicious gossipers may be simply envious of their neighbor's good fortune. Vandals take malicious pleasure in destroying and defacing property.

malign \mə-'līn\ To make harsh and often false or misleading statements about.

• Captain Bligh of the *Bounty* may be one of the most unjustly maligned figures in British naval history.

Malign is related to words like *defame*, *slander*, and *libel*. It implies that the person or group being maligned is the victim of false or misleading statements, but not necessarily that the *maligner* is guilty of deliberate lying. Something that is frequently criticized is often said to be "much maligned," which suggests that the criticism is not entirely fair or deserved.

malnourished \‚mal-'nər-isht\ Badly or poorly nourished.

• When they finally found the children in the locked cabin, they were pale and malnourished but unharmed.

Malnourished people can be found in all types of societies. Famine and poverty are only two of the common causes of *malnutrition*. In more affluent societies, it is often the result of poor eating habits. Any diet that fails to provide the nutrients needed for health and growth can lead to malnutrition, and some of the malnourished are actually fat.

CATA comes from the Greek *kata*, one of whose meanings was "down." A *catalogue* is a list of items put down on paper. A *catapult* is an ancient military weapon for hurling missiles down on one's enemies.

---

cataclysm \'ka-tə-‚kli-zəm\ (1) A violent and massive change of the earth's surface. (2) A momentous event that results in great upheaval and often destruction.

• World War I was a great cataclysm in modern history, marking the end of the old European social and political order.

A cataclysm causes great and lasting changes. An earthquake or other natural disaster that changes the landscape is one kind of cataclysm. We might also speak of the *cataclysmic* changes brought about by a political revolution. Even a new discovery or invention can be seen as cataclysmic if it brings great changes in how people think or work.

catacomb \\'ka-tə-ˌkōm\\ An underground cemetery of connecting passageways with recesses for tombs.

● The early Christian catacombs of Rome provide a striking glimpse into the ancient past for modern-day visitors.

About forty Christian catacombs have been found near the roads that once led into Rome. After the decline of the Roman empire these cemeteries were forgotten, not to be rediscovered until 1578. *Catacomb* has come to refer to different kinds of underground chambers and passageways. The catacombs of Paris are abandoned stone quarries that were not used for burials until 1787.

catalyst \\'ka-tə-list\\ (1) A substance that speeds up a chemical reaction or lets it take place under different conditions. (2) Someone or something that brings about or speeds significant change or action.

● The assassination of Archduke Ferdinand in Sarajevo in 1914 acted as the catalyst for World War I.

Although the Great Depression was a difficult and tragic period in this country, it served as the catalyst for many important social reforms. The Social Security Act of 1935 helped provide security for retired workers; it in turn became the catalyst for a number of laws concerning disabled and unemployed workers, health insurance, on-the-job safety, and dependents of deceased workers. The Depression was also the catalyst of many public-works projects, which were designed to put the unemployed back to work.

catatonic \\ˌka-tə-'tä-nik\\ (1) Relating to or suffering from a form of schizophrenia. (2) Showing an unusual lack of movement, activity, or expression.

● The audience sat in a catatonic stupor while the speaker droned on about the importance of a good vocabulary.

Catatonia is a form of the terrible mental disease known as schizophrenia. A common symptom is extreme muscular rigidity, so that catatonic patients may be "frozen" for hours or even days in a single position. In general use, *catatonic* most often describes people who are not ill but who likewise seem incapable of moving or of changing expression.

Quizzes

A. Choose the closest definition:

1. malevolent   a. wishing evil   b. wishing well   c. blowing violently   d. badly done
2. cataclysm   a. loud applause   b. feline behavior c. natural disaster   d. inspiration
3. malign   a. speak well of   b. speak to   c. speak ill of d. speak of repeatedly
4. catacomb   a. underground road   b. underground cemetery   c. underground spring   d. underground treasure
5. malicious   a. vague   b. explosive   c. confusing   d. mean
6. catatonic   a. refreshing   b. slow   c. motionless   d. boring
7. malnourished   a. fed frequently   b. fed poorly   c. fed excessively   d. fed occasionally
8. catalyst   a. literary agent   b. insurance agent   c. cleaning agent   d. agent of change

B. Indicate whether the following pairs of words have the same or different meanings:

1. catacomb / catastrophe   same ___ / different ___
2. malnourished / overfed   same ___ / different ___
3. cataclysm / disaster   same ___ / different ___
4. malign / slander   same ___ / different ___
5. catatonic / paralyzed   same ___ / different ___
6. catalyst / cemetery   same ___ / different ___
7. malicious / nasty   same ___ / different ___
8. malevolent / pleasant   same ___ / different ___

PROT/PROTO comes from Greek and has the basic meaning "first in time" or "first formed." *Protozoa* are one-celled animals, such as amoebas and paramecia, that are among the most basic members of the biological kingdom. A *proton* is an elementary particle that, along with neutrons, can be found in all atomic nuclei. A *protoplanet* is a whirling mass that is believed to give rise to a planet.

protagonist \prō-'ta-gə-nist\ The main character in a literary work.

● Macbeth is the ruthlessly ambitious protagonist of Shakespeare's play, but it is his wife who pulls the strings.

Struggle, or conflict, is central to drama. The protagonist or hero of a play is involved in a struggle, either against someone or something else or even against his or her own emotions. So the hero is the "first struggler," which is the literal meaning of the Greek word *prōtagōnistēs*. A character who opposes the hero is the *antagonist*, from a Greek verb that means literally "to struggle against."

protocol \'prō-tə-,kȯl\ (1) An original copy or record of a document. (2) A code of diplomatic or military rules of behavior.

● The guests at the governor's dinner were introduced and seated according to the strict protocol governing such occasions.

Protocol comes from a Greek word that refers to the first sheet of a papyrus roll. As an English word, *protocol* originally meant "a first draft or record," after which it came to mean specifically the first draft of a diplomatic document, such as a treaty. The "diplomatic" connection led eventually to its current meaning of "rules of behavior." Someone wearing Bermuda shorts and sandals to a State dinner at the White House would not be acting "according to protocol." *Protocol* is also now used to refer to other kinds of rules, such as those for doing a scientific experiment or for handling computer data.

protoplasm \'prō-tō-,pla-zəm\ The substance that makes up the living parts of cells.

● Protoplasm is a mixture of organic and inorganic substances, such as protein and water, and is regarded as the physical basis of life.

The term *protoplasm* was first used with its present meaning in 1846 by Hugo von Mohl, a German professor of botany. After studying plant cells, he conceived the idea that the nucleus was surrounded by a jellylike material that formed the main substance of the cell. Von Mohl is also remembered for being the first to propose that new cells are formed by cell division.

prototype \\'prō-tō-ˌtīp\\ (1) An original model on which something is patterned. (2) A first, full-scale, usually working version of a new type or design.

• There was great excitement when, after years of top-secret development, the prototype of the new Stealth bomber first took to the skies.

A prototype is someone or something that serves as a model or inspiration. A successful fund-raising campaign can serve as a prototype for future campaigns. The legendary Robin Hood, the *prototypical* kindhearted, honorable outlaw, has been the inspiration for countless other romantic heroes. For over a century Vincent Van Gogh has been the prototype of the brilliant, tortured artist who is unappreciated in his own time.

ANTE is Latin for "before" or "in front of." *Antediluvian*, a word describing something very old or outdated, literally means "before the flood"—that is, the flood described in the Bible. *Antebellum* literally means "before the war," usually the American Civil War. *Antenatal* care is given during the period before birth.

antechamber \\'an-ti-ˌchăm-bər\\ An outer room that leads to another and is often used as a waiting room.

• The antechamber to the lawyer's office was both elegant and comfortable, designed to inspire trust and confidence.

Antechamber suggests a room somewhat more formal than an *anteroom*. One expects to find an antechamber outside the private chambers of a Supreme Court Justice or leading into the great hall of a medieval castle. In the private end of the castle the lord's or lady's bedchamber would have its own antechamber, which served as a dressing room and sitting room, but could also house bodyguards if the castle came under siege.

antedate \\'an-ti-ˌdāt\\ (1) To date something (such as a check) with a date earlier than that of actual writing. (2) To precede in time.

• Nantucket Island has hundreds of beautifully preserved houses that antedate the Civil War.

Antedate is used when talking about things that can be given dates. Dinosaurs antedated the first human beings by about 65 million years, though this stubborn fact has never stopped cartoonists and moviemakers from having the two species inhabit the same story line. The oral use of a word often antedates its appearance in print by a number of years.

ante meridiem \,an-ti-mə-'ri-dē-,em\ Before noon.

• On great ancient sundials the shadow crossed the central line at noon, dramatically marking the shift from ante meridiem to post meridiem.

Ante meridiem is almost always abbreviated as *a.m.* The term is spelled out only in the most formal contexts, such as laws and statutes. There is controversy about the use of *a.m.* and its counterpart *p.m.*, for *post meridiem,* when referring to twelve o'clock. Some people have argued that *12:00 a.m.* means midnight and *12:00 p.m.* means noon; others have insisted the opposite. There has never been any general agreement. If you want to avoid confusion, use *noon* or *midnight,* either alone or preceded by *12:00.*

anterior \an-'tir-ē-ər\ (1) Located before or toward the front or head. (2) Coming before in time or development.

• She joined the first-class passengers in the plane's anterior section and was delighted to recognize the governor in the next seat.

Anterior tends to appear in either technical or learned contexts. Anatomy books refer to the anterior lobe of the brain, the anterior cerebral artery, the anterior facial vein, etc. When used to refer to an earlier position in time or order, *anterior* is a somewhat formal word. Supporters of states' rights point out that the states enjoyed certain rights anterior to their joining the union. Prenuptial agreements are generally designed to protect the assets that one or both parties acquired anterior to the marriage.

Quizzes

A. Fill in each blank with the correct letter:

a.	antedate	e.	prototype
b.	protoplasm	f.	ante meridiem
c.	anterior	g.	protocol
d.	protagonist	h.	antechamber

1. The ____ of *The Wizard of Oz* is a Kansas farm girl named Dorothy.
2. According to official ____, the Ambassador from England precedes the Canadian Consul.
3. A butterfly's antennae are located on the most ____ part of its body.
4. There under the microscope we saw the cell's ____ in all its amazing complexity.
5. She was tempted to ____ the letter to make it seem that she had not forgotten to write it but only to mail it.
6. The engineers have promised to have the ____ of the new sedan finished by March.
7. Please step into the judge's ____; she'll be with you in a few minutes.
8. In Rome there were six "hours" ____ (that is, "before midday"), but the hours were shorter in winter than in summer.

B. Match the definition on the left to the correct word on the right:

1. to date before
2. cell contents
3. morning
4. rules of behavior
5. toward the front
6. model
7. waiting room
8. hero or heroine

a. protocol
b. antechamber
c. protagonist
d. ante meridiem
e. protoplasm
f. antedate
g. prototype
h. anterior

ORTH/ORTHO comes from *orthos*, the Greek word for "straight," "right," or "true." *Orthotics* is a branch of therapy that straightens out the stance or posture of the body by providing artificial support for weak joints or muscles. *Orthograde* animals, such as human beings, walk with their bodies in a "straight" or vertical position.

orthodontics \ˌȯr-thə-'dän-tiks\ A branch of dentistry that deals with the treatment and correction of crooked teeth and other irregularities.

• As much as she dreaded braces, Jennifer decided the time had come to consult a specialist in orthodontics.

Orthodontics of some kind has been practiced since ancient times, but the elaborate techniques and appliances familiar to us today were introduced only in the 20th century. Training to become an *orthodontist* usually consists of a two-year course following dental school. According to a 1939 text on dentistry, "Speech defects, psychiatric disturbances, personality changes, . . . all are correctable through *orthodontic* measures." Many adolescents, having endured the embarrassment of rubber bands breaking and even of entangling their braces while kissing, might disagree.

orthodox \'ȯr-thə-ˌdäks\ (1) Holding established beliefs, especially in religion. (2) Conforming to established rules or traditions; conventional.

• The O'Briens remain orthodox Catholics, faithfully observing the time-honored rituals of their church.

An orthodox religious belief or interpretation is one handed down by the founders or leaders of a church. When capitalized, as in *Orthodox Judaism*, *Orthodox* refers to branches within larger religious organizations that claim to honor the religion's original or traditional beliefs. The steadfast holding of established beliefs that is seen in religious *orthodoxy* is apparent also in other kinds of orthodox behavior. Orthodox medical treatment, for example, follows the established practices of mainstream medicine.

orthopedics \ˌȯr-thə-'pē-diks\ The correction or prevention of deformities of the skeleton.

• The surgery to correct the child's spinal curvature was done by a leading specialist in orthopedics.

Just as an orthodontist corrects crookedness in the teeth, so does an *orthopedist* correct crookedness in the skeleton. The word *orthopedics* is formed in part from the Greek word for "child," and many *orthopedic* patients are in fact children. But adults also often have need for orthopedic therapy, as when suffering from a disease

of the joints like arthritis or when recovering from a broken arm
or leg.

orthography \or-'thä-grə-fē\ (1) The spelling of words according
to standard usage. (2) The part of language study concerned with
letters and spelling.

• George Washington and Thomas Jefferson—and at least one
recent vice president—were deficient in the skill of orthography.

Even as recently as the 19th century, the orthography of the English
language was still unsettled. Not until primers like "McGuffey's
Readers" and dictionaries like Noah Webster's came along did
uniform spelling become established. Before that, there was much
orthographic variation, even among the more educated. Many people, of course, still have problems with spelling. They can take
heart from the words of Mark Twain, who once remarked, "I don't
give a damn for a man that can spell a word only one way."

RECT comes from the Latin word *rectus,* which means
"straight" or "right." A *rectangle* is a four-sided figure whose
parallel, straight sides meet at right angles. *Rectus,* short for Latin
rectus musculus, may refer to any of several straight muscles, such
as those of the abdomen. To *correct* something is to make it right.

---

rectitude \'rek-tə-,tüd\ (1) Moral integrity. (2) Correctness of
procedure.

• The school superintendent wasn't popular, but no one could
question her moral rectitude.

We associate straightness with honesty, so if we think someone is
being misleading we might ask if they are being "straight" with
us. A person whose rectitude is unquestionable is a person whose
straightness, or honesty, is always apparent in his or her dealings
with other people. Such a person might be called *rectitudinous,*
although this uncommon adjective can also suggest an undesirable
quality of self-righteousness.

rectify \'rek-tə-,fī\ (1) To set right; remedy. (2) To correct by
removing errors; revise.

• You must try to rectify this unfortunate situation before anyone
else gets hurt.

We rectify something by straightening it out or making it right. We might rectify an injustice by seeing to it that a wrongly accused person is cleared. An error in a financial record can be rectified by replacing an incorrect number with a correct one. If the error is in our tax return, the Internal Revenue Service will be happy to rectify it for us. We might then have to rectify the impression that we were trying to cheat on our taxes.

rectilinear \,rek-tə-'li-nē-ər\ (1) Moving in or forming a straight line. (2) Having many straight lines.

● After admiring Frank Lloyd Wright's highly rectilinear buildings for years, the public was astonished by the giant spiral of the Guggenheim Museum.

Rectilinear is a term used widely in physics. Rectilinear motion is motion in which the speed remains constant and the path is a straight line. Rectilinear rays, such as light rays, travel in a straight line. Rectilinear patterns or constructions are those in which straight lines are strikingly obvious. The trunks of trees in a forest form a strongly rectilinear pattern.

rector \'rek-tər\ (1) A clergyman in charge of a church or parish. (2) The head of a university or school.

● We asked the rector of our church to perform the marriage ceremony.

The fiery American preacher Jonathan Edwards began as rector of a church in Massachusetts. He was so convinced of his own ideas about *rectitude* and so harsh in condemning those who opposed him that he was eventually dismissed and turned out of the parish *rectory* where he lived. He spent his remaining years attempting to *rectify* the beliefs of Native Americans.

Quizzes

A. Choose the closest definition:

1. orthodox   a. straight b. pier c. conventional
     d. waterfowl
2. rectify   a. redo b. make right c. modify d. make longer
3. orthopedics   a. foot surgery b. children's medicine
     c. medical dictionaries d. treatment of skeletal defects

4. rector   a. warden   b. headmaster   c. direction   d. effect
5. orthography   a. correct color   b. correct map   c. correct direction   d. correct spelling
6. rectitude   a. roughness   b. integrity   c. certainty d. sameness
7. orthodontics   a. dentistry for children   b. dentistry for gums   c. dentistry for crooked teeth   d. dentistry for everyone
8. rectilinear   a. moving in a straight line   b. moving in a curved line   c. moving at a 45° angle   d. moving in a circle

B. Indicate whether the following pairs have the same or different meanings:

1. orthodox / crucial   same ___ / different ___
2. rectitude / honesty   same ___ / different ___
3. orthopedics / broken bones   same ___ / different ___
4. rector / follower   same ___ / different ___
5. orthography / architecture   same ___ / different ___
6. rectilinear / straight   same ___ / different ___
7. orthodontics / fixing of crooked teeth   same ___ / different ___
8. rectify / damage   same ___ / different ___

EU comes from the Greek word for "well"; in English words it can also mean "good" or "true." A person delivering a *eulogy* is full of good words, or praise, for the honoree. *Euthanasia* is regarded as a way of providing a hopelessly sick or injured person a "good" or easy death.

eugenic \yù-'je-nik\ (1) Relating to or fitted for the production of good offspring. (2) Relating to the science of improving the desirable traits of a race or breed through controlled breeding.

● Eugenic techniques have been part of cattle breeding for many years.

The word *eugenic* (like the name *Eugene*) was formed from the prefix *eu-* in combination with *-genes*, which in Greek means "born." Breeders of horses, cattle, and other animals hope that by using scientific, eugenic methods they can have better results, producing horses that run faster, for example, or cattle that provide more meat. Through *eugenics,* Guernsey cows have become one of the world's highest producers of milk. Earlier in this century there was much discussion of human eugenics, an idea that was taken up enthusiastically by the Nazis, with terrible consequences.

euphemism \'yü-fə-,mi-zəm\ (1) The use of an agreeable or inoffensive word or expression for one that may offend or disgust. (2) An expression used in this way.

● The Victorians, uncomfortable with the physical side of human existence, had euphemisms for most bodily functions.

Euphemism is an ancient part of the English language. While particular expressions come into and go out of vogue, the need for euphemism remains constant. *Golly* and *gosh* started out as euphemisms for *God,* and *darn* is a familiar euphemism for *damn. Shoot, shucks,* and *sugar* are all *euphemistic* substitutes for a well-known vulgar word. The standard household bathroom fixture has given rise to a host of euphemistic substitutes, including *convenience, head, john, potty, privy,* and *water closet.*

euphoria \yü-'fȯr-ē-ə\ A feeling of well-being or great elation.

● The whole city was swept up in the euphoria of a Super Bowl victory.

Euphoria describes a temporary, almost overpowering feeling of health or elation. In medical use, it normally refers to abnormal or inappropriate feelings, such as might be caused by a drug or by mental illness. But euphoria can also be natural and appropriate. When the home team wins the championship, or when we win enough money in the lottery to buy a fleet of yachts and several small Pacific islands, we have good reason to feel *euphoric.*

evangelism \i-'van-jə-,li-zəm\ (1) The enthusiastic preaching or proclamation of the Christian gospel. (2) Militant or crusading zeal.

● Their evangelism for the new program won many converts among those who had previously doubted its merits.

Evangelism comes from *euangelion,* the Greek word for "gospel" or "good news." The firm belief that they are bringing "good news" has traditionally filled Christian *evangelists* with fiery zeal. *Evangelism* can now refer to crusading zeal in behalf of any cause. The *evangelical* enthusiasm of some environmentalists has won over some segments of the general public while alienating others.

DYS comes from Greek, where it means "bad" or "difficult." As a prefix in English, it has the additional meanings "abnormal" and "impaired." *Dysphagia* is difficult or labored swallowing, and *dyspnea* is difficult or labored breathing. *Dysphasia,* which literally means "impaired speech," refers to a disorder in which the ability to use and understand language is seriously impaired as a result of injury to or disease of the brain.

---

dysfunctional \dis-'fəŋk-shə-nəl\ Operating or functioning in an impaired or abnormal way.

• His sisters constantly claimed that the family was dysfunctional, but he could never see it.

Neurologists speak of dysfunctional brain stems, and psychiatrists treat patients for dysfunctional sexual response. Political scientists wonder if the American two-party system has become dysfunctional, and sociologists point to the rising crime rate as evidence of a dysfunctional society. Nowadays *dysfunctional* more often describes families than anything else. In popular usage, any family with problems is likely to be characterized as dysfunctional.

dyslexia \dis-'lek-sē-ə\ A disturbance or interference with the ability to read or to use language.

• She managed to deal with her dyslexia through careful tutoring all throughout elementary school.

Dyslexia is a neurological disorder that usually affects people of average or superior intelligence. *Dyslexic* individuals have an impaired ability to recognize and process words and letters. Dyslexia usually shows itself in the tendency to read and write words and letters in reversed order. Sometimes similar reversals occur in the person's speech. Dyslexia has been shown to be treatable through lengthy instruction in proper reading techniques.

dyspeptic \dis-'pep-tik\ (1) Relating to or suffering from indigestion. (2) Having an irritable temperament; ill-humored.

● For decades the dyspeptic columnist served as the newspaper's—and the city's—resident grouch.

Dyspepsia comes from the Greek word for "bad digestion." Interestingly, the Greek verb *pessein* can mean either "to cook" or "to digest"; a lot of bad cooking has been responsible for a lot of dyspepsia. Dyspepsia can be caused by many diseases, but often dyspeptic individuals are the victims of their own habits and appetites. Worry, overeating, inadequate chewing, and excessive smoking and drinking can all bring on dyspepsia. Today we generally use *dyspeptic* to mean "irritable"—that is, in the kind of mood that could be produced by bad digestion.

dystrophy \'dis-tra-fē\ Any of several disorders involving nerves and muscles, especially a hereditary disease marked by a progressive wasting of muscles.

● In cases involving the most devastating type of muscular dystrophy, infections or respiratory failure can result in the victim's death before the age of 30.

Dystrophy in its original sense refers to a disorder brought about through faulty nutrition. (The *-trophy* element in *dystrophy* comes from the Greek word for "nutrition.") Today *dystrophy* most often refers to the progressive wasting away of the muscles that is known as *muscular dystrophy*. Actually, there are several types of muscular dystrophy, the most common of which is Duchenne's, which strikes males almost exclusively. Duchenne's muscular dystrophy occurs in about one out of 3,300 male births.

Quizzes

A. Fill in each blank with the correct letter:

a. euphemism	e. dyslexia
b. dystrophy	f. euphoria
c. evangelism	g. dysfunctional
d. dyspeptic	h. eugenic

1. There is many a _____ for the word *death*, and many more for the word *drunk*.

2. Some pop psychologists claim that every family is _____ and impaired in some way.
3. The organization campaigns against drunk driving with remarkable _____.
4. Because his _____ was discovered early, he was able to receive the special reading instruction he needed.
5. The end of the war was marked by widespread _____ and celebration.
6. Ebenezer Scrooge, in *A Christmas Carol*, is a thoroughly _____ character.
7. Though the dog is the product of generations of _____ breeding, she is high-strung and has terrible eyesight.
8. The symptoms of muscular _____ can be relieved through physical therapy, various supportive devices, or surgery.

B. Match the word on the left to the correct definition on the right:

1. dystrophy	a.	impaired
2. euphemism	b.	beset by indigestion
3. dyslexia	c.	muscular deterioration
4. eugenic	d.	crusading zeal
5. dysfunctional	e.	polite term
6. euphoria	f.	reading disorder
7. dyspeptic	g.	promoting superior
8. evangelism		offspring
	h.	great happiness

Latin Borrowings

a fortiori \ˌä-ˌfȯr-tē-ˈȯr-ē\ All the more certainly.

● If drug users are going to be subject to mandatory sentences, then a fortiori drug dealers should be subject to them also.

A fortiori in Latin literally means "from the stronger (argument)." It is used when drawing a conclusion that is even more obvious or convincing than the one just drawn. Thus, if teaching English grammar to native speakers is difficult, then, a fortiori, teaching English grammar to nonnative speakers is even more challenging.

a posteriori \,ä-,pōs-tir-ē-'òr-ē\ Relating to or derived by reasoning from known or observed facts.

● The President had come to the a posteriori conclusion that the booming economy was entirely due to his economic policies.

A posteriori is a term from logic. It is Latin for "from the latter." *A posteriori* usually refers to reasoning that derives causes from effects. This kind of reasoning can sometimes lead to false conclusions. The rising of the sun following the crowing of a rooster, for example, does not mean that the rooster's crowing caused the sun to rise.

a priori \,ä-prē-'òr-ē\ Relating to or derived by reasoning from self-evident propositions.

● Her colleagues rejected Professor Winslow's a priori argument because it rested on assumptions they felt were not necessarily true.

A priori is Latin for "from the former"; it is traditionally contrasted with *a posteriori*. It is usually applied to lines of reasoning or arguments that proceed from the general to the particular or from causes to effects. Whereas a posteriori knowledge is knowledge based solely on experience or personal observation, a priori knowledge is knowledge derived through the power of reasoning. An a priori argument is based on reasoning from what is self-evident; it does not rely on observed facts for its proof.

bona fide \'bō-nə-,fīd\ (1) Made in good faith, without deceit. (2) Authentic or genuine.

● They made a bona fide and sincere offer to buy the property at its fair market value.

Bona fide means "in good faith" in Latin. When applied to business deals and the like, it stresses the absence of fraud or deception. A bona fide sale of securities is an entirely aboveboard transaction. When used of matters outside of the legal or business worlds, *bona fide* implies sincerity and earnestness. A bona fide promise is one that the promisor has every intention of keeping. A bona fide proposal of marriage is one made by a suitor who isn't kidding around.

carpe diem \'kär-pā-'dē-,em\ Enjoy the pleasures or opportunities of the moment without concern about the future.

● He was convinced he would die young, so he told himself "carpe diem" and lived an adventurous life.

Carpe diem comes from Latin, where it literally means "Pluck the day," though it is usually translated as "Seize the day." A free translation might be "Enjoy yourself while you have the chance." Some people make *carpe diem* a kind of slogan for their lives, feeling that life is too short to spend it worrying about the future, and that we should grab the opportunities life gives us because they may not come again.

caveat emptor \'ka-vē-ˌät-'emp-tər\ Let the buyer beware.

● The best rule to keep in mind when buying anything from a pushcart is: "Caveat emptor."

"Without a warranty, the buyer must take the risk" is the basic meaning of the phrase *caveat emptor*. In olden days when buying and selling was carried on in the local marketplace, the rule was a practical one. Buyer and seller knew each other and were on equal footing. The nature of modern commerce and technology placed the buyer at a disadvantage, however, so a stack of regulations have been written by federal, state, and local agencies to protect the consumer against dangerous, defective, and ineffective products, fraudulent practices, and the like.

corpus delicti \'kȯr-pəs-di-'lik-ˌtī\ (1) The substantial and basic fact or facts necessary to prove that a crime has been committed. (2) The material substance, such as the murdered body, on which a crime has been committed.

● The police believed they had solved the crime, but they couldn't prove their case without the corpus delicti.

Corpus delicti literally means "body of the crime" in Latin. In its original sense the "body" in question refers not to a corpse but to the body of essential facts that taken together prove that a crime has been committed. In popular, nontechnical usage, *corpus delicti* also refers to the actual physical object upon which a crime has been committed. In a case of arson, it would be a ruined building.

In a murder case, as every fan of whodunits knows, it would be the victim's body.

curriculum vitae \kə-'ri-kyu̇-ləm-'vē-ˌtī\ A short summary of one's career and qualifications, typically prepared by an applicant for an academic job; résumé.

● The job advertisement asked for an up-to-date curriculum vitae and three recommendations.

Curriculum vitae is a term usually used in academic circles where teaching positions are the issue. The phrase means "the course of one's life," and is often abbreviated *CV*. In other fields, *résumé* is more commonly used.

Quiz

Fill in each blank with the correct letter:

a.	a priori	e.	carpe diem
b.	curriculum vitae	f.	a fortiori
c.	caveat emptor	g.	corpus delicti
d.	a posteriori	h.	bona fide

1. To ensure that all reservations are _____, the cruise line requires a nonrefundable deposit.
2. If these two medium-sized cars won't hold all of us and our luggage, _____ those smaller cars won't even come close.
3. The philosopher published his own _____ proof of the existence of God.
4. When we're afraid to pursue our dreams, we sometimes have to tell ourselves, _____.
5. She sent out a _____ full of impressive educational and professional credentials.
6. All of the elements were available to establish the _____ of the defendant's crime.
7. This art critic takes the _____ position that if Pablo Picasso painted it, it's a masterpiece of modern art.
8. When you go out to buy a used car, the best advice, warranty or no warranty, is still _____.

Review Quizzes

A. Complete the analogy:

1. antagonist : villain :: protagonist : _____
   a. maiden b. wizard c. knight d. hero
2. radical : rebellious :: orthodox : _____
   a. routine b. conventional c. sane d. typical
3. fake : fraudulent :: bona fide : _____
   a. copied b. certain c. authentic d. desirable
4. slang : vulgar :: euphemism : _____
   a. habitual b. polite c. dirty d. dumb
5. identify : name :: rectify : _____
   a. make over b. make new c. make right d. make up
6. superior : inferior :: anterior : _____
   a. before b. beside c. above d. behind
7. warranty : guarantee :: caveat emptor : _____
   a. explanation b. warning c. endorsement d. contract
8. jovial : friendly :: dyspeptic : _____
   a. grumpy b. sleepy c. dopey d. happy
9. hot : cold :: catatonic : _____
   a. active b. petrified c. feline d. tired
10. benevolent : wicked :: malevolent : _____
    a. evil b. silly c. noisy d. kindly

B. Fill in each blank with the correct letter:

a. antechamber	i. curriculum vitae
b. a posteriori	j. catacomb
c. euphoria	k. dystrophy
d. malign	l. eugenic
e. a fortiori	m. malnourished
f. orthography	n. protoplasm
g. prototype	o. orthodontics
h. rector	

1. Before car makers produce a new model, they always build and test a _____.
2. Please include a _____ so that we can evaluate your qualifications for this position.
3. They were shown into an elegant _____ where they awaited their audience with the king.

4. After graduation from dental school, Kyle took a postgraduate course in _____.
5. The philosopher's conclusion was based on _____ reasoning.
6. The jellylike substance in cells is called _____.
7. These abused and _____ children can't be expected to pay attention in class.
8. With some milder types of muscular _____, victims can function well into adulthood.
9. They felt such _____ that they almost wept with joy.
10. Since they earned high honors for achieving a 3.7 average, _____ we should do so for getting a 3.8.
11. Obsessed with _____, the teacher seemed to care not for what his students wrote, only for how it was spelled.
12. It is common for boxers to _____ each other in crude terms before a big match.
13. The _____ of their church gives excellent sermons full of sensible advice.
14. When they went to Rome, they made sure to visit at least one underground _____.
15. _____ experimentation has produced a new breed of sheep with thick, fast-growing wool.

C. **Indicate whether the following pairs have the same or different meanings:**

1. corpus delicti / basic evidence   same ___ / different ___
2. ante meridiem / after noon   same ___ / different ___
3. malicious / mean   same ___ / different ___
4. protocol / rules of behavior   same ___ / different ___
5. a priori / determined later   same ___ / different ___
6. dyslexia / speech patterns   same ___ / different ___
7. cataclysm / religious teachings   same ___ / different ___
8. antedate / occur before   same ___ / different ___
9. orthopedics / shoe repair   same ___ / different ___
10. rectilinear / curvy   same ___ / different ___
11. evangelism / crusading   same ___ / different ___
12. carpe diem / look ahead   same ___ / different ___
13. dysfunctional / damaged   same ___ / different ___
14. catalyst / distributor   same ___ / different ___
15. rectitude / stubbornness   same ___ / different ___

Unit 6

ROG comes from *rogare*, the Latin verb meaning "to ask." The ancient Romans also used this word to mean "to propose," thinking perhaps that when we propose an idea, we are actually asking someone to consider it. So *interrogate* means "to question systematically," and a *surrogate* (for example, a surrogate mother) is a substitute, someone who is proposed to stand in for another.

abrogate \'a-brə-ˌgāt\ (1) To abolish or annul. (2) To ignore or treat as if nonexistent.

● The proposed constitutional amendment would abrogate fundamental rights of citizens that had long been protected by the courts.

The Latin prefix *ab-* sometimes functions like the English prefix *un-*, so if the ancient Romans wanted to "un-propose" something—that is, propose that something no longer be done—the verb they used was *abrogare*, from which we get *abrogate*. Today, members of our Senate might consider abrogating a treaty if serious questions were raised about the way in which it was negotiated. Similarly, a manufacturer faced with large increases in the cost of materials may feel justified in abrogating contracts with its customers. And policies requiring doctors to give out information about their patients are said to abrogate the confidential patient-doctor relationship.

arrogate \'ar-ə-ˌgāt\ To claim or seize without justification.

● With this legislation, Governor Burns insisted, the federal government was trying to arrogate powers previously held by the states.

A project team will probably succeed best if individual members do not try to arrogate decision-making authority to themselves. And many of us are annoyed when television evangelists try to arrogate to themselves the right to decide what kind of faith is acceptable. (Because of their similarity, it is all too easy to confuse *arrogate* with *abrogate*—and with *arrogant,* for that matter. Study them carefully.)

derogatory \di-'rä-gə-ˌtór-ē\ Expressing a low or poor opinion of someone or something.

● The radio talk-show host tried to discredit the politician by making derogatory remarks about his appearance.

Derogatory also comes from the "propose" sense of *rogare.* When Romans wanted to propose that something be taken out of a law, the verb they used was *derogare,* and this word developed the general meaning of "take away from." A derogatory comment is one that takes away because it detracts from a person's reputation or lowers the person in the eyes of others. Derogatory remarks are a specialty of some comedians, though their meanness sometimes detracts from their humor.

prerogative \pri-'rä-gə-tiv\ A special or exclusive right, power, or privilege that sets one apart from others.

● It is the prerogative of governors and presidents to grant reprieves and pardons.

In some meetings in ancient Rome, the person asked to vote first on an issue was called the *praerogativus.* Voting first was considered a privilege, and so the Romans also had the word *praerogativa,* meaning "preference" or "privilege," from which we get our word *prerogative,* meaning a special right that one has because of one's office, rank, or character. So a company's president may have the prerogative to occupy the largest office with the best view. In a less official sense, a successful writer may claim the prerogative to invent new words. Speaking frankly is sometimes thought to be the prerogative of the senior citizen, but it is probably best exercised with caution.

QUIS is derived from the Latin verb *quaerere*, meaning "to seek or obtain." You can see it in our word *acquisitive*, which means "having a strong wish to possess things." The roots *quer*, *quir*, and *ques* are also derived from this word and give us words such as *inquiry*, "a search or request for information," and *question*, "something asked."

inquisition \,in-kwə-'zi-shən\ A questioning or examining that is often harsh or severe.

● The President's choice for the cabinet position turned down the appointment, fearing that the confirmation hearings would turn into an inquisition into her past.

While *inquiry* is a general term and can apply to almost any search for truth, *inquisition* suggests an ongoing search for hidden facts that is thorough and involves long and harsh questioning. Originally *inquisition* had about the same meaning as *inquiry*, but our current use is very much influenced by the Spanish Inquisition, an ongoing trial which began in the Middle Ages and was conducted by church-appointed *inquisitors* who sought out nonbelievers and Jews and sentenced thousands of them to torture and to burning at the stake. Because of this historical connection, the word today almost always means ruthless questioning conducted with complete disregard for human rights.

perquisite \'pər-kwə-zət\ (1) A privilege or profit that is provided in addition to one's base salary. (2) Something claimed as an exclusive possession or right.

● A new car, a big house, and yearly trips to Europe were among the perquisites that made the presidency of Wyndam College such an attractive position.

A perquisite, often referred to simply as a *perk*, is usually something of value to which the holder of a particular job or position is entitled. The President of the United States, for instance, enjoys the perquisites of the use of the White House, Camp David, and Air Force One. Perhaps because perquisites are usually available to only a small number of people, the word sometimes refers to non-job-related privileges that are claimed as exclusive rights. It often is very close in meaning to *prerogative* (see above).

acquisitive \ə-'kwi-zə-tiv\ Eager to acquire; greedy.

• With each year the couple became more madly acquisitive, buying jewelry, a huge yacht, and two country estates.

Many have observed that we live in an acquisitive society, a society devoted to getting and spending, unlike most tribal societies and some older nations. America often makes successfully acquisitive people into heroes; even Ebenezer Scrooge, that model of miserly greed and *acquisitiveness,* was once defended by the White House chief of staff. An acquisitive nation may seek to *acquire* other territories by force. But mental *acquisition* of specialized knowledge or skills—or new vocabulary!—doesn't deprive others of the same information.

requisition \re-kwə-'zi-shən\ A demand or request (such as for supplies) made with proper authority.

• The teachers had grown impatient with having to submit a requisition for even routine classroom supplies.

Requisition is both a noun and a verb. We can speak of sending a requisition to the purchasing department, but we also refer to soldiers *requisitioning* food from civilians. The word has a bureaucratic flavor, but one of Hollywood's bittersweet love stories begins when Omar Sharif, playing a World War II freedom fighter, says to Ingrid Bergman, who is the owner of a stately old yellow Rolls Royce, "I've come to requisition your car."

Quizzes

A. Choose the word that does not belong:

1. derogatory   a. critical b. unflattering c. admiring
     d. scornful
2. inquisition   a. examination b. interrogation
     c. pardon d. inquiry
3. abrogate   a. neglect b. abolish c. steal d. ignore
4. perquisite   a. privilege b. bonus c. salary d. right
5. prerogative   a. right b. persuasion c. power
     d. privilege
6. acquisitive   a. grateful b. grasping c. grabby d. greedy

7. requisition   a. purchase order   b. receipt   c. request
   d. demand
8. arrogate   a. claim   b. seize   c. grab   d. release

B. Fill in each blank with the correct letter:

a.	prerogative	e.	arrogate
b.	requisition	f.	acquisitive
c.	derogatory	g.	abrogate
d.	perquisite	h.	inquisition

1. She decided to _____ her family obligations for one day
   to go to the fair.
2. You couldn't even get a pencil unless you filled out
   a _____.
3. Rodney made _____ remarks about Philip's intelligence
   that insulted and angered him.
4. Jeannette discovered that a _____ to membership in
   Frank's family was the privilege of participating in all
   their quarrels.
5. The mayor tried to _____ to himself sole control of local
   political activity.
6. The whole family was _____ by nature, and there were
   bitter legal battles over the will.
7. His status as newcomer did carry the special _____ of
   being able to ask a lot of questions.
8. Louisa feared an _____ into her background and previous
   involvements.

PLE comes from a Latin word meaning "to fill." It can be seen
in the word *complete*, meaning "possessing all necessary parts."
The *ple* root has a Greek equivalent, *pleth*, seen in the word *pleth-
ora*, which means "multitude or abundance."

---

complement \'käm-plə-mənt\ (1) Something that fills up or
makes perfect; the amount needed to make something complete.
(2) A counterpart.

● In an inventive mind, imagination often serves as a necessary
complement to reason.

A complement fills out or balances something. Salt is the complement of pepper, and the right necktie is a perfect complement to a good suit. *Complement* can also mean "the full quantity, number, or amount." A ship's complement of officers and crew is the whole force necessary for full operation. (Do not confuse with *compliment*, which means an expression of respect or affection.)

deplete \di-'plēt\ To reduce in amount by using up.

● Years of farming on the same small plot of land had left the soil depleted of minerals.

The *de-* prefix often means "do the opposite of," so *deplete* means the opposite of "fill." It can mean merely a lessening in amount; thus, food supplies can be rapidly depleted by hungry teenagers in the house. However, *deplete* usually suggests a reduction that endangers the ability to function. Desertions can deplete an army; layoffs can deplete an office staff; and too much exercise without rest can deplete a body's strength.

implement \'im-plə-,ment\ To take steps to fulfill or put into practice.

● Senators and cabinet members were called in to discuss how to implement the President's new foreign policy.

Implement is usually used in connection with bills that have been passed, proposals that have been accepted, or policies that have been adopted. When companies develop new corporate strategies, they will often hire a new management team to implement the strategy; and when strategies succeed, credit should go to those responsible for both the original idea and its *implementation*.

replete \ri-'plēt\ Fully or abundantly filled or supplied.

● The retired professor's autobiography was a fascinating book, replete with details and anecdotes about academic life in the 1930s.

Replete implies that something is filled to capacity. Most people enjoy autumn weekends in New England, replete with colorful foliage, the smell of wood smoke, and a little chill in the air. Supermarket tabloids are usually replete with more details of stars' lives than anyone has any use for. After a big meal of lobster and all the trimmings, we feel replete and drowsy; better wait till later for any more volleyball.

METR comes to us from Greek by way of Latin; in both languages it refers to "measure." A *thermometer* measures heat; a *perimeter* is the measure around something; and things that are *isometric* are equal in measure.

---

metric \'me-trik\ (1) Relating to or based on the metric system. (2) Relating to or arranged in meter.

● Many Americans are beginning to become accustomed to metric units such as the liter, milligram, and kilometer.

The metric system, used in most of the world to measure distance, weight, and volume, is built in part on a unit length called the *meter*, from which it takes its name. Other metric units are the kilogram (the basic unit of weight) and the liter (the basic unit of volume). *Metric* can also refer to the meter, or rhythm, in songs and poetry, although the word *metrical* is used more often for this meaning. So while the scientists' measurements are usually metric, the poets' are usually metrical.

odometer \ō-'dä-mə-tər\ An instrument used to measure distance traveled.

● Jennifer watched the odometer to see how far she would have to drive to her new job.

Odometer includes the root from the Greek word *hodos*, meaning "road" or "trip." The odometer is what unscrupulous car salesmen illegally tamper with when they want to reduce the mileage a car registers as having traveled. One of life's little pleasures is watching the odometer when all of the numbers change at the same time.

symmetrical \sə-'me-tri-kəl\ (1) Having or exhibiting balanced proportions or the beauty that results from such balance. (2) Corresponding in size, shape, or other qualities on opposite sides of a dividing line or plane or around a center.

● Noting the dents in both front fenders, Robert comforted himself that at least his car was now symmetrical.

A key element in the appeal of most formal gardens is their symmetrical design, and *symmetry* plays a large part in the timeless beauty of Greek temples. Of course, the opposite can also be true. Cindy Crawford was not the first person to discover that a certain lack of symmetry can add interest to the human face.

tachometer \ta-'kä-mə-tər\ A device used to measure speed of rotation.

● Even though one purpose of having a tachometer is to help drivers keep their engine speeds down, most of us occasionally try to see how high we can make the needle go.

A tachometer is literally a "speed-measurer," since the Greek root *tach-* means "speed." This is clear in the name of the *tachyon*, a particle of matter that travels faster than the speed of light. If it exists, it is so fast that it is impossible to see. *Tachycardia* is a medical condition in which the heart races uncontrollably. Since the speed that a tachometer measures is speed of rotation, the numbers it reports are usually revolutions per minute, or rpm's.

Quizzes

A. Match the word on the left to the correct definition on the right:

1.	symmetrical	a.	drain
2.	tachometer	b.	put to use
3.	metric	c.	counterpart
4.	replete	d.	balanced
5.	odometer	e.	distance measurer
6.	deplete	f.	speed measurer
7.	implement	g.	full
8.	complement	h.	relating to a measuring system

B. Choose the closest definition:

1. deplete   a. straighten out   b. draw down   c. fold
   d. abandon
2. replete   a. refold   b. repeat   c. abundantly provided
   d. fully clothed
3. odometer   a. intelligence measurer   b. heart-rate
   measurer   c. height measurer   d. distance measurer

4. tachometer   a. speed measurer b. sharpness measurer
   c. fatigue measurer d. size measurer
5. complement   a. praise b. number required
   c. abundance d. usual dress
6. metric   a. relating to poetic rhythm b. relating to ocean
   depth c. relating to books d. relating to particles of
   matter
7. implement   a. put to death b. put to pasture c. put into
   practice d. put to sleep
8. symmetrical   a. uncomplicated b. measured
   c. unattractive d. balanced

AUD, from the Latin verb *audire,* is the root that has to do with hearing. What is *audible* is hearable, and an *audience* is a group of people that listens, sometimes in an *auditorium.*

auditor \\'ȯ-də-tər\\ A person who formally examines and verifies financial accounts.

● It seems impossible that so many banks could have gotten themselves into so much trouble in the 1980s if their auditors had been doing their jobs.

We don't normally associate auditors with listening—looking and adding up numbers seems more their line of work. But auditors do have to listen to people's explanations, and perhaps that is the historical link. Both Latin and some old forms of French had words similar to our *auditor* which meant "hearer," "judge's assistant," and "one who examines accounts." So listening and judging have been intertwined with looking at the books for hundreds of years.

auditory \\'ȯ-də-ˌtȯr-ē\\ (1) Perceived or experienced through hearing. (2) Of or relating to the sense or organs of hearing.

● With the new sophisticated sound systems that are now available, going to a movie has become an auditory experience almost as much as a visual one.

Auditory is close in meaning to *acoustic* and *acoustical* as they all relate to the hearing of sounds. *Auditory,* however, usually refers more to hearing than to sound. For instance, many dogs have great auditory powers. The nerve that allows us to hear by connecting the inner ear to the brain is the auditory nerve. *Acoustic* and *acoustical* refer especially to instruments and to the conditions under which sound can be heard. So architects concern themselves with the acoustic (or acoustical) properties of an auditorium, and instrument makers with those of a clarinet or piano.

audition \ȯ-'di-shən\ A trial performance to evaluate a performer's skills.

● Auditions for Broadway shows attract so many hopeful unknown performers that they are referred to as "cattle calls."

Most stars are discovered at auditions, where a number of candidates read the same part and the director chooses. Lana Turner, on the other hand, skipped the audition process altogether; once she was discovered sipping a soda at Schwab's, her future was secure. *Audition* can also be a verb. After Miss Turner won her stardom, the prize was the opportunity to audition to be her leading man.

inaudible \i-'nȯ-də-bəl\ Not heard or capable of being heard.

● The coach spoke to the young gymnast in a low voice that was inaudible to the rest of the team.

Inaudible adds the negative prefix *in-* to the adjective *audible* and turns it into its opposite. Modern spy technology (if movies like *Three Days of the Condor* or *Patriot Games* are accurate) can turn inaudible conversations into audible ones with the use of high-powered directional microphones. So if you think you're being spied on, make sure there's a lot of other noise around you.

SON is the Latin root meaning "sound," as in our word *sonata*, meaning a kind of music usually played by one or two instruments, and *sonorous*, usually meaning full, loud, or rich in sound.

---

dissonant \'di-sə-nənt\ (1) Clashing or discordant, especially in music. (2) Incompatible or disagreeing.

● Critics of the health-care plan pointed to its two seemingly dissonant goals: cost containment, which would try to control spending, and universal coverage, which could increase spending.

Dissonant includes the negative prefix *dis-*. What is dissonant sounds or feels unresolved, unharmonic, and clashing. Twentieth-century composers such as Arnold Schoenberg and his students Alban Berg and Anton Webern developed the use of *dissonance* in music as a style in itself. To many, such visual and jarring sounds are still unbearable; most listeners prefer music based on traditional tonality.

resonance \'re-zə-nəns\ (1) A continuing or echoing of sound. (2) A richness and variety in the depth and quality of sound.

• Audiences for both *Star Wars* and CNN are drawn to the resonance in the voice of James Earl Jones.

Many of the finest musical instruments possess a high degree of resonance which, by producing additional vibrations and echoes of the original sound, enriches and amplifies it. Violins made by the masters Stradivari and Guarneri, for example, possess a quality of resonance that modern violinmakers have not been able to duplicate.

sonic \'sä-nik\ (1) Having to do with sound. (2) Having to do with the speed of sound in air (about 750 miles per hour).

• With a sonic depth finder, they determined the depth of the lake by bouncing a sound signal off the bottom.

In 1947 a plane burst the sound barrier and created a sonic boom for the first time. Now even commercial jetliners, including the Concorde, leave sonic booms in their wake as they exceed the speed of sound.

ultrasound \'əl-trə-ˌsaund\ The use of sound vibrations above the limits of human hearing to produce images with which to diagnose internal bodily conditions.

• His doctor, who loved new technology, used CAT scans, MRI, and ultrasound to view his various organs.

The root *son-* came to be spelled *soun-* in medieval English, which led to *sound* and all the English words that now contain it. Ultra-sound, or *ultrasonography*, works on the principle that sound is reflected at different speeds by tissues or substances of different densities. *Sonograms*, the pictures produced by ultrasound, can reveal heart defects, tumors, and gallstones, but are most often used to display fetuses during pregnancy in order to make sure they are healthy.

Quizzes

A. Indicate whether the following pairs of words have the same or different meanings:

1. dissonant / jarring   same ___ / different ___
2. inaudible / invisible   same ___ / different ___
3. resonance / richness   same ___ / different ___
4. audition / tryout   same ___ / different ___
5. ultrasound / harmony   same ___ / different ___
6. auditor / performer   same ___ / different ___
7. sonic / loud   same ___ / different ___
8. auditory / hearing   same ___ / different ___

B. Match the word on the left to the correct definition on the right:

1. inaudible   a. involving sound
2. auditory   b. impossible to hear
3. ultrasound   c. diagnostic technique
4. resonance   d. a critical hearing
5. auditor   e. relating to hearing
6. sonic   f. unharmonious
7. dissonant   g. financial examiner
8. audition   h. continuing or echoing sound

ERR, from the Latin verb *errare*, means "to wander" or "to stray." This root is easily seen in the word *error*, which means a wandering or straying from what is correct or true. We also use the word *erratum* to mean "a mistake" in a book or other printed material; its plural is *errata*, and the *errata* page is the book page that lists mistakes found too late to correct before publication.

---

aberrant \ə-'ber-ənt\ Straying or differing from the right, normal, or natural type.

● Richard's aberrant behavior began to make his colleagues fear that the stress of the project was getting to be too much for him.

Something that is aberrant has wandered away from the usual or normal path or form. Aberrant behavior is usually bad behavior and may be a symptom of other problems. However, in biology, the discovery of an aberrant variety of a species can be exciting news, and in medical research the discovery of an aberrant gene can lead the way to new cures for diseases.

errant \'er-ənt\ (1) Wandering or moving about aimlessly. (2) Straying outside proper bounds, or away from an accepted pattern or standard.

● Modern-day cowboys have been known to use helicopters to spot errant calves.

Errant means both "wandering" and "mistaken." A *knight-errant* was a wandering knight going about slaying dragons or rescuing damsels in distress. *Arrant* is a rarely used variant of *errant*, but we sometimes hear it in the phrase *arrant knave*, which comes from Shakespeare and refers to an extremely untrustworthy individual. More typical is the errant cloud or breeze that just happens along or the errant child that requires discipline.

erratic \i-'ra-tik\ (1) Having no fixed course. (2) Lacking in consistency.

● In the 1993 World Series, the Phillies weren't helped by the erratic performance of their ace relief pitcher, "Wild Thing."

Erratic can refer to literal "wandering." A missile that loses its guidance system may follow an erratic path, and a river with lots of twists and bends is said to have an erratic course. *Erratic* can also mean "inconsistent" or "irregular." So a stock market that often changes direction is said to be acting *erratically*. And Wild Thing's problem was erratic control: he could throw strikes but he also threw a lot of wild pitches.

erroneous \i-'rō-nē-əs\ Mistaken, incorrect.

● The chess wizard's parents formed an erroneous idea of his intelligence because he didn't talk until he was six.

Erroneous seems to be used most often with words that suggest mental activity. "Erroneous assumptions" and "erroneous ideas" are two very common phrases in English, perhaps because we suffer from so many of them. "Erroneous information" is also very common, and it leads to erroneous decisions, erroneous theories, and erroneous conclusions.

CED/CESS, from the Latin verb *cedere,* meaning "to go" or "to proceed," produces many English words, from *procession,* meaning something that goes forward, to *recession,* which is a moving back or away.

---

accede \ak-'sēd\ (1) To give in to a request or demand. (2) To give approval or consent.

● Voters tend to worry when Congress seems to be acceding to the demands of too many special-interest groups.

To accede usually means to yield, often under pressure, to the needs or requests of others. Sometimes this is a good thing, as when family members accede to the needs of others or we accede to our curiosity and take the peaceful back road to our destination. *Accede* often also implies reluctance. Patients may accede to surgery, and voters may accede to a tax increase, but eager shoppers do not accede to price reductions—they welcome them.

antecedent \an-tə-'sē-dənt\ (1) A preceding event, state, or cause. (2) One's ancestor or parent.

● The harsh terms of the treaty that ended World War I are often said to have been antecedents of World War II.

Antecedents can be persons, conditions, or events that are responsible, if only in part, for a later person, condition, or event. So the rhythm-and-blues music of the 1940s and 1950s is an antecedent of today's rock and roll. And the breakup of the Soviet Union was surely an important antecedent of the war in Yugoslavia. Since our parents and ancestors are responsible for our existence, they are our own antecedents.

concession \kən-'se-shən\ (1) The yielding of a point or privilege, often unwillingly. (2) An acknowledgment or admission.

• When the company agreed to pay millions of dollars in damage claims, the payments were seen as a concession that somebody had done something wrong.

When the baseball strike of the 1980s was settled, both players and management had to make concessions. This meant that each side *conceded* (gave up or reduced) some of its demands until they reached agreement. *Concede* can also mean simply "admit." So your boss may concede that she is at fault for something, or you may have to concede that your opponent in an argument has some good points.

precedent \'pre-sə-dənt\ Something done or said that may be an example or rule to guide later acts of a similar kind.

• When Judy bought Christmas presents for all her relatives one year she claimed that it set no precedent, but it did.

The Supreme Court relies on precedents, earlier laws or decisions that provide some example or rule to guide them in the present case. Sometimes, as in the famous 1954 ruling that ordered public schools desegregated, the precedent lies in the Constitution and its Amendments.

Quizzes

A. Complete the analogy:

1. descending : ascending :: errant : _____
   a. moving b. wandering   c. fixed d. straying
2. abundance : plenty :: antecedent : _____
   a. ancestor   b. descendant c. relative d. protector
3. fruitful : barren :: erroneous : _____
   a. productive b. pleasant c. targeted d. correct
4. collision : hit :: concession : _____
   a. drive b. hover c. yielding d. refuse
5. stable : constant :: erratic : _____
   a. fast b. invisible c. mistaken d. unpredictable
6. swerve : veer :: accede : _____
   a. assent b. descent c. reject d. demand

7. typical : normal :: aberrant : _____
   a. burdened b. roving c. odd d. missing
8. etiquette : manners :: precedent : _____
   a. courtesy b. tradition c. rudeness d. behavior

B. Fill in each blank with the correct letter:

a. aberrant   e. erratic
b. errant   f. erroneous
c. precedent   g. antecedent
d. concession   h. accede

1. Her unfair opinion of him was based on several _____ assumptions.
2. They could find no _____ for this offense to guide them in deciding how to deal with it.
3. Doctors traced the _____ changes in his temperature to the attack of malaria.
4. Willy Loman lived the _____ life of the traveling salesman.
5. In agreeing to end the bombing, the rebels made only a single _____.
6. After repeated incidents of criminally _____ behavior, he finally got sent to jail.
7. After lengthy negotiations, the union will probably _____ to several of the company's terms.
8. She proudly claimed Booker T. Washington as her _____.

Words from Mythology and History

Augean stable \ȯ-'jē-ən-'stā-bəl\ A condition or place marked by great accumulation of filth or corruption.

● Leaders of many of the newly formed nations of Eastern Europe found that the old governments of their countries had become Augean stables that they must now clean out.

Augean stable most often appears in the phrase "clean the Augean stable," which usually means "clear away corruption" or "perform a large and unpleasant task that has long called for attention." Augeus, the mythical king of Elis, kept great stables that held 3,000 oxen and had not been cleaned for thirty years when Hercules was assigned the job. Thus, the word *Augean* by itself has come to mean "extremely difficult or distasteful," so we can also refer to Augean tasks or Augean labor, or even Augean clutter. By the way, Hercules cleaned the stables by causing two rivers to run through them.

Croesus \'krē-səs\ A very rich person.

● H. Ross Perot's many successful business ventures have made him an American Croesus.

Croesus most often appears in the phrase "rich as Croesus," which means "extremely rich." Bill Gates, founder of Microsoft, could fairly be called "rich as Croesus." Croesus himself was a sixth-century B.C. king of Lydia, an ancient kingdom in what is now Turkey. He conquered many surrounding regions, grew wealthy, and became the subject of many legends.

dragon's teeth \'dra-gənz-'tēth\ Seeds of conflict.

● We should realize that we sow dragon's teeth when we neglect the education of our children.

This term often appears in the phrase "sow dragon's teeth," which means to create the conditions for future trouble. In an ancient Greek legend, Cadmus killed a dragon and planted its teeth in the ground. Armed men immediately sprang up from where the teeth were sown and tried to kill him. The goddess Athena directed him to throw a precious stone into their midst and they proceeded to slaughter each other until only the five greatest warriors were left, and these became Cadmus's generals.

Hades \'hā-dēz\ The underground home of the dead in Greek mythology.

● Always careful not to offend, the angry Senator bellowed, "Who in Hades gave out this information about me?"

Hades is both the land of the dead and the god who rules there. Hades (Pluto) the god is the brother of Zeus (Jupiter) and Poseidon (Neptune), who rule the skies and the seas respectively. His own realm is Hades, the region under the earth, full of mineral wealth and fertility and home of the dead. There he rules with his wife Persephone (Proserpina). *Hades* has become a polite term for *Hell* and often appears in its place, as in the sentence "The restaurant became hotter than Hades after the air conditioner broke down."

lethargic \lə-'thär-jik\ (1) Lazily sluggish. (2) Indifferent or apathetic.

● Once again the long Sunday dinner had left most of the family feeling stuffed and lethargic.

The Greek philosopher Plato wrote that before a dead person could leave Hades to begin a new life, he or she had to drink from the River Lethe, whose name means "forgetfulness" in Greek. One would thereby forget all aspects of one's former life and the time spent in Hades (usually pretty awful, according to Plato). But our word *lethargic* and the related noun *lethargy* usually refer not to forgetting but rather to the weak, ghostly state of those who have drunk from Lethe as dead spirits—so weak that they may require a drink of blood before they can even speak.

Midas touch \'mī-dəs-'təch\ The talent for making money in every venture.

● For much of his career Donald Trump seemed to possess the Midas touch.

Midas was the legendary king of Phrygia who, when granted one wish by the god Dionysus, asked for the power to turn everything he touched into gold. When he found that even his food and drink turned to gold, he begged Dionysus to take back his gift. The moral of this tale of greed is usually ignored when the term is used today.

Pyrrhic victory \'pir-ik-'vik-tə-rē\ A victory won at excessive cost.

● The coach regarded their win as a Pyrrhic victory, as his best players sustained injuries that would sideline them for weeks.

Pyrrhic victories take their name from Pyrrhus, the king of Epirus, an ancient country in northwest Greece. Pyrrhus defeated the Romans at the Battle of Ausculum (279 B.C.) but lost all of his best officers and many men. He is said to have exclaimed after the battle, "One more such victory and we are lost."

stygian \'sti-jē-ən\ Extremely dark, dank, gloomy, and forbidding, like the River Styx.

• When the power went out in the building, the halls and stairwells were plunged in stygian darkness.

The word *stygian* comes from the name of the River Styx, which was the chief river of the Greek underground world of the dead and which had to be crossed in order to enter this world.

Quiz

Choose the word that does not belong:
1. lethargic   a. lazy b. sluggish c. energetic d. indifferent
2. Croesus   a. rich b. powerful c. impoverished
      d. successful
3. Midas touch   a. talented b. unsuccessful c. rich
      d. prosperous
4. Pyrrhic victory   a. unqualified b. costly
      c. dangerous d. destructive
5. Augean stable   a. purity b. corruption c. filth
      d. Herculean
6. Hades   a. underworld b. heaven c. dead d. eternity
7. dragon's teeth   a. dangerous b. troublesome
      c. sensible d. conflict
8. stygian   a. glamorous b. gloomy c. grim d. dank

Review Quizzes

A. **Match each word on the left to its antonym on the right:**

1.	antecedent	a.	true
2.	erroneous	b.	generous
3.	dissonant	c.	energetic
4.	lethargic	d.	fill
5.	symmetrical	e.	admiring
6.	acquisitive	f.	typical
7.	deplete	g.	descendant
8.	derogatory	h.	hearable
9.	inaudible	i.	unbalanced
10.	aberrant	j.	harmonious

B. Complete the analogies:

1. arrogate : _____ :: implement : _____
   a. question / serve b. surrogate / tool c. claim /
   accomplishment d. arrogant / rake

2. precedent : _____ :: prerogative : _____
   a. example / privilege b. sample / rule c. governor /
   request d. forerunner / introduction

3. odometer : _____:: Croesus : _____
   a. alphabet / dog b. intelligence / loyalty c. surprise /
   monster d. distance / wealth

4. audition : _____ :: inquisition : _____
   a. hearing / asking b. trying / cooking c. affecting /
   reflecting d. listening / seeing

5. ultrasound : _____ :: ultraviolet : _____
   a. loud / colorful b. inaudible / invisible c. medical /
   artistic d. excessive / exaggerated

6. concession : _____ :: perquisite : _____
   a. edible / necessary b. affordable / bearable
   c. reluctant / welcome d. appreciative / greedy

7. resonance : _____ :: replete : _____
   a. reworking / refilling b. echoing / full c. divided /
   united d. continuing / exhausted

8. stygian : _____ :: aberrant : _____
   a. muddy / angry b. dark / abnormal c. gloomy /
   bright d. light / simple

9. requisition : _____ :: errant : _____
   a. regular / stable b. demand / wandering
   c. refreshed / roving d. routine / usual

10. sonic : _____:: auditory : _____
    a. sound / hearing b. jet-propelled / taped c. tonic /
    radial d. audible / visual

C. Fill in each blank with the correct letter:

a.	abrogate	f.	erratic
b.	tachometer	g.	Midas touch
c.	dragon's teeth	h.	accede
d.	complement	i.	Pyrrhic victory
e.	Croesus	j.	metric

1. Through shrewd investing, she had become as rich as
   _____ .

2. The French use the _____ system to calculate volume.
3. If you want respect, you must never _____ your responsibilities.
4. The triumphant corporate takeover proved to be a _____, since the debt that resulted crippled the corporation for years.
5. The children made only _____ progress because they kept stopping to pick flowers.
6. At last the teachers decided to _____ to the students' request for less homework.
7. He knew that with her mean gossip in the office she was sowing _____, but he did nothing to stop her.
8. The _____ showed that the engine was racing much too fast.
9. Fresh, hot bread is the perfect _____ to any dinner.
10. He skipped his class reunion, preferring to avoid any successful former classmates who clearly had the _____.

Unit 7

VID/VIS comes from the Latin verb *videre*, and appears in words having to do with seeing and sight. A *videotape* is a collection of *visual* images—that is, images *visible* to our eyes. But this root does not always involve eyes. To *envision* something, for instance, is to see it with your imagination.

visage \'vi-zij\ The face or appearance of a person.

● A kindly man, he had a bright, cheerful visage that people found attractive.

Visage is one of several words for the human face. *Countenance* and *physiognomy* are two others. *Countenance* is usually used to refer to the face as it reveals mood or character, and *physiognomy* is used when referring to the shape or contour of the face. *Visage* is a more literary term and may refer either to the shape of the face or the impression it gives or the mood it reveals. FBI Most Wanted posters seem to emphasize the threatening visages of the suspects. Unlike *countenance* and *physiognomy*, the use of *visage* is not restricted to humans. We can speak, for instance, of the grimy visage of a mining town.

vis-à-vis \ˌvē-zä-'vē\ In relation to or compared with.

● Many financial reporters worry about the loss of U.S. economic strength vis-à-vis our principal trading partners.

Vis-à-vis comes from Latin by way of French. It means literally "face-to-face"; things that are face-to-face can easily be compared or contrasted. So, for example, the Red Sox have often fared badly vis-à-vis the Yankees, and a greyhound is very tall vis-à-vis a Scottie.

visionary \'vi-zhə-,ner-ē\ (1) A person with foresight and imagination. (2) A dreamer whose ideas are often impractical.

● His followers regarded him as an inspired visionary; his opponents saw him as either a con man or a lunatic.

A visionary is someone who vividly imagines the future, whether accurately or not, with ideas that may either work brilliantly or fail miserably. Martin Luther King, Jr., was a visionary in his hopes and ideas for a just society; but this, like so many visions, has proved easier to *envision* than to achieve.

visitation \,vi-zə-'tā-shən\ (1) A visit or short stay, often for some definite, official purpose such as inspection. (2) A parent's privilege to have temporary access to or care of a child.

● The local ministers dreaded the annual visitation from the bishop's evaluation committee.

Visit and *visitation* share some meanings, since both refer to a fairly short call or stay. But *visit* is the more general word, while a visitation is normally a visit that is somehow out of the ordinary, such as by being formal or official. Faithful followers of religious leaders such as the Pope or the Dalai Lama look forward to visitations from these holy figures. Businesspeople, on the other hand, could probably do without annual visitations from the tax auditors.

SPIC/SPEC comes from the Latin verb *specere* or *spicere*, meaning "to look at or behold." Closely related is the root *specta-*, which comes from a slightly different verb and produces such words as *spectator*, *spectacles*, and *spectacular*.

---

auspicious \ȯ-'spi-shəs\ (1) Promising success; favorable. (2) Fortunate, prosperous.

● Martha was mildly superstitious, so breaking her mirror didn't seem an auspicious start to the day.

In ancient Rome there was an entire order of priests, the *auspices*, whose job it was to watch birds fly across the Roman sky. After noting what kinds of birds and how many had flown in which direction, they delivered prophecies according to what they had seen. For example, two eagles flying from east to west was usually considered auspicious, or favorable; two or more vultures flying west to east was *inauspicious,* unless the Romans were looking forward to a war. Thus, the auspices were birdwatchers, although not quite like birdwatchers today.

conspicuous \kən-'spi-kyù-wəs\ Obvious or noticeable; striking in a way that attracts attention.

• Soon after the shooting, "No Trespassing" signs appeared in conspicuous colors at conspicuous locations around the preserve.

Conspicuous usually refers to something so obvious that it cannot be missed by the eye or mind. We often speak, for instance, of conspicuous bravery or conspicuous generosity. It also frequently describes something that draws attention by being unpleasant or unusual. Businesspeople try to avoid making themselves conspicuous by their clothes or their personal habits. The phrase "conspicuous consumption" is often used to describe lavish spending intended to increase one's social prestige, a well-known aspect of American life.

introspection \ˌin-trō-'spek-shən\ A looking within oneself to examine one's own thoughts and feelings.

• The poet Sylvia Plath's journals are filled with the results of her constant introspection.

Introspection is a valuable resource of writers. In her autobiography, *The Road from Coorain,* Jill Ker Conway produces a fascinating, highly *introspective* portrayal of her life's journey from an Australian sheep farm to the president's office of a major American women's college, and beyond. We learn not only what her life was like but how she felt about it along the way and also in *retrospect*— that is, looking back.

perspicacious \ˌpər-spi-'kā-shəs\ Having acute or shrewd mental vision or judgment.

• Successful poker players are usually perspicacious judges of human character.

Perspicacious is derived from the Latin word *perspicere,* meaning "to look through" or "to see clearly," so *perspicacious,* usually means having unusual power to see through or understand. You tend to admire the *perspicacity* of the person who understands what a fine human being you are. (The confusingly similar word *perspicuous* comes from the same Latin word but means "plain to the understanding" or simply "clear." A writer will strive for a perspicuous style, for example, and a lawyer will try to present perspicuous arguments to a judge.)

Quizzes

A. Fill in each blank with the correct letter:

a. introspection
b. vis-à-vis
c. perspicacious
d. conspicuous
e. visitation
f. auspicious
g. visionary
h. visage

1. When she considered Cleveland _____ other cities where she might have to live, she always chose Cleveland.
2. The couple were _____ by their absence from the meeting.
3. His plans for the new city marked him as a true _____.
4. The beautiful sunrise provided an _____ start to their camping trip.
5. She was a _____ woman of rare judgment, who always seemed to know the right thing to say in even the most delicate situation.
6. The _____ of Marlene Dietrich gazed out from movie posters throughout Europe and America in the 1930s.
7. After the confrontation, both devoted themselves to long periods of _____ to try to understand their own feelings.
8. A visit from her mother-in-law always felt like a _____ of the plague.

B. Match the definition on the left to the correct word on the right:

1. compared to   a. introspection
2. shrewd   b. visitation
3. prophet   c. vis-à-vis
4. appearance   d. auspicious
5. self-examination   e. perspicacious

6. noticeable	f. visionary
7. favorable	g. conspicuous
8. official call	h. visage

VOC/VOK, from the Latin noun *vox* and the verb *vocare*, has to do with speaking and calling and the use of the voice. So a *vocation* is a special calling to a type of work; an *evocative* sight or smell calls forth memories and feelings; and a *vocal* ensemble is a singing group.

equivocate \i-'kwi-və-ˌkāt\ (1) To use ambiguous language, especially in order to deceive. (2) To avoid giving a direct answer.

● As the company directors continued to equivocate, the union prepared to return to the picket lines.

Equivocate contains the root *equi*, meaning "equal." It thus suggests that whatever is said has two equally possible meanings. The person who equivocates avoids giving a clear, *unequivocal* message. Politicians are often said to equivocate, but equivocating is also typical of used-car salesmen or nervous witnesses in a courtroom. Sometimes even husbands and wives will equivocate to avoid a quarrel.

irrevocable \i-'re-və-kə-bəl\ Impossible to call back or retract.

● By throwing her hat into the presidential race, the young governor made the irrevocable decision to put her family into the public eye.

The word *irrevocable* has a legal sound to it, and in fact is often used in legal contexts. Irrevocable trusts are trust funds that cannot be dissolved by the people who create them. An irrevocable credit is an absolute obligation from a bank to provide credit to a customer. Under U.S. tax law, irrevocable gifts are gifts that are given by one living person to another and that cannot be reclaimed by the giver. But we all have had to make irrevocable decisions, decisions that commit us absolutely to something.

provoke \prə-'vōk\ (1) To call forth or stimulate a feeling or action. (2) To anger.

● Before every boxing match, Cassius Clay (Muhammad Ali) would provoke his opponent with poetic taunts.

To provoke a response is to call for that response to happen. Funny stories should provoke laughter; angry comments can provoke a fight; and taking controversial stands may provoke opposition. Something is *provocative* if it has the power to produce a response. The provocative clothing and behavior of some rock-music performers seem designed to provoke criticism as much as admiring attention.

vociferous \vō-'si-fə-rəs\ Making noisy or emphatic outcries.

● Parents at soccer games are often known to make vociferous protests when they think the referee has made a bad call.

Someone who is vociferous shouts loudly and insistently. The group U2 draws vociferous crowds whose noisy din at times makes it hard to hear the music. And as at any rock concert, there are vociferous objections when the music ends.

PHON is a Greek root meaning "sound," "voice," or "speech." It is similar to the Latin *voc* in meaning but typically means only "sound" when used in such words as *telephone* ("far sound"), *microphone* ("small sound"), or *xylophone* ("wood sound").

---

cacophony \kə-'kä-fə-nē\ Harsh or unpleasant sound.

● To some people, much recent jazz sounds more like cacophony than like real music.

Cacophony employs the Greek prefix *caco-*, meaning "bad," but not everything we call *cacophonous* is necessarily bad. Open-air food markets may be marked by a cacophony of voices but also by wonderful sights and sounds. Heavy metal is probably the most cacophonous form of modern music but it is still very popular. On the other hand, few people can really enjoy, for more than a few minutes, the cacophony of jackhammers, car horns, and truck engines that assaults the city pedestrian on a hot day in August.

phonetic \fə-'ne-tik\ Relating to or representing the sounds of the spoken language.

● Some school systems teach first-graders to read by the phonetic method.

The English alphabet is phonetic; that is, the letters represent sounds. Certain other alphabets, such as Chinese, are not phonetic, since their symbols represent ideas rather than sounds. But even in English a letter does not always represent the same sound; the "a" in *cat, father,* and *mate,* for example, represents three different sounds. Because of this, books about words often use specially created phonetic alphabets in which each symbol stands for a single sound in order to represent pronunciations. So in this book, *cat, father,* and *mate* would be *phonetically* represented as \'kat\, \'fä-thər\, and \'māt\.

polyphonic \ˌpä-lē-'fä-nik\ Referring to a style of music in which two or more melodies are sung or played against each other in harmony.

● The polyphonic chants of the monks punctuated the ceremony at important intervals.

Since *poly-* means "many," polyphonic music has "many voices." In *polyphony,* each part has its own melody. It reached its height during the 16th century with Italian madrigals and the sacred music of such composers as Palestrina, Tallis, and Byrd.

symphony \'sim-fə-nē\ A usually long and complex musical composition for orchestra.

● Beethoven, Bruckner, Mahler, and possibly Schubert completed nine symphonies each before their deaths.

Symphony includes the prefix *sym-* ("together") and thus means "a sounding together." The symphonies of Beethoven, most of which have four separate movements, are among the greatest ever composed. From the First, which is almost like the music of Mozart, to the magnificent choral Ninth, few other pieces of music compare to them in controlled intensity. "*Symphonic* poems" by such composers as Franz Liszt and Richard Strauss usually attempt to paint a picture or tell a dramatic story by means of music alone. Both require a symphony orchestra (sometimes called simply a "symphony" itself) made up of stringed, woodwind, brass, and percussion instruments.

Quizzes

A. Complete the analogy:

1. initial : beginning :: irrevocable : _____
     a. usual b. noisy c. final d. reversible
2. novel : literature :: symphony : _____
     a. dance b. poetry c. film d. music
3. soothe : quiet :: provoke : _____
     a. prevent b. project c. produce d. protect
4. multistoried : floor :: polyphonic : _____
     a. poetry b. melody c. story d. harmony
5. reject : accept :: equivocate : _____
     a. decide b. specify c. detect d. delay
6. melodic : notes :: phonetic : _____
     a. sounds b. signs c. ideas d. pages
7. monotonous : boring :: vociferous : _____
     a. vegetarian b. angry c. favorable d. noisy
8. stillness : quiet :: cacophony : _____
     a. melodious b. dissonant c. creative d. birdlike

B. Indicate whether the following pairs have the same or different meanings:

1. provoke / annoy   same __ / different __
2. phonetic / phonelike   same __ / different __
3. equivocate / refuse   same __ / different __
4. polyphonic / many-voiced   same __ / different __
5. irrevocable / unalterable   same __ / different __
6. cacophony / din   same __ / different __
7. vociferous / calm   same __ / different __
8. symphony / heavy metal   same __ / different __

CUR, from the Latin verb *curare*, means basically "care for."
Our verb *cure* comes from this root, as do *manicure* ("care of the
hands") and *pedicure* ("care of the feet").

---

curative \'kyu̇r-ə-tiv\ Having to do with curing diseases.

● As soon as the antibiotic entered his system, he imagined he could
begin to feel its curative effects.

Medical researchers are finding curative substances in places that surprise them. Folklore has led to some "new" *cures* of old diseases, and natural substances never before tried have often proved effective. Taxol, a drug used in treating some cancers comes from the bark of a certain yew tree; the challenge now is to produce this *curative* synthetically, since natural supplies are limited.

curator \'kyur-,ā-tər\ Someone in charge of something where things are on exhibit, such as a collection, a museum, or a zoo.

• Curators of zoos continually try to make the animals' surroundings more and more like their natural homes.

A curator cares for some sort of collection, usually works of art or animals. Thomas Hoving, in his years as director of the Metropolitan Museum of Art, was responsible for supervising the curators of all the separate art collections and seeing that all *curatorial* duties were carried out: acquiring new artworks, caring for and repairing objects already owned, discovering frauds and counterfeits, returning some pieces to their country of origin, and mounting exhibitions of everything from Greek sculpture to 20th-century clothing.

procure \prō-'kyur\ To get possession of; obtain.

• In an era of Defense Department cutbacks, military planners have had to look for more economical ways to procure the supplies they need.

While *procure* has the general meaning of "come into possession of," it usually implies that some effort is required. It may also suggest getting something through a formal set of procedures. In many business offices, there is a particular person responsible for procuring supplies, and many government agencies have formal *procurement* policies designed to prevent unauthorized spending. However, it sometimes seems that such policies cost more money to administer than they could possibly save.

sinecure \'si-nə-,kyur\ A job or position requiring little work but usually providing some income.

• The job of Dean of Students at any college is no sinecure; the hours can be long and the work draining.

Sinecure contains the Latin word *sine,* "without," and thus means "without care." Many view the positions occupied by British royalty as sinecures, in which they earn enormous sums of money and inherit enormous amounts of property in return for nothing at all. But their many supporters defend them by pointing to the amount of public-service, charitable, and ceremonial work they perform, not to mention the effort they put into promoting Britain and all things British. Sinecure or not, many of us would probably like to try being king or queen for a day.

PERI usually means "going around something." With a *periscope,* you can see around corners. *Peristalsis* is the bodily function that moves food around the intestines; without it, digestion would grind to a halt. The moon's *perigee* is the point in its orbit where it is closest to the earth. The point in the earth's orbit around the sun that brings it closest to the sun is its *perihelion.*

---

perimeter \pə-'ri-mə-tər\ The boundary or distance around a body or figure.

● All along the city's perimeter the guerrillas kept up their attack night after night.

The perimeter of a prison is ringed with high walls and watchtowers, and the entire perimeter of Australia is bounded by water. To measure the perimeter of a square, multiply the length of one of its sides by four. Try not to confuse this word with *parameter,* which usually means a characteristic element or factor or a limit or boundary.

periodontal \per-ē-ō-'dän-təl\ Surrounding the teeth; concerning or affecting the tissues around the teeth.

● Years of bad living had filled his teeth with cavities, but it was periodontal disease that finished them off.

There are dentists called *periodontists* who specialize in the treatment of periodontal problems. These specialists do their best to save a patient's teeth by making sure the periodontal tissues do not degenerate to the point where they can no longer hold the teeth in place. The *-odont-* root comes from the Greek word for "tooth," so the *endodontist,* unlike the periodontist, is concerned with problems inside the tooth.

peripatetic \per-ə-pə-'te-tik\ (1) Having to do with walking. (2) Moving or traveling from place to place.

● She spent her early adult years as a peripatetic musician, traveling from one engagement to another.

Peripatetic was the name given to the philosopher Aristotle and his followers, since he used to teach them while walking up and down in a covered walkway called the *Peripatos.* The word kept this sense of traveling or moving about. Johnny Appleseed is a good example of a peripatetic soul, wandering far and wide while he planted his apple trees. Today peripatetic executives and salespeople move from one job to the next and stare into laptop computers while flying from city to city.

peripheral \pə-'ri-fə-rəl\ (1) Having to do with the outer edges, especially of the field of vision. (2) Auxiliary or supplemental.

● The teacher seemed to have eyes in the back of her head, but what she really had was excellent peripheral vision and a thorough knowledge of how ten-year-olds behave.

Driving into or out of Chicago during rush hour requires excellent peripheral vision, especially when switching lanes. Peripheral vision relates to the outer area of the field of vision, where one can still detect movement and shape. Issues in a discussion may also be called peripheral—that is, not of primary importance. And *peripheral* now can act as a noun: computer peripherals are the added components that increase a computer's capacities.

Quizzes

A. Fill in each blank with the correct letter:

a. curative	e. peripheral
b. sinecure	f. perimeter
c. procure	g. peripatetic
d. curator	h. periodontal

1. The _____ benefits of antibiotics have saved many lives.
2. Testing _____ vision is part of most eye tests done in a doctor's office.

3. What he had hoped was an undemanding ＿＿ turned out to be the hardest and most rewarding job of his career.
4. She knew she needed to put up a fence along the ＿＿ of the garden.
5. We asked our purchasing manager to ＿＿ new chairs for the office.
6. With tents and backpacks ready, the young couple were ready to become ＿＿ vacationers.
7. At the museum we spoke to the ＿＿ of African art.
8. Regular use of dental floss will prevent many kinds of ＿＿ diseases.

B. Choose the closest definition:

1. sinecure   a. hopeful sign   b. fruitless search   c. careless act   d. easy job
2. curator   a. doctor   b. lawyer   c. caretaker   d. spectator
3. periodontal   a. visual   b. inside a tooth   c. around a tooth   d. wandering
4. peripatetic   a. wandering   b. unemployed   c. surrounding   d. old-fashioned
5. procure   a. say   b. obtain   c. look after   d. heal
6. curative   a. purifying   b. healing   c. saving   d. repairing
7. perimeter   a. factor   b. characteristic   c. supplement   d. boundary
8. peripheral   a. supplementary   b. around a tooth   c. wandering   d. dangerous

---

SENT/SENS, from the Latin verb *sentire*, meaning "to feel," or the noun *sensus*, meaning "feeling" or "sense," can signify different kinds of feeling. *Sentimental* has to do with emotions, whereas *sensual* relates more to physical *sensations*.

---

sensational \sen-'sā-shə-nəl\ (1) Exciting an intense but usually brief interest or emotional reaction. (2) Extremely or unexpectedly excellent.

● The sensational newspaper accounts of the marital problems of the royal couple fascinated many readers but made others a little uncomfortable.

The photos sent back from Jupiter by the Voyager satellite were sensational—both excellent and exciting. The murder of a pregnant woman by her husband was sensational also, although in a very different sense, since it was picked up by the tabloid press and *sensationalist* TV journalists, who thrive on such sordid tales and *sensationalize* every detail. Both stories, however, can be said to have created a *sensation*.

sentient \'sen-chənt\ Aware of and responsive to sense impressions.

● The planet Earth supports the only sentient beings that we yet know of in the universe.

Sentient describes beings that perceive and respond to sensations of whatever kind—sight, hearing, touch, taste, smell. The science of robotics is now capable of creating machines that *sense* things in much the way living beings do and respond in pretty much the same way as well; however, few of us are yet ready to refer to robots as sentient beings. Mary Shelley, in her novel *Frankenstein*, was among the first to suggest the possibility of creating sentient beings out of used parts.

sentiment \'sen-tə-mənt\ (1) A thought or attitude colored by feeling; opinion. (2) Tender feelings of affection.

● We don't care whose nephew he is; hiring decisions must be based on merit, not sentiment.

"My sentiments exactly!" expresses agreement to someone else's opinion. A sentiment is usually of gentle to moderate intensity. The refined women of Jane Austen's novels are full of sentiment that occasionally spills over into deep emotion but usually remains subdued and controlled. Similarly, a *sentimental* journey, as the old popular song suggests, satisfies feelings of longing and romantic homesickness rather than intense craving. *Sentiment* is used less today than it once was, and *sentimental* now usually means excessively emotional.

sensuous \'sen-shù-wəs\ (1) Highly pleasing to the senses. (2) Relating to the senses.

• A chef like Craig Claiborne takes sensuous pleasure in the smell and taste of well-prepared food.

Sensuous and *sensual* are closely related in meaning but not identical. *Sensuous* usually implies gratification of the senses for the sake of aesthetic pleasure; great music, for example, can be a source of sensuous delight. *Sensual*, on the other hand, usually describes gratification of the senses or physical appetites as an end in itself; thus we often think (perhaps unfairly) of wealthy Roman aristocrats leading lives devoted to sensual pleasure.

SOPH is a Greek root from the word meaning "wise" or "wisdom." In our language, the root often appears in words where the wisdom concerned is of the "wiseguy" variety. But in words such as *philosophy* we see a more respectful attitude toward wisdom.

---

sophistry \'sä-fə-strē\ Cleverly deceptive reasoning or argument.

• The defendant's claim that he wasn't guilty of the crime because he didn't actually pull the trigger was dismissed as pure sophistry.

Our words *sophist* and *sophistry* come from the name of a group of Greek teachers of rhetoric and philosophy who were famous during the 5th century B.C. Originally, the Sophists represented a respectable school of philosophy and were involved in serious educational efforts. But in time they fell into disrepute and gained a reputation for their abilities to persuade more by means of clever and often misleading arguments than by the merits of their positions. It is not difficult to see the Sophists as the natural ancestors of many of today's politicians.

sophisticated \sə-'fis-tə-ˌkā-təd\ (1) Having a thorough and refined knowledge of the ways of society. (2) Highly complex or developed.

• In *Woman of the Year* Katharine Hepburn plays a sophisticated newspaperwoman who can handle everything except Spencer Tracy.

A satellite is a sophisticated piece of technology, intricate and complex and designed to accomplish difficult tasks. A sophisticated argument is thorough and well-worked-out. A sophisticated person, such as Humphrey Bogart in *Casablanca,* knows how to get around in the world and is able to get pretty much what he or she wants; such *sophistication* can produce a bored, blasé attitude, as it does with Bogie until his long-lost love appears.

sophomoric \ˌsä-fə-ˈmȯr-ik\ Overly impressed with one's own knowledge, but in fact undereducated and immature.

● The kids at summer camp played the usual sophomoric pranks—short-sheeted beds, salt in the sugar bowl, shaving cream on the light switch, water bucket balanced on the door.

Sophomoric seems to include the roots *soph-,* "wise," and *moros,* "fool," so the contrast between wisdom and ignorance is built right into the word. A high-school or college *sophomore* has delusions of wisdom—but only the seniors are truly wise, as we all know. Sophomoric behavior and sophomoric jokes are typical of those who have gotten a small taste of experience but think they have experienced a lot.

theosophy \thē-ˈä-sə-fē\ A set of teachings about God and the world based on mystical insights into their nature and workings.

● She experimented with a number of beliefs, starting with theosophy and ending with a variety of Hinduism.

The best-known religious movement associated with theosophy began in the 19th century under the leadership of Helena Blavatsky. She combined elements of Platonic thought, Christian mysticism, and Hindu belief in a way she claimed had been divinely revealed to her. *Theosophical* beliefs include oneness with nature and reincarnation. The Theosophical Society, founded in 1875 to promote her beliefs, still exists, although scientific experiments had disproved many of her claims by the 20th century.

Quizzes

A. Indicate whether the following pairs of words have the same or different meanings:

1. sophisticated / worldly-wise   same ___ / different ___
2. sensuous / sophisticated   same ___ / different ___
3. theosophy / mythology   same ___ / different ___

4. sentiment / feeling   same ___ / different ___
5. sophistry / wisdom   same ___ / different ___
6. sentient / romantic   same ___ / different ___
7. sophomoric / wise   same ___ / different ___
8. sensational / enormous   same ___ / different ___

B. Match the word on the left to the correct definition on the right:

1. theosophy   a. immaturely overconfident
2. sentiment   b. outstandingly excellent
3. sensuous   c. doctrine of God and the
4. sophomoric   world
5. sophistry   d. gratifying the senses
6. sentient   e. false reasoning
7. sophisticated   f. opinion colored by
8. sensational   emotion
                       g. receiving perceptions
                       h. highly complex

Words from Mythology and History

Achilles' heel \ə-'ki-lēz-'hēl\ A vulnerable point.

● Grafton had been an excellent manager in his first years there, but his Achilles' heel turned out to be his addiction to increasingly damaging drugs.

When the hero Achilles was an infant, his sea-nymph mother dipped him into the river Styx to make him immortal. But since she held him by one heel, this spot did not touch the water and so remained mortal and vulnerable. It was this heel where Achilles was eventually mortally wounded. Today, the tendon that stretches up the calf from each heel is called the *Achilles tendon*; however, the term *Achilles' heel* is only used figuratively; thus, it can refer to the weakest point in a country's military defenses, or a person's tendency to drink too much, for example.

arcadia \är-'kā-dēə\ A region or setting of rural pleasure and peacefulness.

• The Pocono Mountains of Pennsylvania are a vacationer's arcadia.

Arcadia, a beautiful rural area in Greece, became the favorite setting for poems about naive and ideal innocence unaffected by the passions of the larger world. There, shepherds play their pipes and sigh with longing for flirtatious nymphs; shepherdesses sing to their flocks, and goat-footed nature gods cavort in the fields and woods.

Cassandra \kə-'san-drə\ A person who predicts misfortune or disaster.

• The newspaper columnist was accused of being a Cassandra who always looked for the worst and predicted disaster, despite the fact that his predictions often came true.

Cassandra, the daughter of King Priam of Troy, was one of those beautiful young maidens with whom Apollo fell in love. He gave her the gift of prophecy in return for the promise of her sexual favors, but at the last minute she refused him. Though he could not take back his gift, he pronounced that no one would ever believe her predictions. Thus, her prophecy of the fall of Troy and the death of its heroes were laughed at by the Trojans. A modern-day Cassandra goes around predicting gloom and doom, like many current economists with their constant pessimistic forecasts.

cyclopean \ˌsī-klə-'pē-ən\ Huge or massive.

• The scale of the new ten-block high-rise medical center was cyclopean.

The Cyclops of Greek mythology were huge, crude giants, each with a single eye in the middle of his forehead. Odysseus had a terrible encounter with one of these creatures in his travels, and escaped being devoured only by blinding the monster with a burning stick. The great stone walls at such places as Troy, Tiryns, and Mycenae are called cyclopean because the stones are so massive and the construction so expert that it was assumed that only a superhuman race such as the Cyclops could have achieved such a feat.

draconian \drə-'kō-nē-ən\ Extremely severe or cruel.

• The new president thinks that only draconian spending limits and staff cutbacks can save the ailing company.

The word *draconian* comes from *Draco,* the name of a 7th-century B.C. Athenian legislator. Legends and stories about Draco hold that he created a very severe code of laws, which were sometimes said to have been written in blood rather than ink. Today, we use the word *draconian* in a wide variety of ways, sometimes even referring to something as minor as parking policies. (Because the word is derived from a person's name, *draconian* is often spelled with a capital *D.*)

myrmidon \\'mər-mə-ˌdän\\ A loyal follower, especially one who executes orders unquestioningly.

● Wherever the corporate tycoon went, he was surrounded by myrmidons all too eager to do his bidding.

Achilles' troops in the Trojan War, called Myrmidons, were created from ants. This insect origin explained their blind obedience to him, their willingness to carry out any order—such as refusing to fight even when it meant many lives would be lost. The Nazis expected all Germans in uniform to exhibit this same unquestioning loyalty and obedience; the postwar Nuremberg trials established the principle that the utter, unthinking obedience of a myrmidon does not excuse committing certain crimes against humanity in wartime.

nemesis \\'ne-mə-səs\\ A powerful, frightening opponent or rival who is usually victorious.

● During the 1970s and 1980s Japanese carmakers became the nemesis of the U.S. auto industry.

The Greek goddess Nemesis doled out rewards for noble acts and vengeance for evil ones. The Greeks believed that Nemesis did not always punish an offender right away, but might wait as much as five generations to avenge a crime. But whenever she worked, her cause was always just and her victory sure. Today, a nemesis may or may not be believed to be working justice. So most people agree that the weak economy was George Bush's nemesis in 1992, even if they voted for him.

Trojan horse \\'trō-jən-'hȯrs\\ Someone or something that works from within to defeat or undermine.

● Like a Trojan horse, she came back to school with a bad case of the flu that spread rapidly among the other students.

After besieging the walls of Troy for ten years, the Greeks built a huge, hollow wooden horse, secretly filled it with armed warriors, and presented it to the Trojans as a gift for the goddess Athena. The Trojans accepted the offering and took the horse inside the city's walls. That night, the armed Greeks swarmed out and captured and burned the city. A Trojan horse is thus anything that looks innocent but, once accepted, has power to harm or destroy— for example, a computer program that seems helpful but actually works to wipe out data and functions.

Quiz

Fill in each blank with the correct letter:

a. myrmidons	e. Achilles' heel
b. draconian	f. nemesis
c. cyclopean	g. Cassandra
d. Trojan horse	h. arcadia

1. The CEO expected immediate and absolute obedience from his ____, no matter what he asked.

2. Shortly after hiring him, they discovered that he was actually a ____, sent by a rival company to destroy the workers' faith in the company's plans.

3. The architect surrounded the pool and garden with a great stone wall modeled on the ____ walls of ancient Greece.

4. They considered their little corner of New Hampshire a true ____ in its freedom from the pressures of the modern world.

5. In eighth grade his ____ was a disagreeable girl named Rita who liked playing horrible little tricks.

6. In times of national crisis, each news commentator sounds more like a ____ than the next.

7. Historians point to the ____ treaty terms as one of the causes of the next war.

8. Believing the flattery of others and enjoying the trappings of power have often been the ____ of successful politicians.

Review Quizzes

A. Choose the correct synonym and the correct antonym:

1. auspicious   a. bad b. birdlike c. good d. likely
2. sensational   a. kindly b. exciting c. ordinary
    d. odoriferous
3. provoke   a. soothe b. incite c. veto d. announce
4. curative   a. drug b. poison c. recreation d. antidote
5. irrevocable   a. final b. retractable c. unbelievable
    d. vocal
6. perimeter   a. essence b. edge c. center d. spurt
7. nemesis   a. ally b. no one c. enemy d. sibling
8. sophomoric   a. silly b. sage c. cacophonous d. languid
9. Achilles' heel   a. paradise b. heroism c. immortality
    d. vulnerability
10. peripatetic   a. immobile b. exact c. wandering
    d. imprecise
11. conspicuous   a. shrewd b. invisible c. noticeable
    d. promising
12. vociferous   a. speechless b. steely c. pliant d. noisy
13. visionary   a. idealist b. cinematographer
    c. conservative d. writer
14. sentient   a. frantic b. unaware c. alert d. tranquil
15. sophisticated   a. rejected b. advanced c. worldly
    wise d. naive

B. Choose the closest definition:

1. phonetic a. called b. twitched c. sounded
    d. remembered
2. sophistry a. deception b. musical composition c. sound
    reasoning d. pleasure
3. procure a. appoint b. obtain c. decide d. lose
4. visage a. imagination b. citation c. expression
    d. depression
5. symphony a. piano recital b. complex rhythm c. unison
    chant d. orchestral composition

6. vis-à-vis a. compared to b. allowed to c. rented to
   d. talked to
7. introspection a. critical judgment b. self-examination
   c. inquisition d. detention
8. peripheral a. auxiliary b. central c. relating to the
   sun d. philosophical
9. draconian a. rustic b. massive c. disastrous d. severe
10. polyphonic a. multi-melodic b. uniformly harmonic
    c. relatively boring d. intentionally imitative
11. cyclopean a. serpentine b. gigantic c. infinitesimal
    d. circular
12. visitation a. journey b. prayer c. official visit
    d. stimulation
13. periodontal a. relating to feet b. around the sun
    c. around the teeth d. around a corner
14. curator a. caretaker b. watcher c. doctor d. purchaser
15. Cassandra a. optimist b. economist c. pessimist
    d. oculist

C. Fill in each blank with the correct letter:

a. equivocate   f. Trojan horse
b. sensuous   g. arcadia
c. cacophony   h. theosophy
d. sentiment   i. sinecure
e. myrmidon   j. perspicacious

1. The job turned out to be a ___, and no one cared if he
   played golf twice a week.
2. The huge Senate bill was a ___, filled with items that
   almost none of the senators were aware of.
3. We opened the door onto a haze of cigarette smoke and
   a ___ of music and laughter.
4. In the old book on ___ she found a philosophy very
   similar to the one she and her friends were exploring.
5. One ___ after another scurried in and out of the
   boardroom on errands for the chairman.
6. It didn't require a ___ eye to see that their marriage
   was a difficult one.

7. The letter described their new Virginia farm as a kind of
    _____ of unspoiled nature.
8. Whenever they asked for a definite date, he would _____
    and try to change the subject.
9. She lay in the bath with her eyes closed in a kind of _____
    daydream.
10. He always tried to end his letters with an appropriate
    _____ and a warm closing.

Unit 8

TEND/TENT, from the Latin *tendere,* meaning "to stretch, extend, or spread," can be seen most simply in the English word *tent,* meaning a piece of material stretched or extended over a frame. It can also be seen in the word *extend,* which means "to stretch forth or stretch out," and in *tendon,* the word for a tough band of tissue that stretches from a muscle to a bone.

contentious \kən-'ten-chəs\ Having a tendency to pick fights; quarrelsome.

● The school board meeting lasted late into the night as contentious parents argued over every detail of the new bus routes.

Someone who is contentious seems to enjoy arguing and sometimes goes to great lengths to start a fight. Some legislative battles in Congress seem to be caused as much by contentious politicians as by the issues involved. The word *contentious* can also mean "likely to cause an argument." Reform of the health-care system, for instance, has been a very contentious issue.

distend \di-'stend\ To swell or become expanded.

● Television viewers were shocked to see the distended bellies of the young children, usually a sign of malnutrition and starvation.

Distend is generally used in medical or technical contexts, and it usually refers to swelling caused by pressure from within. A doctor examining a patient complaining of intestinal pain will look to see if the abdomen is distended. Hoses distend and straighten when water is pumped through them.

portend \pȯr-'tend\ (1) To give a sign or warning beforehand. (2) To indicate or signify.

● Although the warm spell in February was welcome, the huge puddles by the melting snowbanks portended the spring floods that were likely to follow.

Portend comes directly from the Latin verb *portendere*, meaning "to foretell or predict," both of which suggest a stretching out into the future. Predicting often involves interpreting signs and omens. When the Cubs lose on opening day at Wrigley Field it often portends another season of heartbreak for Chicago fans. *Portend* may be used for both favorable and unfavorable outcomes, but it usually indicates a threat of evil or disaster. Some foreign-policy experts saw that the breakup of the Soviet Union portended chaos and strife for many countries in Eastern Europe.

tendentious \ten-'den-shəs\ Leaning toward a particular point of view; biased.

● In his later years, the professor wrote a series of tendentious essays attacking many modern novelists and praising authors from earlier eras.

Political speeches can often be as tendentious as they are *contentious*. Politicians will adopt a particular philosophy, and from that day on they will tend to view matters from that point of view. Facts are replaced by tendentious claims, and debates become predictable and unproductive.

PEND/PENS, meaning "to hang, weigh, or cause to hang down," comes from the Latin verb *pendere*. We find it in English in words like *pensive*, meaning "thoughtful," and *appendix*, that useless and sometimes troublesome piece that hangs from the intestine.

---

appendage \ə-'pen-dij\ (1) Something joined on to a larger or more important body or thing. (2) A subordinate body part, such as an arm or a leg.

● Wives complain justifiably when they are treated by others as mere appendages of their husbands.

Appendage refers to an attachment that is less important than the thing to which it is attached. A controversial speaker, for instance, may add a few soothing remarks as an appendage to an otherwise fiery speech. Some appendages are important in their own right, but may not be viewed that way by some people. So residents of Staten Island don't like having their borough viewed as simply an appendage of New York City. And many Canadians fear that their U.S. neighbors view Canada, despite its size, as an appendage to the United States.

expend \ik-'spend\ (1) To pay out. (2) To use up.

● The company was taking steps to limit the funds it was expending on health-care costs and disability benefits.

Expend comes straight from the Latin word *expendere*, meaning "to weigh out" or "to spend." *Expend* is close in meaning to *spend*, but it is usually used more in reference to business, industry, finance, or government, and it therefore usually also implies larger sums of money. We have a deficit in this country because government expends more dollars than it collects. In its nonfinancial sense, *expend* suggests an unnecessary waste of something. The deficit may continue because more ink and paper are expended on stories of gossip and scandal than on the day-to-day operations of government.

propensity \prə-'pen-sə-tē\ An often intense natural inclination or preference.

● In-laws have a natural propensity to offer advice, especially when it hasn't been requested.

A propensity is a leaning toward something. We have a propensity for something when we have a natural tendency or are driven by a natural appetite. Good reporters have a propensity to ask questions; good politicians have a propensity for avoiding them. Small children have a propensity for getting sticky, and, for some reason, spilled food has a propensity for landing on new ties.

stipend \'stī-pənd\ A sum of money paid at regular intervals in return for services or to cover expenses.

● David's fellowship to graduate school included a stipend to cover his basic living expenses.

A stipend is a little like a salary, but there are differences. A stipend may be intended more to cover expenses than to pay for a service. A stipend may arrive weekly or annually, but the amount of money is usually small. Stipends are normally paid to people involved in noncommercial activities, such as scholars, artists, and amateur athletes. One very generous stipend is the one paid by the MacArthur Foundation, which often runs into the hundreds of thousands of dollars, with no strings attached. The only catch is that you need to be a genius to get one.

Quizzes

A. Complete the analogy:

1. calculate : count :: expend : _____
   a. stretch b. speculate c. pay d. explode
2. distort : warp :: distend : _____
   a. swell b. notice c. display d. shrink
3. abode : dwelling :: stipend : _____
   a. study b. salary c. mortgage d. advance
4. sensational : great :: tendentious : _____
   a. opinionated b. neutral c. important d. promotional
5. imaginary : unreal :: propensity : _____
   a. idea b. opinion c. inclination d. artistry
6. passionate : loving :: contentious : _____
   a. competitive b. continuous c. collected
   d. quarrelsome
7. laugh : giggle :: portend : _____
   a. bend b. indicate c. argue d. stretch
8. passage : opening :: appendage : _____
   a. hanger b. hangar c. limb d. branch

B. Fill in each blank with the correct letter:

a. contentious   e. appendage
b. distend   f. expend
c. tendentious   g. propensity
d. portend   h. stipend

1. These departments _____ the largest amount of money on new computers.
2. The bodies of snakes _____ as they eat their prey.

3. The eager assistant was willing to be seen as the necessary _____ to his boss.
4. Life with a disagreeable, _____ neighbor is not easy.
5. Her unusual talent and _____ for chess was obvious before she was five.
6. The senator made a highly _____ speech about U.S. involvement overseas.
7. As part of his scholarship, he received a small _____ to cover living expenses.
8. Those dark clouds rolling in _____ bad weather to come.

PAN comes from Greek with its spelling and meaning intact. It simply means "all" in Greek; as an English prefix it can also mean "completely," "whole," or "general." A *panoramic* view is a complete view in every direction. *Panchromatic* film is sensitive to the reflected light of all colors in the spectrum. *Pantheism* is the worship of all gods. A *pantheon* is a temple dedicated to all the gods of a particular religion. A *pandemic* outbreak of a disease may not literally affect the entire human population, but enough to create catastrophic problems.

---

panacea \ˌpa-nə-'sē-ə\ A remedy for all ills or difficulties; cure-all.

● Educational reform is sometimes viewed as the panacea for all of society's problems.

Panacea combines *pan-* and the Greek word *akos,* "remedy." A panacea is a magical medicine that can cure whatever ails you, or a magical solution that can solve a whole set of problems. But since no such medicine or solution exists, the word *panacea* almost always occurs in contexts where the writer is criticizing a single solution to an array of problems ("There is no panacea for the problems of the inner city"). *Panacea* is also applied to easy solutions to individual problems, although this use loses the original "cure-all" sense of the word. In the view of its opponents, for example, the proposed legalization of street drugs is a panacea doomed to create far more problems than it would solve.

pandemonium \pan-də-'mō-nē-əm\ A wild uproar or commotion.

• Pandemonium erupted in the football stadium as the underdogs scored an upset victory in the final seconds.

In *Paradise Lost,* the fallen Satan has his heralds proclaim "A solemn Councel forthwith to be held / At Pandaemonium, the high Capital / Of Satan and his Peers." John Milton got the name for his capital of hell from linking *pan* with the Latin word *daemonium,* "evil spirit," thus indicating the place where Satan gathered together all the demons. For later writers, *pandemonium* became a synonym for hell itself, since a traditional image of hell was of a place where noise and confusion abound. *Pandemonium* also came to be used of any wicked, lawless, or riotous place. But nowadays, it is used to refer to the uproar itself rather than the place where it occurs.

panegyric \pa-nə-'jir-ik\ A formal speech or statement giving high praise to someone or something.

• Lincoln's "Gettysburg Address" is as much a panegyric celebrating American democratic ideals as it is a eulogy for the brave soldiers who died on the battlefield.

American presidents at their inaugurations typically deliver a panegyric in praise of their great nation and the people who have had the wisdom to elect them. Probably few of them have realized that in delivering their praise-filled speeches before a vast throng they have remained true to our cultural roots in ancient Greece. In Athens *panēgyris* was the name for a public assembly, the word coming from *pan-* plus *agyris,* "assembly." A chosen speaker would deliver a set oration in praise of those who had served the state. With time the Greek word *panēgyrikos* shifted from meaning "of or for a festival assembly" to "a praise-filled oration." Today a panegyric need not be a public speech—many panegyrics are private or written—but the word continues to suggest praise that is elaborate, highflown, and perhaps a bit excessive.

panoply \'pa-nə-plē\ (1) A magnificent or impressive array. (2) A display of all appropriate accessory items.

• The full panoply of a royal coronation was a thrilling sight for the throngs of sidewalk onlookers and the millions of television viewers.

Panoply originally referred to the full suit of armor donned by a soldier or knight in preparation for combat. In fact, *panoply* comes from a Greek word that includes the noun *hopla,* "arms or armor." *Panoply* may refer to full ceremonial dress of any kind or to something resembling a suit of armor in being protective. More commonly, *panoply* refers to striking spectacle: the breathtaking panoply of the autumn foliage, or the stirring panoply of a military parade, for example. Or it can mean an extensive array or succession of things, as in "The display windows of the electronics store feature the complete panoply of equipment that is now thought necessary for home entertainment."

EXTRA places words outside or beyond their usual or routine territory. *Extraterrestrial* and *extragalactic* affairs take place beyond the earth or the galaxy. Something *extravagant,* such as an *extravaganza,* goes beyond the limits of reason or necessity. And of course *extra* itself is a word, a shortening of *extraordinary,* "beyond the ordinary."

---

extramundane \ek-strə-,mən-'dān\ Situated in or relating to a region beyond the material world.

● Communism is atheistic, and admits no extramundane authority.

Extramundane uses an older meaning of *mundane,* "relating to this world" or "earthly." The events described in Dante's 14th-century *Divine Comedy,* where the author is taken on a tour through hell, purgatory, and heaven, are entirely extramundane. At the end of his journey, in the highest heaven, he has a vision of extramundane harmony and bliss, the reward of the blessed for their holy earthly lives. As you can see, when *extra-* is a prefix it never means "extremely" (as in "Go extra slow through here") but instead always means "outside or beyond."

extrapolate \ik-'stra-pə-,lāt\ To extend or project facts or data into an area not known in order to make assumptions or to predict facts or trends.

● Economists try to predict future buying trends by extrapolating from current economic data.

Scientists worry about the greenhouse effect because they have extrapolated the rate of carbon dioxide buildup and predicted that its effect on the atmosphere will become increasingly severe. On the basis of their *extrapolations,* they have urged governments and businesses to limit factory and automobile emissions, and have cautioned that the burning and clearing of the Amazon rain forest must stop. Other scientists, extrapolating from the same conditions, trends, and data, have concluded that the greenhouse effect is less dangerous than we have been led to believe. The problem is that by the time either extrapolation is proved to be true, we may be at a point where further damage cannot be prevented. Notice that it is acceptable to speak of extrapolating existing data (to produce new data), extrapolating *from* existing data (to produce new data), or extrapolating new data (from existing data)—in other words, it isn't easy to use this word wrong.

extrovert \'ek-strə-ˌvərt\ A person mainly concerned with things outside him- or herself; a sociable and outgoing person.

● A complete extrovert, she made friends easily and lived one day at a time.

Extrovert (sometimes spelled *extravert*) means basically "turned outward"—that is, toward things outside oneself. The opposite personality type is the *introvert,* which naturally means "turned inward." Some psychologists have said that the only personality traits that can be identified in newborn infants are shyness and lack of shyness, which are rather close to *introversion* and *extroversion.*

extraneous \ek-'strā-nē-əs\ (1) Existing or coming from the outside. (2) Not forming an essential part; irrelevant.

● Your essay should be well-focused and should not contain any extraneous material.

Homework is difficult enough with extraneous distractions: the television, the radio, phone calls, or a pesky brother or sister. The library may be a good place to study since librarians try to limit extraneous noise. But even under ideal conditions, you can still be diverted by extraneous thoughts: the weather conditions, what to have for dinner, or a really good joke you heard recently.

Quizzes

A. Fill in each blank with the correct letter:

a.	extrapolate	e.	extramundane
b.	panoply	f.	panegyric
c.	extraneous	g.	extrovert
d.	panacea	h.	pandemonium

1. From these figures, economists can _____ data that shows a steady increase in employment.
2. Being a natural _____, he took to his new career as a salesman easily.
3. The new voice-mail system, with its full _____ of options, impressed the whole staff.
4. _____ broke out at the news of the victory.
5. The pope's address stressed that concern with worldly things must not lead us to forget spiritual and _____ matters.
6. He locked himself in his studio to ensure that there would be no _____ distractions.
7. She had been thinking of vitamins as a _____, but they weren't able to fight off infections.
8. Then he launched into a _____ to his father, calling him brilliant, loving, and saintly.

B. Indicate whether the following pairs of terms have the same or different meanings:

1. panacea / antibiotic   same ___ / different ___
2. pandemonium / chaos   same ___ / different ___
3. panegyric / pep talk   same ___ / different ___
4. panoply / display   same ___ / different ___
5. extrapolate / project   same ___ / different ___
6. extraneous / necessary   same ___ / different ___
7. extramundane / very ordinary   same ___ / different ___
8. extrovert / schizophrenic   same ___ / different ___

PHOS/PHOT comes from the Greek word for "light." *Phos* can be seen in the word *phosphorus*, which refers generally to anything that glows in the dark and also to a particular glowing chemical element. *Phot,* the more familiar root, appears in words like *photography,* which is the use of light to create an image on film or paper.

---

phosphorescent \,fäs-fə-'re-sənt\ (1) Giving off a glow that continues after an energy source has stopped transmitting energy. (2) Giving off a glow over a period of time without producing noticeable heat.

• The boat's wake glittered in the night with phosphorescent sea creatures stirred up by its passing.

The waters of the Caribbean Sea are phosphorescent in some places and glow with beautiful glimmering twinkles at night. The effect is created by tiny marine organisms that give off light in the warm tropical seas. Some minerals are naturally phosphorescent as well, and new chemical combinations can produce long-lasting *phosphorescence* without heat. One popular use is in Halloween "torches" that can be carried safely by children in costume.

photogenic \,fō-tə-'je-nik\ Very suitable for being photographed.

• Visitors to New England are often disappointed to find that the photogenic small towns with white churches and tidy houses are actually few and far between.

Photogenic originally meant "produced by light" or "producing light" and was used mostly in scientific or technical contexts. During the 20th century *photogenic* developed its now most common sense, perhaps because the original technical meaning was simply ignored. So now we use *photogenic* to describe scenery, baby animals, and presidential candidates.

photon \'fō-,tän\ A tiny particle or bundle of radiant energy.

• The idea that light consists of photons is difficult until you begin to think of a ray of light as being caused by a stream of very small particles.

It was Albert Einstein who first theorized that the energy in a light beam exists in small bits or particles called photons, and scientists now realize that light sometimes behaves like a wave (somewhat like sound or water) and sometimes like a stream of particles. The amazing power of lasers is the result of a concentration of photons

that have been made to travel together in order to hit their target
at the same time.

photosynthesis \ˌfō-tō-'sin-thə-sis\ The process by which green
plants use light to produce organic matter from carbon dioxide and
water.

• Sagebrush survives in harsh climates because it is capable of
carrying on photosynthesis at very low temperatures.

The Greek roots of *photosynthesis* combine to produce the basic
meaning "to put together with the help of light." Sunlight splits
the water molecules held in a plant's leaves and releases the oxygen
in them into the air. (Photosynthesis is what first produced oxygen
in the atmosphere billions of years ago, and it is still what keeps it
there.) What is left over combines with carbon dioxide to produce
carbohydrates, which the plant uses as food.

LUC comes from the Latin noun *lux,* "light," and the verb *lucere,*
"to shine or glitter." *Lucid* prose is clear in meaning, as if light
were shining through it. *Lucifer,* a name for the devil, means
"Light-bearer," the name he had before he fell from heaven.

---

elucidate \i-'lü-sə-ˌdāt\ To clarify by explaining; explain.

• A good doctor should always be willing to elucidate any medical
jargon he or she uses.

Elucidate means "to shed light on." When you elucidate, you
make transparent or clear something that was formerly murky or
confusing. Carl Sagan, the astrophysicist, has a gift for elucidating
to a large audience information about the objects in the universe.
Through his *lucid* explanations he has made clear how stars are
born and die, how the universe may have begun, and much more.

lucent \'lü-sənt\ (1) Giving off light. (2) Easily seen through.

● Their romance began under a lucent moon on a Mediterranean island.

Lucent is most often used in poetry or literature, where its meaning is usually close to that of *luminous*. The lucent petals of buttercups are one of the joys of a bright summer's day. Brightly polished stones have a lucent appearance. And we may even admire the lucent performance of a gifted musician.

lucubration \,lü-kyü-'brā-shən\ (1) Hard and difficult study. (2) The product of such study.

● By the end of the semester our professor admitted that he wasn't looking forward to reading through any more of our lucubrations on novels that no one enjoyed.

Lucubration came to mean "hard study" because it originally meant study done by lamplight, which in a world without electric lights was likely to be hard work. Abe Lincoln is known for having engaged in lucubration of this sort. The word has a literary feel to it and is often used with a touch of sarcasm.

translucent \tranz-'lü-sənt\ Partly transparent; allowing light to pass through but diffusing it so that objects beyond cannot be seen clearly.

● Architects have recently used industrial glass bricks in designing buildings because their translucent quality gives light but guards privacy.

Frosted glass is probably the most familiar translucent material. Stained glass is also translucent. Some red wines prove to be translucent when poured into a crystal goblet and held before a candle in a dark corner of a quiet restaurant.

Quizzes

A. Indicate whether the following pairs have the same or different meanings:

1. photogenic / glittering	same ___ / different ___
2. lucent / flashing	same ___ / different ___
3. photon / light particle	same ___ / different ___
4. translucent / beaming	same ___ / different ___

5. phosphorescent / pulsing   same __ / different __
6. lucubration / vacation   same __ / different __
7. photosynthesis / twinkling   same __ / different __
8. elucidate / explain   same __ / different __

B. Match the definition on the left to the correct word on the right:

1. glowing
2. production of organic matter
3. clarify
4. passing diffused light
5. elemental particle
6. brightly clear
7. hard study
8. visually appealing

a. lucubration
b. phosphorescent
c. translucent
d. elucidate
e. photogenic
f. photosynthesis
g. photon
h. lucent

MOR/MORT comes from the Latin *mori,* "to die," and *mort-,* the stem of *mors,* meaning "death." A *mortuary* is a place where dead bodies are kept until burial. A *postmortem* examination is one conducted on a recently dead body. And a *memento mori* (a Latin phrase meaning literally "Remember that you must die") is a reminder of death; the death's head carved onto an old gravestone is an example.

---

immortality \ˌi-ˌmȯr-'ta-lə-tē\ (1) Deathless or unending existence. (2) Lasting fame.

● Michelangelo achieved immortality with his painting and sculpture, Beethoven with his music.

Most of the world's religions deal with the issue of immortality and give advice on how to achieve it. For Achilles and the Greek heroes, immortality and *mortality* existed side by side: the *mortal* bodies of heroes died, but their *immortal* fame lived on in song and story.

moribund \'mȯr-ə-bənd\ (1) In the process of dying or approaching death. (2) Inactive or becoming outmoded.

● Many economists believe that America must replace its moribund smokestack industries with businesses based on new technology.

Moribund can be used in its original literal sense of "approaching death." Doctors will speak of a moribund patient going into a coma or a deep stupor. But *moribund* is much more commonly used to refer to things. When the economy goes bad, we hear about moribund mills and factories and towns, and the economy itself may be called moribund. People who worry about culture will speak of the moribund state of poetry or the moribund film industry—which may just mean they haven't seen a good movie lately.

mortician \mȯr-'ti-shən\ A person who prepares the dead for burial or cremation and manages the funeral.

● Every town needs a mortician, but the job only seems popular at Halloween.

Modern morticians employ skills somewhat different from those of Egyptian times. In ancient Egypt, morticians removed the organs and placed them in ornamental jars, drained the blood, and set the dead body in a solution to dry it out. The body was then wrapped in linen and placed in a mummy case, which was in turn placed in a tomb. The Great Pyramids were the most magnificent of the Egyptian tombs.

mortify \'mȯr-tə-ˌfī\ (1) To subdue or deaden (the body) especially by self-discipline or self-inflicted pain. (2) To embarrass greatly; humiliate.

● Teenagers are often mortified by their parents' attempts to act youthful.

Mortify once meant "put to death," but no longer. The "subdue or deaden" sense of *mortify* is most familiar to us in the phrase "mortifying the flesh," which refers to an old custom once followed by devout Christians, who would starve themselves, deprive themselves of every comfort, and even whip themselves in order to subdue their bodily desires. But the most common use of *mortify* today is the "humiliate" sense, and its connection with death is still apparent when we speak of "dying of embarrassment."

NEC/NIC/NOX, from the Latin verb *necare* and the noun *noxa*, have to do with killing or slaying. These roots are related to the Greek *nekros*, "corpse," found in such words as *necrology*, "a list of the recently dead," and *necromancy*, "the art of conjuring up spirits of the dead."

internecine \ˌin-tər-'ne-ˌsēn\ (1) Deadly; mutually destructive. (2) Involving conflict within a group.

● The downfall of the radical political group came as it succumbed to internecine struggles for power and influence.

The Latin word *internecinus* meant "to the death." An internecine battle, then, was simply a very bloody one. Over the years, the English word developed the sense of "mutually destructive." And during the 20th century the word developed its main meaning of "conflict within a group." So now internecine warfare seldom refers to bloody battles but instead to the internal bickering and fighting that go on within a political party, government, profession, or family.

necrosis \ne-'krō-səs\ The usually localized death of living tissue.

● One danger for young athletes is that prolonged use of some pain medications can cause necrosis in the kidney.

Many kinds of injuries and ailments can cause the death of bodily tissue. A heart attack can cause necrosis of heart tissue, and one stage in appendicitis is necrosis of the appendix. Cirrhosis and hepatitis can cause the liver to become *necrotic*, and other kinds of diseases can cause necrotic gallbladders, corneas, or intestines. Infections resulting from injuries can create necrotic tissue that may have to be surgically removed in order for the injury to heal.

noxious \'näk-shəs\ Harmful to or destructive of living things.

● The bombing of the World Trade Center caused noxious fumes and smoke to spread through the structure and cause injury to hundreds of people.

The Environmental Protection Agency regulates the disposal of noxious chemicals or wastes that would harm the environment or the creatures living in it. Such noxious residues of modern technological processes are proving harder and harder to get rid of safely. No one wants them nearby, and a way of making them disappear has simply not been found. The meaning of *noxious* is sometimes close to *obnoxious,* though it's not so often applied to people.

pernicious \pər-'ni-shəs\ Extremely harmful or destructive.

● The debate goes on about whether censorship or pornography has the more pernicious effect on society.

Pernicious usually implies serious harm done by an evil or corrupting force. Violence on television may have a pernicious influence on children. Welfare is seen as a pernicious institution by those who believe it discourages individual initiative. And AIDS is rightly referred to as a pernicious disease.

Quizzes

A. Complete the analogy:

1. immortality : _____ :: heaven : hell
   a. eternity b. god c. death d. life
2. necrosis : _____ :: disease : sickness
   a. medicine b. cure c. damage d. prescription
3. mortician : _____ :: physician : doctor
   a. grave digger b. gardener c. underwear
   d. undertaker
4. internecine : _____ :: international : domestic
   a. external b. extracurricular c. extroverted
   d. extraordinary
5. mortify : _____ :: appeal : request
   a. paralyze b. humiliate c. embalm d. slay
6. noxious : _____ :: successful : failing
   a. noisy b. beautiful c. beneficial d. noticeable
7. moribund : _____ :: cautious : fearful
   a. concerned b. obstinate c. grim d. obsolete
8. pernicious : _____ :: fruitful : productive
   a. healthful b. particular c. deadly d. demanding

B. Fill in each blank with the correct letter:

a. pernicious   e. moribund
b. internecine   f. mortify
c. necrosis   g. immortality
d. noxious   h. mortician

1. As the textile industry moved south, mill towns in New England became ___.
2. When fire broke out in the hallway, ___ fumes from the burning carpet filled every room.
3. Achilles chose ___ in legend over a long, happy life.
4. The police turned the body over to a ___ when they had finished their examination.
5. The doctor said he had to stop drinking to avoid further ___ of the liver.
6. Some religious zealots still engage in acts designed to ___ the flesh.
7. The ___ effects of a teacher's constant criticism may show in her students' unwillingness to volunteer in class.
8. The wise leader guarded against ___ conflict by providing many opportunities for cooperation among his followers.

Words from Mythology and History

aeolian harp \ē-'ō-lē-ən-'härp\ A box with strings that produce musical sounds when wind blows on them.

● Poets have long been fascinated by the aeolian harp because it is an instrument that produces music without a human performer.

Aeolus was the king or guardian of the winds, according to the ancient Greeks. He lived in a cave with his many, many sons and daughters, and sent forth whatever wind Zeus asked for. When Odysseus stopped there on his way home from Troy, he received a bag of winds to fill his sails. His men, however, opened the bag and released them all while he was asleep, and the raging winds blew them all the way back to their starting point. An aeolian harp produces enchanting harmonies when the wind passes over it. According to Homer, it was the god Hermes who invented the harp, by having the wind blow over the dried sinews attached to a tortoise shell.

cynosure \\'sī-nə-₁shùr\ (1) A guide. (2) A center of attention.

● Whenever the latest hot young rock star enters the nightclub, he becomes the cynosure of the assembled crowd.

Cynosure means "dog's tail" in Greek and Latin. In those languages it was the name for the constellation Ursa Minor, or the Little Bear, whose tail is formed by the North Star. The North Star has always been a trusty guide for travelers, especially sailors, because unlike the other stars, it always remains in the same position in the northern sky. So cynosure came to mean both "guide" and "center of attention."

laconic \lə-'kä-nik\ Using extremely few words.

● Male movie stars usually don't have a lot of dialogue to learn because most scripts seem to call for laconic leading men who avoid conversation.

Ancient Sparta was located in the region known as Laconia. The disciplined and militaristic Spartans were known for using no more words than they had to. So this terse, abrupt way of speaking became known as *laconic* after them and their territory.

mnemonic \ni-'mä-nik\ Having to do with the memory; assisting the memory.

● Sales-training courses recommend mnemonic devices as a way of remembering peoples' names.

The Greek word for memory is *mnemosyne*; something that helps the memory is therefore a mnemonic aid. Such snappy mnemonic devices as KISS (Keep It Simple, Stupid) or Every Good Boy Does Fine (for the notes on the lines of a musical staff with a treble clef) help to recall simple rules or complicated series that might otherwise slip away.

platonic \plə-'tä-nik\ (1) Relating to the philosopher Plato or his teachings. (2) Involving a close relationship from which romance and sex are absent.

● The male and female leads in many situation comedies keep their relationship platonic for the first few seasons, but romance almost always wins out in the end.

The philosopher Plato taught that all objects here on earth are pale imitations of their ideal form, just as a shadow is a weak imitation of the real object or a painting fails to capture true reality. This true form has come to be called the "platonic form." Plato presented his theories in a series of dramatic conversations between the philosopher Socrates and other people, which became known as the "Platonic dialogues." Because these philosophers and their students were all male, and because Socrates in the dialogues sometimes goes to great lengths to avoid committing homosexual acts, despite his desires, close but nonsexual friendship between two people who might be thought to be romantically attracted to each other is today known as platonic love or friendship.

sapphic \\'sa-fik\\ (1) Lesbian. (2) Relating to a poetic verse pattern associated with Sappho.

● The Roman poets Catullus and Horace composed wonderful love poems in sapphic verse.

Sappho wrote poems of passion and self-reflection, some of them directed to the women attending the school she conducted on the Greek island of Lesbos around 600 B.C. The poems were written in an original rhythmical pattern, which has become known as sapphic verse. The island of Lesbos also gave its name to lesbianism, which is sometimes called sapphic love.

Socratic \\sō-'kra-tik\\ Having to do with the philosopher Socrates or with his teaching method, in which he systematically questioned the student in conversation in order to draw forth truths.

● The professor fascinated some students but annoyed others with her Socratic method of teaching, which required them to listen, think, and participate in class.

Socrates lived in Greece in the 5th century B.C. He left no writings behind, so all that we know of him is through the writings of his disciple Plato. Today he is most remembered for his method of teaching by asking questions. His name survives in terms such as *Socratic induction*, which is a method of gradually arriving at generalizations through a process of questions and answers, and *Socratic irony*, in which the teacher pretends ignorance, but questions his students skillfully to make them aware of their errors in understanding.

solecism \'sō-lə-ˌsi-zəm\ (1) A grammatical mistake in speaking or writing. (2) A blunder in etiquette or proper behavior.

● The poor boy committed his first solecism immediately on entering by tracking mud over the Persian rug in the dining room.

In ancient Asia Minor, there was a city called Soloi where the inhabitants spoke Greek that was full of grammatical errors. Any lapse in grammar or in formal social behavior has hence come to be known as a solecism. Such things as saying "ain't" or "they was" or using the hostess's best bath towel to dry off the dog are solecisms. The earth won't shatter from such acts, but sometimes a few nerves will.

Quiz

Fill in each blank with the correct letter:

a. solecism   e. cynosure
b. sapphic   f. aeolian harp
c. platonic   g. mnemonic
d. Socratic   h. laconic

1. The teacher quickly learned the students' names by using her own ____ devices.
2. We all were fascinated as breezes raised a tune from the ____.
3. New Yorkers tend to think of their city as the ____ of the nation.
4. The ____ method is inappropriate for normal courtroom interrogation.
5. After encountering the fifth ____ in the report, we began to lose faith in the writer.
6. Her father-in-law was ____ in her presence but extremely talkative around his son.
7. She knew he loved her when a love poem in ____ verse appeared on her desk.
8. The dinner was good, but saying that it approached the ____ ideal of a meal was probably too much.

Review Quizzes

A. Choose the correct antonym *and* the correct synonym

1. elucidate   a. confuse b. count c. clarify d. describe
2. contentious   a. continental b. quarrelsome
    c. conscious d. agreeable
3. solecism   a. correctness b. love poem c. death wish
    d. error
4. noxious   a. harmful b. beneficial c. intrusive
    d. annoying
5. pernicious   a. dangerous b. large c. gentle
    d. impressive
6. laconic   a. glad b. quiet c. beneficial d. talkative
7. moribund   a. obsolete b. sashed c. delay d. healthy
8. distend   a. shrink b. swell c. seek d. hold
9. immortality   a. eternal damnation b. eternal flame
    c. eternal life d. eternal death
10. tendentious   a. opinionated b. suitable c. common
    d. objective

**B. Indicate whether the following pairs of words have
the same or different meanings:**

1. mnemonic / ideal	same ___ / different ___
2. necrosis / infection	same ___ / different ___
3. extrapolate / project	same ___ / different ___
4. mortify / stiffen	same ___ / different ___
5. appendage / attachment	same ___ / different ___
6. cynosure / beacon	same ___ / different ___
7. pernicious / destructive	same ___ / different ___
8. propensity / projectile	same ___ / different ___
9. mortician / philosopher	same ___ / different ___
10. lucent / glittering	same ___ / different ___
11. phosphorescent / sea green	same ___ / different ___
12. translucent / cross-lighted	same ___ / different ___
13. solecism / goof	same ___ / different ___
14. elucidate / explain	same ___ / different ___
15. distend / swell	same ___ / different ___
16. lucubration / nightmare	same ___ / different ___
17. photosynthesis / reproduction	same ___ / different ___

18.	panacea / remedy	same ___ / different ___
19.	photogenic / appealing	same ___ / different ___
20.	internecine / impassioned	same ___ / different ___

C. Match the definition on the left to the correct word on the right:

1.	question-and-answer	a.	contentious
2.	elementary particle of light	b.	expend
		c.	sapphic
3.	allowance	d.	portend
4.	use up	e.	translucent
5.	argumentative	f.	platonic
6.	nonsexual	g.	photon
7.	foretell	h.	Socratic
8.	dying	i.	stipend
9.	lesbian	j.	moribund
10.	light-diffusing		

Unit 9

HER/HES, from the Latin verb *haerere,* means "to stick" or "to get stuck." This has produced words with two kinds of meaning. A word such as *adhesive* means basically "sticking," whereas a word such as *hesitate* means more or less "stuck in one place."

adherent \ad-'hir-ənt\ (1) Someone who follows a leader, a party, or a profession. (2) One who believes in a particular philosophy or religion.

● The general's adherents heavily outnumbered his opponents and managed to shout them down repeatedly.

A plan for cutting the deficit without raising taxes or reducing spending will usually attract adherents easily. In the 1992 presidential elections, Ross Perot inspired an army of enthusiastic adherents, more than any third-party candidate in U.S. history.

cohesion \kō-'hē-zhən\ The act or state of sticking together.

● Successful athletic teams usually achieve their victories through tight cohesion among the players.

Cohesion, which contains the prefix *co-,* "together," generally refers to similar things sticking together. *Adhesion,* on the other hand, usually means sticking to something of a different kind, in the way that *adhesive* tape or an *adherent* does. So a company may desire to create cohesion among its employees, and psychologists may seek to promote *cohesive* family units.

incoherent \,in-kō-'hir-ənt\ (1) Unclear or difficult to understand. (2) Loosely organized or inconsistent.

● She was tired of her boss's angry lectures, which usually turned into incoherent ranting and raving.

Incoherent is the opposite of *coherent*, and both commonly refer to words and thought. Just as *coherent* means well-ordered and clear, *incoherent* means disordered and hard to follow. *Incoherence* in speech may result from emotional stress, especially anxiety or anger. Incoherence in writing may simply result from poor planning; a twelve-page term paper that isn't written until the night before it is due will almost certainly suffer from incoherence.

inherent \in-'hir-ənt\ Part of something by nature or habit.

● A guiding belief behind our Constitution is that individuals have certain inherent rights that ought to be protected from governmental interference.

Inherent literally refers to something that "sticks in" or is "stuck in" something else. A plan may have an inherent flaw that will cause it to fail; a person may have inherent virtues that will bring him or her love and respect. Something inherent cannot be removed: the plan with inherent flaws may simply have to be thrown out, but the person with inherent virtues will never lose them.

FUG comes from the Latin verb *fugere*, meaning "to flee or escape." A *refugee* flees from some threat or danger to a *refuge*, which is a place that provides shelter and safety.

---

centrifugal \sen-'tri-fyù-gəl\ Moving outward from a center or central focus.

● Their favorite ride was the Round-up, in which centrifugal force flattened them against the outer wall of a rapidly spinning cage.

Part of an astronaut's training occurs in a *centrifuge*, a spinning machine that generates force equal to several times the force of gravity. The force sends the astronaut away from the machine's center; his or her sense of direction and balance as well as muscular strength thus become used to some of the centrifugal forces that will be at work during a real space mission.

fugitive \\'fyü-jə-tiv\\ A person who flees or tries to escape.

● The United States sometimes makes special allowances for refugees who are fugitives from persecution in their homelands.

The young outlaws Bonnie Parker and Clyde Barrow were high-spirited fugitives from justice for two years in the Depression era, fleeing and robbing banks across the Southwest, barely escaping the long arm of the law. Fugitives with Robin Hood-like style and glamour have always attracted interest and sympathy, especially from the poor.

fugue \\'fyüg\\ A musical form in which a theme is echoed and imitated by voices or instruments that enter one after another and interweave as the piece proceeds.

● For his debut on the new organ, the church organist chose a fugue by J. S. Bach.

Bach and Handel composed many fugues for harpsichord and organ in which the various parts (or voices) seem to flee from and chase each other in an intricate dance. Each part, after it has stated the theme or melody, apparently flees from the next part, which takes up the same theme and sets off in pursuit. Somewhat the same effect can be had by singing a round such as "Three Blind Mice" or "Row, Row, Row Your Boat."

subterfuge \\'səb-tər-ˌfyüj\\ (1) A trick designed to help conceal, escape, or evade. (2) A deceptive trick.

● The students employed every kind of subterfuge they knew to keep the substitute teacher from assigning homework.

Subterfuge contains the prefix *subter-* (related to *sub-*), meaning "under" or "secretly," so a subterfuge is something done secretly or "under the table." The spies depicted in John LeCarré's novels employ all kinds of subterfuge to accomplish their missions. The life of a spy sometimes seems appealing, but few of us have much experience with subterfuges more elaborate than claiming to have a previous engagement in order to avoid having dinner with our relatives.

Quizzes

A. Fill in each blank with the correct letter:

a. cohesion   e. centrifugal
b. fugitive   f. adherent
c. incoherent   g. subterfuge
d. fugue   h. inherent

1. The first-year students were sent off on a camping trip to create a greater sense of ____ within the class.
2. By ____ they had managed to infiltrate the enemy ranks and blow up the bridge.
3. The Christian Scientist philosophy of Mary Baker Eddy continued to attract many an ____.
4. Federal agents were pleased to have apprehended the ____.
5. By the time his fever reached 105°, the boy was mumbling ____ sentences.
6. A rock tied to a string and whirled about exerts ____ force on the string.
7. Mahatma Gandhi believed goodness was ____ in humans.
8. They chose a grand ____ by Bach as their wedding march.

B. Choose the closest definition:

1. inherent   a. part of   b. inherited   c. confused   d. loyal
2. fugue   a. mathematical formula   b. musical form   c. marginal figure   d. masonry foundation
3. adherent   a. sticker   b. stinker   c. follower   d. flower
4. centrifugal   a. moving upward   b. moving backward   c. moving downward   d. moving outward
5. cohesion   a. unity   b. thoughtfulness   c. uniformity   d. thoughtlessness
6. subterfuge   a. overhead serve   b. underhanded plot   c. powerful force   d. secret supporter
7. incoherent   a. attached   b. constant   c. controlled   d. confused
8. fugitive   a. traveler   b. sailor   c. escapee   d. drifter

COSM, from the Greek word meaning both "ornament" and "order," gives us two different groups of words. *Cosmetics* are the stuff we use to ornament our faces. The "order" meaning combines with the Greek belief that the universe was an orderly place, so words in this group relate to the universe and the worlds within it. *Cosmonaut,* for instance, is the word for a space traveler from the former Soviet Union.

cosmetic \käz-'me-tik\ Done or made for the sake of beauty or appearance.

• Renovating the house would involve more than just cosmetic changes such as fresh paint and new curtains.

Constant exposure to modern standards of beauty through advertisements prompts more and more people to make cosmetic changes in their appearance: a straightened nose, a lifted face, a tucked tummy. The cosmetic surgery that people undergo to achieve their new look does nothing to improve their underlying state of health. In fact, another meaning of *cosmetic* is "lacking substance, superficial." A company accused of corrupt practices may try to improve its image by making cosmetic changes, such as issuing idealistic policy statements or replacing a few guilty-looking executives.

cosmology \käz-'mä-lə-jē\ (1) A theory that describes the nature of the universe. (2) A branch of astronomy that deals with the origin and structure of the universe.

• Many New Age philosophies propose a cosmology that differs greatly from the traditional Jewish, Christian, or Islamic ways of viewing the universe.

Most religions and cultures include some kind of cosmology to explain the nature of the universe. In modern astronomy, the leading cosmology is still the Big Bang theory, which claims that the universe began with a huge explosion that sent matter and energy spreading out in all directions. One of the reasons fans watch "Star Trek" is for the various cosmologies depicted in the show, such as different conceptions of space, time, and the meaning of life.

cosmopolitan \,käz-mə-'pä-lə-tən\ (1) Having international sophistication and experience. (2) Made up of persons, elements, or influences from many different parts of the world.

● New York, like most cosmopolitan cities, offers a wonderful array of restaurants featuring cooking styles from around the world.

Cosmopolitan includes the root *polit-*, meaning "citizen"; thus, someone who is cosmopolitan is a "citizen of the world." She may be able to read the morning paper in Rio de Janeiro and attend a lecture in Madrid with equal ease. And a city or a country that is cosmopolitan has aspects and elements that come from various countries.

cosmos \'käz-,mōs\ (1) The universe, especially when it is viewed as orderly and systematic. (2) Any orderly system that is complete in itself.

● The biologist, the philosopher, and the astronomer all try in their own ways to understand the mysteries of the cosmos.

In some of its uses, *cosmos* simply means "universe." So we can say that the invention of the telescope helped us learn more about our cosmos. But usually *cosmos* is used to suggest an orderly or harmonious universe. Thus it may be the philosopher, or even the religious mystic, that helps put us in touch with the cosmos. In a similar way, *cosmic* rays come from outer space, but cosmic questions come from human attempts to find order in the universe.

SCI comes from the Latin verb *scire*, "to know" or "to understand." This root appears in the word *science*, which refers to factual knowledge, and in *conscience*, which refers to moral knowledge. And to be *conscious* is to be in a state where you are able to know or understand.

---

conscientious \,kän-chē-'en-chəs\ (1) Governed by morality; scrupulous. (2) Resulting from painstaking or exact attention.

● New employees should be especially conscientious about turning in all of their assignments on time.

Conscience and *conscientious* both come from a Latin verb meaning "to be aware of guilt." A conscientious person is one with a strong moral sense and one who has feelings of guilt when he or she violates it. *Conscientious* indicates extreme care, either in observing moral laws or in performing assigned duties. A conscientious public official has a moral code that is not easily broken. A conscientious worker has a sense of duty that forces him or her to do a careful job. A conscientious report shows painstaking work on the part of the writer.

omniscience \äm-'ni-shəns\ Infinite awareness, understanding, and insight.

● It was comforting to believe in the omniscience of a Supreme Being, and it kept him on his best behavior.

Omniscience includes another root, *omni-*, from a Latin word meaning "all," and literally means "knowing all." Omniscience is usually only possible for a god or supernatural being. However, the narrator in many novels is *omniscient*—able to see everything that is happening, no matter where or when, and able to know and understand everything going on in the minds of all the characters. For ordinary mortals such omniscience may sound attractive but would probably actually be quite a burden.

prescient \'pre-shənt\ Having or showing advance knowledge of what is going to happen.

● For years she had read *The Wall Street Journal* every morning in hopes of finding prescient warnings about future crashes, crises, and catastrophes.

Like being omniscient, being truly prescient would require supernatural powers. But well-informed people may have such good judgment as to appear prescient, and *prescient* is often used to mean "having good foresight." U.S. presidents hope to have prescient advisers or, at least once in a while, to receive a prescient analysis of world and domestic affairs. Some newspaper columnists appear to be prescient in their predictions, but we may suspect that leaks rather than *prescience* are the secret.

unconscionable \ən-'kän-chə-nə-bəl\ (1) Not guided by any moral sense; unscrupulous. (2) Shockingly excessive, unreasonable, or unfair.

● The used-car dealer was convicted of rolling back odometers and other unconscionable business practices.

The word *unconscionable* comes from *conscience*. An unconscionable person is one whose conduct is not guided by conscience. Unconscionable acts are immoral. Unconscionable things are those that cannot be tolerated in good conscience. The owner of a new house may not expect perfection, but if it has an unconscionable number of defects, it's a lemon.

Quizzes

A. Complete the analogy:

1. present : absent :: prescient : _____
   a. evil b. blind c. far-sighted d. painstaking
2. cosmic : universal :: cosmetic : _____
   a. decorative b. organized c. planetary d. starred
3. bold : shy :: cosmopolitan : _____
   a. planetary b. naive c. unique d. nearby
4. shining : glowing :: conscientious : _____
   a. careful b. all-seeing c. well-informed d. scientific
5. description : illustration :: cosmology : _____
   a. sophistication b. universe c. explanation
   d. appearance
6. truth : fiction :: omniscience : _____
   a. morality b. ignorance c. foresight d. worldliness
7. woods : forest :: cosmos : _____
   a. stars b. planets c. orbits d. universe
8. solid : liquid :: unconscionable : _____
   a. orderly b. attractive c. universal d. moral

B. Match the definition on the right to the correct word on the left:

1. cosmopolitan   a. having foresight
2. omniscience   b. universe
3. cosmetic   c. universal knowledge
4. conscientious   d. sophisticated
5. unconscionable   e. for the sake of appearance
6. cosmology   f. scrupulous
7. prescient   g. inexcusable
8. cosmos   h. description of the universe

JUNCT, from the Latin verb *jungere,* means "join." A *junction* is a place where things come together. A *conjunction* is a word (such as *and* or *or*) that joins two other words or groups of words: "this *and* that," "to be *or* not to be."

---

adjunct \'a-,jəŋkt\ Something joined or added to another thing of which it is not a part.

● The technical school promised formal classroom instruction that would be a valuable adjunct to the on-the-job training and experience.

The roots of *adjunct,* which includes the prefix *ad-,* meaning "to or toward," imply that one thing is "joined to" another. A car wash may be operated as an adjunct to a gas station. Teachers often take on advising students as an adjunct to their regular classroom duties. And anyone truly interested in expanding his or her vocabulary will find that daily reading of a newspaper or magazine is a valuable adjunct to studying this book.

disjunction \dis-'jəŋk-shən\ A break, separation, or sharp difference between two things.

● The best English teachers see no disjunction between theory and practice when it comes to good writing.

A disjunction is often simply a lack of connection between two things. For example, there is frequently a disjunction between what people expect from computers and what they actually know about them. Sometimes this takes the form of an abrupt break. In this sense, Ronald Reagan's policies seemed to represent a disjunction with the politics of the previous twenty years. And sometimes *disjunction* is used to suggest that two things are very different in some important way, and so we speak of a disjunction between science and morality, between doing and telling, or between knowing and explaining.

injunction \in-'jəŋk-shən\ (1) A warning, direction, or prohibition regarding an activity. (2) A court order commanding or forbidding the doing of some act.

• Her new fitness program included no injunctions against drinking beer and wine, she was glad to see.

Injunctions can either require or forbid something. "Eat your vegetables" and "Drive safely" are orders to do something. But injunctions are more frequently prohibitions. For instance, some English teachers uphold the injunction against beginning a sentence with "and." Similarly, legal injunctions can command or forbid; an injunction may require that a contract be honored, or may forbid a strike from taking place.

junta \'hùn-tə\ A committee that controls a government, especially after a revolution.

• Hopes for democratic reforms ended when the military junta took power and closed down the country's major newspaper.

The Latin root is a little hard to see in this word, because it comes into English through Spanish. Though we may think of a junta as a group that seizes power illegally, the word basically refers to the joining together of the group; in fact, the oldest meaning of *junta* is "a council or committee for political or governmental purposes." But today it generally means a close-knit group of people who dominate a government after seizing power in a revolution. Given the way juntas come to power, it should be no surprise that most are made up of military officers and few are overly concerned with protecting human rights.

PART, from the Latin word *pars*, meaning "part," comes into English most obviously in our word *part* but also in words like *apartment*, *compartment*, and *particle*, all of which are parts of a larger whole.

---

impart \im-'pärt\ (1) To give from one's store or abundance. (2) To make known; disclose.

• As a dedicated teacher, her primary goal was always to impart knowledge.

When we impart something, we give a piece of it, sometimes a big piece. The yellow corn in chicken feed imparts the yellow color to chickens that eat it. A speaker's manner of delivery can impart authority to what he or she says. To impart is also to say or communicate: "He finally decided to impart his plans to his family"; "She imparted her displeasure regarding absences to her staff in no uncertain terms."

impartial \im-'pär-shəl\ Fair and not biased; treating or affecting all equally.

● Representatives of labor and management agreed to have the matter decided by an impartial third party.

To be partial toward someone or something is to be somewhat biased or prejudiced, which means that a person who is partial really only sees part of the whole picture. To be impartial is the opposite of this. The United Nations sends impartial observers to monitor elections in troubled countries. We hope that juries will be impartial when they render verdicts. Grandparents, on the other hand, are not expected to be impartial when describing the good looks of a new grandchild.

participle \'pär-tə-ˌsi-pəl\ A word that is formed from a verb but used like an adjective.

● "Crying" in the phrase "the crying child" is a present participle; "guaranteed" in "satisfaction guaranteed" is a past participle.

English verbs can take several basic forms, which we call their principal parts: the infinitive ("to move," "to speak"), the past tense ("moved," "spoke"), the past participle ("moved," "spoken"), and the present participle ("moving," "speaking"). Past and present participles act like adjectives since they can modify nouns ("the spoken word," "a moving experience"). A grammatical error called a *dangling participle* occurs when a sentence begins with a participle that doesn't modify the subject. In the sentence "Climbing the mountain, the cabin came in view," "climbing" is a dangling participle since it doesn't modify "cabin."

partisan \'pär-tə-zən\ (1) A person who is strongly devoted to a particular cause or group. (2) A guerrilla fighter.

● The retiring Supreme Court justice was an unashamed partisan of the cause of free speech.

A partisan is one who supports one *part* or *party*. Sometimes the support takes the form of military action, as when guerrilla fighters engage in harassing government forces. *Partisan* can also be used as an adjective. In some families, the World Series can arouse partisan passions; most frequently, however, *partisan* refers to support of a political party, as in the phrase "partisan politics."

Quizzes

A. Choose the closest definition:

1. injunction   a. order   b. position   c. fact   d. connection
2. impartial   a. fair   b. biased   c. accurate   d. opinionated
3. adjunct   a. warning   b. addition   c. disclosure
   d. difference
4. participle   a. verb part   b. warning   c. supplement
   d. guerrilla fighter
5. junta   a. dance   b. point   c. group   d. symphony
6. impart   a. separate   b. support   c. favor   d. disclose
7. disjunction   a. prohibition   b. break   c. requirement
   d. intersection
8. partisan   a. judge   b. teacher   c. supporter   d. leader

B. Indicate whether the following pairs of words have the same or different meanings:

1. impart / give   same ___ / different ___
2. junta / guerrilla   same ___ / different ___
3. participle / verb part   same ___ / different ___
4. impartial / supportive   same ___ / different ___
5. adjunct / supplement   same ___ / different ___
6. injunction / warning   same ___ / different ___
7. partisan / fighter   same ___ / different ___
8. disjunction / connection   same ___ / different ___

MIT/MIS, from the Latin verb *mittere*, "to send," appears in such English words as *missionary*, *missile*, and *emit*. A missionary is sent out to convert others to a new faith; a missile is sent to explode on some far spot; and to emit is to send something out.

emissary \\'e-mə-ˌser-ē\ Someone sent out to represent another; an agent.

● The senior diplomat had served as a presidential emissary to many troubled regions of the world.

Like *missionaries*, emissaries are sent out on *missions*. However, emissaries are more likely to be representing governments, political leaders, or institutions other than churches. The mission of an emissary is usually to negotiate or to carry or collect information. Presidents send out emissaries to discuss peace terms. Politicians send out emissaries to lure major supporters. And advertising agencies find attractive models to act as emissaries for companies and products on television.

manumission \\ˌman-yù-'mi-shən\ The act of freeing from slavery.

● Frederick Douglass, William Lloyd Garrison, and Harriet Tubman were major forces in the movement that led to the manumission of slaves in this country.

The verb *manumit* comes from a Latin verb made up of *manus*, meaning "hand," and *mittere*, which can mean both "let go" and "send." So *manumission*, like *emancipation*, suggests the "freeing of hands." *Emancipate* can mean to free from any kind of control or domination, but *manumit* and *manumission* always refer to liberation from slavery or servitude.

missive \\'mi-siv\ A letter or written communication.

● We await further missives from your mother as to her health and sanity.

Missive simply means "letter," and its connection to the *mit-/mis-* root is that letters, after all, are meant to be sent. *Missive* is a rather formal word and is generally used humorously. A parent or grandparent teasing a college student for not writing home might say, "I've enjoyed your many missives," or might even begin a letter, "I hope this missive finds you in good health."

remittance \\ri-'mi-təns\ (1) Money sent in payment. (2) The sending of money, especially to a distant place.

● The hardest part of April 15 is putting the remittance into the envelope with the 1040 form.

When we pay our bills and include a remittance, we are sending something back to pay for what we received. *Remittance* is a slightly formal word (in most cases, *payment* is just as good), but some bills do include the statement "Please remit" or "Please enclose remittance." Another common use of *remittance* is for payments that workers send back to their families when they are working outside of their home countries. The economies of many poor countries rely on such remittances from workers employed in more industrialized countries.

PEL/PULS comes from the Latin verb *pellere,* meaning "to move or drive." A *propeller* moves an airplane forward. When soldiers *repel* an enemy charge, they drive it back. And to *dispel* something is to drive it away.

---

compel \kəm-'pel\ To drive or urge with force.

● After learning more about the sufferings of the refugees, they felt compelled to make contributions to the relief agencies.

To compel is to drive powerfully. *Compulsion* is the noun form; in other words, a thing that compels. Most commonly a compulsion is a powerful inner urge—a *compelling* urge. You may feel compelled to speak to a friend about his drinking. But a compelling film is simply one that seems serious and important.

expel \ik-'spel\ (1) To drive or force out. (2) To force to leave, usually by official action.

● The doctor had him take a deep breath and then expel all the air from his lungs.

To expel is to drive out, and the noun associated with it is *expulsion*. *Expel* is similar in meaning to *eject,* except that *expel* suggests pushing out while *eject* suggests throwing out. Also, to expel usually means to force out permanently, whereas ejecting may only be temporary. The player ejected from the game may be back tomorrow; the student expelled from school is probably out forever.

impel \im-'pel\ To urge or drive forward by strong moral force.

• As the meeting wore on without any real progress being made, she felt impelled to stand and speak.

Impel is very similar in meaning to *compel* but suggests even more strongly an inner drive to do something, and often greater urgency in the desire to act. People who believe in civil disobedience feel impelled to resist unjust laws. True civil libertarians feel impelled to tolerate even what they intensely dislike.

repulsion \ri-'pəl-shən\ (1) The act of driving away or rejecting. (2) A feeling of great dislike; disgust.

• She overcame her feeling of repulsion long enough to notice the snake's beautiful diamond patterning.

Repulsion basically means "driving back" or the feeling that one wants to drive back something. So the goal of an armed attack is the repulsion of an enemy, and magnets exhibit both attraction and repulsion. But we generally use *repulsion* to mean strong dislike, which is also described by the adjectives *repellent* and *repulsive* (though *repellent* often appears in phrases like "water-repellent"). For example, "She considered most modern art to be meaningless and repellent," and "He said that the food at college was repulsive."

Quizzes

A. Fill in each blank with the correct letter:

a.	manumission	e.	expel
b.	missive	f.	impel
c.	emissary	g.	repulsion
d.	remittance	h.	compel

1. They knew that hunger would eventually ＿＿ the grizzly to wake up.
2. An ＿＿ was sent to the Duke with a new offer.
3. Children find the feeling of ＿＿ caused by reptiles exciting.
4. Please enclose your ＿＿ in the envelope provided.
5. Though the Senate can ＿＿ a member for certain crimes, it has almost never been done.

6. His elegant Christmas _____ was always eagerly awaited.
7. Let your conscience _____ you to make the right choice.
8. Military victory of the Union forces was required to make _____ of the slaves a reality.

B. Match the definition on the left to the correct word on the right:

1. force by moral pressure   a. remittance
2. letter   b. compel
3. drive irresistibly   c. repulsion
4. disgust   d. manumission
5. agent   e. expel
6. payment   f. missive
7. drive out   g. impel
8. emancipation   h. emissary

Words from Mythology

arachnid \ə-'rak-ˌnid\ A member of the class Arachnida, which principally includes animals with four pairs of legs and no antennae, such as spiders, scorpions, mites, and ticks.

● My interest in arachnids began when I used to watch spiders build their gorgeous webs in the corners of the porch.

The Greek word for "spider" is *arachne*. According to Greek mythology, the original arachnid was a girl, Arachne. Like all good Greek girls, she spent much of her time weaving, but she made the mistake of claiming she was a better weaver than the goddess Athena. In a contest between the two, she angered the goddess by showing the gods at their worst in the pattern she wove. As punishment, Athena changed Arachne into a spider, fated to spend her life weaving.

calliope \kə-'lī-ə-pē\ A musical instrument similar to an organ in which whistles are sounded by steam or compressed air.

● The town's old calliope, with its unmistakable sound, summoned them to the fair every summer.

To the ancient Greeks, the muses were nine goddesses, each of whom was the spirit of one or more of the arts and sciences. Calliope was the muse of heroic or epic poetry and responsible for inspiring poets to write epics such as the *Iliad* and the *Odyssey*. Since these were generally sung and were usually very long, she was responsible for a great deal of musical reciting. When the hooting musical calliope was invented in America around 1855, her name seemed natural for it. Calliopes gave a festive air to river showboats; the loudest of them could supposedly be heard eight miles away. Today they are only heard on merry-go-rounds and at circuses.

dryad \\'drī-əd\\ A wood nymph.

● The Greeks' love of trees can be seen in their belief that every tree contained a dryad, which died when the tree was cut.

The term *dryad* comes from the Greek word for "oak tree." As the Greeks saw it, every tree (not only oaks) had a spirit. The myth of Daphne tells of a young woman who chose to become a dryad in order to escape an unwanted suitor, the god Apollo. Pursued by Apollo, she transformed herself into a laurel tree.

fauna \\'fò-nə\\ Animal life, especially the animals that live naturally in a given area or environment.

● In biology class they examined the fauna of the meadow next to the school.

Faunus and Fauna were the Roman nature god and goddess, part goat and part human, who were in charge of animals. Their helpers, who look just like them, are called *fauns*. Perhaps the most famous depiction of a faun is Debussy's orchestral work "Prelude to the Afternoon of a Faun," which was turned into a ballet by the great Russian dancer Nijinsky.

flora \\'flòr-ə\\ Plant life, especially the flowering plants that live naturally in a specific area or environment.

● Scientists are busily identifying the flora of the Amazon rain forest before the rapid expansion of the commercial interests consumes it.

The Roman Flora, which means "flower," was the goddess of spring and flowering plants, especially wildflowers and plants not raised for food. She was shown as a beautiful young woman in a long, flowing dress with flowers in her hair and cascading across her shoulders. English preserves her name in such words as *floral*, *floret*, and *flourish*.

herculean \ˌhər-kyù-'lē-ən\ (1) Extremely strong. (2) Extremely extensive, intense, or difficult.

● The whole family now faced the herculean task of cleaning out the attic.

The hero Hercules (in Greek, Heracles) had to perform twelve enormously difficult tasks, or "labors," to pacify the wrath of the god Apollo. Any job or task that is extremely difficult or calls for enormous strength, therefore, is called herculean.

Pandora's box \pan-'dòr-əz-'bäks\ A source of many troubles.

● Raising the issue of a new tax opened a real Pandora's box of related economic problems.

The beautiful woman Pandora was created by the gods to punish the human race because Prometheus had stolen fire from heaven. As a gift, Zeus gave Pandora a box, but told her never to open it. However, as soon as he was out of sight she took off the lid, and out swarmed all the troubles of the world. Only Hope was left in the box, stuck under the lid. Anything that seems harmless but when opened or investigated brings forth problems is called a Pandora's box.

Scylla and Charybdis \'si-lə-and-kə-'rib-dəs\ Two equally dangerous alternatives.

● As always, they feel caught between Scylla and Charybdis as they try to hold down costs while still investing for the future.

Scylla and Charybdis were two monsters in Greek mythology who endangered shipping in the Strait of Messina between Italy and Sicily. Scylla, a female monster with twelve feet and six heads, each with pointed teeth, barked like a dog from the rocks on the Italian side. Charybdis lived under a huge fig tree on the Sicilian side and caused a whirlpool by swallowing the waters of the sea. Being caught between Scylla and Charybdis is a lot like being between a rock and a hard place.

Quiz

Complete the analogy:

1. hobgoblin : ghost :: dryad : _____
   a. moth b. oak tree c. nymph d. dragonfly
2. difficult : simple :: herculean : _____
   a. intense b. easy c. mammoth d. strong
3. wrath : anger :: Scylla and Charybdis : _____
   a. rage b. peril c. ferocity d. whirlpool
4. piano : nightclub :: calliope : _____
   a. organ b. circus c. church d. steam
5. canine : dog :: flora : _____
   a. oak trees b. wood nymphs c. plants d. animals
6. reptile : snake :: arachnid : _____
   a. toad b. salamander c. bird d. scorpion
7. cabinet : china :: Pandora's box : _____
   a. pleasures b. troubles c. taxes d. music
8. cattle : livestock :: fauna : _____
   a. meadows b. flowers c. wildlife d. trees

Review Quizzes

A. Choose the correct antonym:

1. impartial   a. fair b. biased c. cautious d. undecided
2. cosmopolitan   a. bored b. intelligent
   c. inexperienced d. well-traveled
3. incoherent   a. clear b. garbled c. confused d. unknown
4. manumission   a. prohibition b. blockade
   c. liberation d. enslavement
5. compel   a. drive b. prevent c. eject d. compare
6. inherent   a. native b. inherited c. acquired d. internal
7. cosmos   a. chaos b. order c. universe d. beauty
8. impart   a. send b. stick c. combine d. withhold
9. adjunct   a. added feature b. sharp break c. tight
   connection d. central core
10. repulsion   a. disgust b. attraction c. offense d. battle

B. Match the definition on the right to the correct word on the left:

1.	emissary	a.	verb part
2.	junta	b.	cause to move
3.	participle	c.	equal perils
4.	impel	d.	agent
5.	dryad	e.	letter
6.	missive	f.	attachment
7.	Scylla and Charybdis	g.	ruling group
8.	cosmetic	h.	very difficult
9.	herculean	i.	beautifying
10.	adjunct	j.	tree spirit

C. Fill in each blank with the correct letter:

a.	adherent	f.	flora
b.	centrifugal	g.	cohesion
c.	conscientious	h.	prescient
d.	arachnid	i.	disjunction
e.	remittance	j.	subterfuge

1. The candidate's wife, his staunchest _____, was overjoyed by the victory.
2. The successful stockbroker won a reputation for being _____
3. The philosopher saw no _____ between science and morality.
4. _____ force keeps the roller-coaster cars from crashing to the ground.
5. Please send your _____ immediately or we will be forced to take legal action.
6. The plateau is home to various members of the _____ family.
7. The _____ of the family was strengthened with each reunion.
8. She won praise for her _____ handling of details.
9. We managed to get hold of tickets for the Grateful Dead concert only by _____.
10. The _____ of the West Creek Valley includes at least a dozen rare species.

Unit 10

PUT, from the Latin verb *putare*, meaning "to think, consider, or believe," has come into English in a variety of forms. A *reputation*, for example, is what others think of you; a *deputy* is someone "considered as" the person who appointed him or her.

disputatious \ˌdis-pyù-'tā-shəs\ Inclined to argue or debate.

• Because both sides were so disputatious, it seemed as if a peace accord would never be reached.

A discussion may be called disputatious, and so may a subject about which people disagree, but normally we use the word to describe individuals. For example, Beethoven was the first composer of genius who dared to be disputatious with the European nobles who were the source of his income. Trial lawyers often cultivate a disputatious style, though at home they may argue no more than balloonists or lion tamers.

impute \im-'pyüt\ To attribute.

• The British imputed motives of piracy to American ships trying to prevent them from interfering with American trade during the War of 1812.

Imputing something to someone (or something) usually means observing something invisible in that person (or thing). We may impute meaning to a play or novel, or even to a casual remark by a friend, that was never intended. Imputing a particular character to a whole country—calling the Germans militaristic or the Italians amorous, for example—is very common but always risky. And many of us like to impute bad motives to others, while always regarding our own motives as pure.

putative \'pyü-tə-tiv\ Generally supposed; assumed to exist.

● To strengthen the case for the defense, a putative expert took the stand.

Putative is almost always used to express doubt or skepticism about a common belief. Thus, Tintagel Castle in Cornwall, a picturesque ruin, is the putative fortress of King Arthur. The residents of New York City are *putatively* rude, neurotic, chic, and dangerous. And in the era of Senator Joseph McCarthy, the State Department became the putative home of hundreds of Communists.

reputed \ri-'pyü-təd\ Believed to be a certain way by popular opinion.

● A 15th-century Romanian prince, Vlad the Impaler, is reputed to have been the inspiration for the character Dracula.

Reputed is used constantly today by reporters, almost always to describe suspected criminals—"a reputed mobster," "the reputed drug kingpin." But someone may equally well be reputed to have four dead husbands or a fortune in emeralds or an obsession with medieval catapults.

LOG, from the Greek word *logos,* meaning "word, speech, reason," is found particularly in English words that end in *-logy* and *-logue*. The ending *-logy* often means "the study of": *biology* is the study of life, and *anthropology* is the study of humans. The ending *-logue* usually indicates a type of discussion: *dialogue* is conversation between two people or groups, and an *epilogue* is an author's last words on a subject.

---

eulogy \'yü-lə-jē\ A speech in praise of someone, often someone who has died.

● At President Kennedy's funeral, Chief Justice Earl Warren delivered a moving eulogy.

Since the prefix *eu-* means "well or good," a eulogy speaks well of a person or thing. A speech at a funeral or memorial service is generally called a eulogy, but you may also *eulogize* a living person. At a party you may bore everyone with your eulogies to your hometown, your dog, or your favorite vitamin.

monologue \'mä-nə-ˌlóg\ (1) A speech or dramatic scene spoken by one person or one actor. (2) Talk that dominates a conversation.

• Myra's loud and endless monologue about her travels was still ringing in our ears when we got home.

Dramatic monologues have often been used to let a character talk openly about himself or herself; the most famous of all is probably Hamlet's "To be or not to be." James Joyce and Virginia Woolf wrote long and memorable monologues for characters in their novels. Garrison Keillor, Lily Tomlin, and Bette Midler are present-day masters of the live comic monologue.

neologism \nē-'ä-lə-ˌji-zəm\ A new word, usage, or expression.

• Such neologisms as *cyberspace* and *virtual reality* come from computer technology.

Neologisms are appearing in English all the time, originating from a variety of sources. Though *-log-* means "word" (and *neo-* means "new"), a neologism doesn't have to be an entirely new word. *Rap*, a very old word, was first used in the 1920s to mean "talk," and in the 1970s to describe a new type of "talk music," and each new use was also a neologism in its time.

genealogy \ˌjē-nē-'a-lə-jē\ (1) The descent of a person or family from an ancestor, or a history of such descent. (2) The study of family history.

• In ancient Rome, prominent senators could trace their genealogies almost to the founding of the city.

In 1976, Alex Haley, Jr., published a partly fictional genealogy of his family in the form of a novel. *Roots* was not only a *genealogical* work but a history of the United States and colonial slavery told from an African-American standpoint. When its television version became the hugest success in the history of television, amateur genealogy became widely popular among both white and black Americans.

Quizzes

A. Indicate whether the following pairs of words have the same or different meanings:

1. putative / supposed   same ___ / different ___
2. neologism / terminology   same ___ / different ___
3. reputed / questioned   same ___ / different ___
4. genealogy / genetics   same ___ / different ___
5. disputatious / dysfunctional   same ___ / different ___
6. monologue / discussion   same ___ / different ___
7. impute / compute   same ___ / different ___
8. eulogy / praise   same ___ / different ___

B. Choose the closest definition:

1. monologue   a. speech   b. drama   c. catalog   d. boredom
2. impute   a. imply   b. revise   c. attribute   d. defy
3. reputed   a. rethought   b. accused   c. determined
   d. believed
4. neologism   a. new day   b. new word   c. new way
   d. new thought
5. putative   a. assumed   b. appointed   c. solved   d. ignored
6. genealogy   a. generation   b. inheritance   c. family
   history   d. height
7. disputatious   a. courageous   b. disproved
   c. unknown   d. argumentative
8. eulogy   a. high praise   b. high flight   c. high times
   d. high jump

TERR comes from the Latin *terra*, "earth." *Terra firma* is a Latin phrase that means "firm ground" as opposed to the swaying seas; a *terrace* is a leveled area along a sloping hill; the French call potatoes *pommes de terre*, literally "apples of the earth"; *territory* is a specific piece of land.

---

parterre \pär-'ter\ (1) A decorative garden with paths between the beds of plants. (2) The back area of the ground floor of a theater, often under the balcony.

• The city's park boasts a beautiful parterre with many varieties of roses.

Parterre comes to English by way of French, where it means "on the ground." In Shakespeare's day, the parterre of an English theater was filled with rowdy spectators whose response to the plays was noisy and often crude.

subterranean \ˌsəb-tə-'rā-nē-ən\ Underground.

• Carlsbad Caverns National Park has a subterranean chamber over half a mile long.

A subway is a subterranean railway; a tunnel can provide a subterranean pathway; the subterranean vaults at Fort Knox hold billions of dollars of gold reserves. Throughout New England are subterranean reservoirs, called *aquifers,* that are tapped for water. The pressure is great enough to push the subterranean water to the surface once a well provides an outlet; such wells are called *artesian.*

terrarium \tə-'rar-ē-əm\ An enclosure, usually transparent, with a layer of dirt in the bottom in which plants and sometimes small animals are kept indoors.

• When no one was watching, they dropped their snake in the fifth-grade terrarium, and then waited in the hall to hear the screams.

The turtle exhibit at a zoo is often in the form of a terrarium, as are some of the exhibits at a plant conservatory. Terrariums try to create conditions as close as possible to a natural habitat. A covered terrarium can often sustain itself for months on the moisture trapped inside.

terrestrial \tə-'res-trē-əl\ Having to do with the earth or its inhabitants.

• Although a largely terrestrial bird, the roadrunner can take to wing for short periods when necessary.

Everything on or having to do with the earth is terrestrial, although from the top of Mount Everest or K2 it may not seem that way, since the air is so thin that climbers need to carry extra oxygen to breathe. Something *extraterrestrial* comes from beyond the earth and its atmosphere; though the word is probably most familiar from science fiction, *extraterrestrial* can be used to describe anything " out of this world," from moon rocks to meteors. But Mercury, Venus, and Mars are often called the terrestrial planets, since they are rocky balls somewhat like Earth rather than great globes consisting largely of gas like most of the outer planets. In another usage of the word, animals may be divided into the terrestrial (land-living) and the aquatic (water-living).

MAR, from the Latin word *mare*, meaning "sea," brings its salty tang to English in words like *marine*, "having to do with the sea," and *submarine*, "under the sea."

---

aquamarine \ă-kwə-mə-'rēn\ (1) A pale blue or greenish blue that is the color of clear seawater in sunlight. (2) A transparent gem that is blue or blue-green.

● Many of the houses on the Italian Riviera are painted aquamarine to match the Mediterranean.

Aquamarine includes the root *aqua*, "water," and accurately describes limpid, clear seawater such as laps the shores of the islands of Greece or those of the Caribbean. The semiprecious gem called aquamarine, a form of beryl, is named for its color.

marina \mə-'rē-nə\ A dock or harbor where pleasure boats can be moored securely, often with facilities offering supplies or repairs.

● The coast of Florida has marinas all along it for the use of anything from enormous powerboats to the flimsiest sailboats.

The word *marina* comes straight from Latin, where it means "of the sea." At a marina sailors can acquire whatever they need for their next excursion, or they can tie up their boats until the next weekend comes along. John D. MacDonald's detective hero Travis McGee lives on his boat in Miami and rarely leaves the marina.

mariner \'mar-ə-nər\ A seaman or sailor.

● When he signed on as a mariner, the young Ishmael never suspected that the ship would be pursuing a great white whale.

In Coleridge's *Rime of the Ancient Mariner,* an old seaman tells the story of how he shot a friendly albatross and brought storms and disaster to his ship. As punishment, his shipmates hung the great seabird around the mariner's neck and made him wear it until it rotted.

maritime \'mar-ə-,tīm\ (1) Bordering on or having to do with the sea. (2) Having to do with navigation or commerce on the sea.

● Canada's Maritime Provinces—New Brunswick, Nova Scotia, and Prince Edward Island—have a late spring but a mild winter as a result of the ocean.

The maritime countries of Portugal and England produced many explorers during the 16th and 17th centuries, many of whom, like Ferdinand Magellan and Henry Hudson, sailed under the flags of other countries. Magellan sailed for Spain and captained the ship that was the first to circle the world, charting many new maritime routes as it went. Hudson, funded by the Dutch, sailed up what is now called the Hudson River in New York, claiming that maritime area for the Netherlands.

Quizzes

A. Complete the analogy:

1. crepe : pancake :: parterre : _____
   a. balcony b. planet c. garden d. parachute
2. motel : motorist :: marina : _____
   a. dock b. pier c. sailor d. boat
3. aquarium : water :: terrarium : _____
   a. plants b. turtles c. rocks d. earth
4. urban : city :: maritime : _____
   a. beach b. dock c. sea d. harbor
5. aquatic : water :: terrestrial : _____
   a. sea b. land c. forest d. mountain
6. pink : red :: aquamarine : _____
   a. blue b. watery c. turquoise d. yellow
7. submarine : wet :: subterranean : _____
   a. blue b. dark c. hollow d. full
8. logger : lumberjack :: mariner : _____
   a. doctor b. lawyer c. chief d. sailor

B. Match the definition on the left to the correct word on the right:

1. theater area   a. mariner
2. blue-green gem   b. terrestrial
3. under the ground   c. marina
4. near the sea   d. terrarium
5. contained habitat   e. maritime
6. seaman   f. parterre
7. small harbor   g. subterranean
8. earthly   h. aquamarine

PATH comes from the Greek word *pathos*, which means "suffering." A *pathetic* sight moves us to pity. *Pathos* itself is used in English to describe the intense emotions produced by tragedy.

---

apathetic \a-pə-'the-tik\ (1) Showing or feeling little or no emotion. (2) Having no interest.

● His apathetic response to the victory bewildered his friends.

Apathy, or lack of emotion, is central to Albert Camus's famous novel *The Stranger*, in which the main character's indifference toward almost everything, including his mother's death, results in his imprisonment. We feel little *sympathy* for him, and may even feel *antipathy*, or dislike. The American voter is often called apathetic; of all the industrial democracies, only in America does more than half the adult population fail to vote in major elections.

empathy \'em-pə-thē\ The feeling of, or the ability to feel, the emotions and sensations of another.

● Her maternal empathy was so strong that she often seemed to be living her son's life emotionally.

In the 19th century Charles Dickens counted on producing a strong *empathetic* response in his readers so that they would be involved enough to buy the next newspaper installment of each novel. Today, when reading a novel such as *A Tale of Two Cities*, only the hardest-hearted reader does not feel empathy for Sidney Carton as he approaches the guillotine. One who *empathizes* suffers along with the one who feels the sensations directly. Empathy is similar to *sympathy,* but empathy usually suggests stronger, more instinctive feeling. We may feel sympathy, or pity, for victims of a war in Asia, but we may feel empathy for a close friend going through a divorce, even though it is a much smaller disaster.

pathology \pa-'thä-lǝ-jē\ (1) The study of diseases. (2) The abnormalities that are characteristic of a disease.

• Scientists understood the pathology of smallpox long before they found a vaccine to prevent it.

Based on its roots, *pathology* would mean literally "the study of suffering," but it is actually used to describe the study of diseases. Scientists have found vaccines or cures for diseases from chicken pox to diphtheria by studying their pathology. In this role, the researchers are called *pathologists*. However, a psychiatrist might speak of pathologies of behavior, meaning only that the behavior in question is abnormal.

sociopath \'sō-shē-ō-ˌpath\ A mentally ill or unstable person who acts in a way that harms people and society; a psychopath.

• Controlling its sociopaths is a goal of every society.

One of the most famous sociopaths of history was Jack the Ripper, the mysterious serial killer who murdered at least seven London prostitutes in 1888. But a sociopath doesn't have to be a murderer; almost any person who is destructive or potentially dangerous can be described as a sociopath. Today psychiatrists use the bland term "antisocial personality" in place of *psychopath* or *sociopath*.

PEN/PUN comes from the Latin words *poena,* "penalty," and *punire,* "to punish." From them come such English words as *penalty* and *repentance*; when a penalty is given to someone, it is expected that he or she will be moved to repentance.

---

impunity \im-'pyü-nǝ-tē\ Freedom from punishment, harm, or loss.

● Under the flag of truce, the soldiers crossed the field with impunity.

Impunity is protection from punishment, just as immunity is protection from disease. Tom Sawyer, in Mark Twain's novel, broke his Aunt Polly's rules with near impunity because he could usually sweet-talk her into forgiving him; if that failed, he had enjoyed himself so much he didn't care what *punishment* she gave him.

penal \\'pē-nəl\\ Having to do with punishment or penalties, or institutions where punishment is given.

● The classic novels *Les Misérables* and *The Count of Monte Cristo* portray the terrible conditions in French penal institutions in the last century.

A state or country's *penal code* defines its crimes and describes its punishments. During the 18th and 19th centuries, many countries established penal colonies, where criminals were sent as punishment. Often these were unbearably severe; but it was to such colonies that some of Australia's and the United States' early white inhabitants came, and the convicts provided labor for the European settlement of these lands.

penance \\'pe-nəns\\ An act of self-punishment or religious devotion to show sorrow or regret for sin or wrongdoing.

● In the Middle Ages bands of pilgrims would trudge to distant holy sites as penance for their sins.

Penance as a form of apology for a mistake can be either voluntary or ordered by someone else. Many religions include penance among the ways in which believers can show *repentance* or regret for a misdeed. The Christian season of Lent, 40 days long, is traditionally a time for doing penance.

punitive \\'pyü-nə-tiv\\ Giving, involving, or aiming at punishment.

● The loser in a court case is often directed to pay punitive damages, money over and above the actual cost of the harm done to the other party.

Trade sanctions, which limit one country's trade with another, are a form of punitive action that may be taken against a government for its human-rights violations or for acts of war, among other reasons. On a smaller scale, a school principal may take punitive measures against a misbehaving football team.

Quizzes

A. Fill in each blank with the correct letter:

a.	impunity	e.	empathy
b.	apathetic	f.	penal
c.	punitive	g.	pathology
d.	sociopath	h.	penance

1. Speeders seem to feel they can break the speed limit with ____.
2. Louis Pasteur studied the ____ of rabies in order to produce a vaccine.
3. In some households, grounding is a severe form of ____ action.
4. The mildest of the federal ____ institutions are the so-called "country club" prisons.
5. The ____ crowd responded to the singer with weak applause.
6. As ____ the wrongdoers were made to wash all the windows, except the one their ball had shattered.
7. Almost everyone feels some ____ for a child's misery.
8. A brutal dictator is the most destructive kind of ____.

B. Complete the analogy:

1. passionate : emotional :: apathetic : ____
   a. caring b. unjust c. indifferent d. dominant
2. fine : speeding :: penance : ____
   a. misdeed b. credit card c. fee d. behavior
3. psychology : mind :: pathology : ____
   a. suffering b. maps c. life d. disease
4. immunity : sickness :: impunity : ____
   a. death b. flood c. harm d. sleep
5. station wagon : car :: empathy : ____
   a. bus b. emotion c. idea d. pity
6. social : studies :: penal : ____
   a. violence b. attitude c. colony d. dream

7. composer : music :: sociopath : _____
   a. crime b. illness c. harmony d. dread
8. constructive : idea :: punitive : _____
   a. place b. damages c. focus d. outlet

MATR/METR comes from the Greek and Latin words for "mother." A *matron* is a mature woman with children; *matrimony* is marriage itself, traditionally a first step toward motherhood; and a *matrix* is something in which something else is embedded or takes form, like a baby.

---

maternity \mə-'tər-nə-tē\ The state of being a mother; motherhood.

• Some think the Mona Lisa's smile is the result of her maternity.

Maternity is used as both a noun and an adjective. *Maternity benefits* are benefits specially provided by employers for women having babies, and usually include *maternity leave*, time off work. With maternity come *maternal* feelings. All species of warm-blooded animals show maternal instincts, as do a few reptiles such as crocodiles and alligators.

matriculate \mə-'tri-kyù-,lāt\ To enroll as a member of a group, especially a school or college.

• They matriculated together at both boarding school and college, but after college they disappeared entirely from each other's life.

Matriculate comes into English from *matrix*, which in Latin meant a female animal used for breeding purposes, or a plant that was used to produce other plants. It later acquired the meaning "list" or "register," for in ancient times a list might be thought of as the source or parent of the names appearing on it. A student who matriculates at a school basically signs up on a list of students. (And the school or college attended will become his or her *alma mater*, Latin for "fostering mother.")

matrilineal \,ma-trə-'li-nē-əl\ Based on or tracing the family through the mother.

● Many of the peoples of Ghana in Africa trace their family through matrilineal connections.

Matrilineal means basically "through the mother's line"; *patrilineal* means "through the father's line." Most families that follow the European model take the father's name and are therefore patrilineal; many other peoples follow a matrilineal pattern. Under either system (but especially the latter) there can be *matriarchs,* mothers who rule (*arch*) or head their families or descendants.

metropolitan \,me-trə-'pä-lə-tən\ Having to do with a large, important city and sometimes also its surrounding suburbs.

● The Los Angeles metropolitan area is among the largest in the world and continues to grow.

Metropolis means basically "mother city," and in ancient Greece a metropolis was usually the original city of a colony—thus the mother from which the colony was born, so to speak. A modern *metropolitan area* can be immense, and in poor countries everywhere peasants are flooding into metropolitan centers in search of jobs, often simply exchanging one form of poverty for another even worse form.

MONI comes from the Latin verb *monere,* "to warn" or "to scold." Warning and scolding often are rather similar, since many warnings could be called "pre-scoldings."

---

admonish \ad-'mä-nish\ To warn or criticize mildly.

● The daydreaming student was admonished by the teacher, who told him to pay attention in the future.

The Senate may admonish, or "reprimand," a senator who has misbehaved, but this is far less serious than being "condemned" or actually expelled from the Senate. An *admonition* or *admonishment* usually is less severe than a scolding; it may simply caution against something, and it can even include encouragement.

monitory \'mä-nə-,tȯr-ē\ Giving warning; cautionary.

● Through the fog they could hear the mournful, monitory note of the foghorn.

A professor may start class with a monitory comment about final exams. A president may make a monitory speech addressed to a country that is ignoring its trade obligations. And a pope may issue a monitory message to the world on the subject of war or morality.

monitor \'mä-nə-tər\ To keep track of or watch, usually for a special reason.

● The North's armored ship the *Monitor* was designed to monitor the South's naval activities in the coastal waters.

Monitor can be both a verb and a noun. A heart monitor monitors a patient's heartbeat and warns of any problems. A hall monitor monitors students behavior in the hallways. Both machine and human monitors observe or supervise and give warnings if something goes wrong.

premonition \pre-mə-'ni-shən\ (1) A previous warning or notice; forewarning. (2) A feeling about an event or situation before it happens.

● He now remembered how the birds had been restless and noisy, as though they had felt a premonition of the coming earthquake.

A premonition is literally a forewarning. A story about Abraham Lincoln holds that he had a premonition of his death in a dream shortly before he was assassinated, but the *premonitory* dream did not prevent him from going to Ford's Theatre on April 14, 1865. John Kennedy flew to Dallas in 1963 ignoring the dark premonition expressed by the statesman Adlai Stevenson. And Martin Luther King delivered a great speech containing premonitions of his death only days before he was murdered in 1968.

Quizzes

A. Choose the closest definition:

1. matriculate   a. give birth   b. enroll   c. tickle   d. adjust
2. premonition   a. introduction   b. scolding
      c. prematurity   d. forewarning
3. matrilineal   a. through the mother's family
      b. graduating   c. adopted   d. female
4. monitory   a. monetary   b. mean   c. cautionary
      d. enthusiastic

5. metropolitan   a. urban b. suburban c. rural d. oceanic
6. monitor   a. think b. persuade c. avoid d. watch
7. maternity   a. motherhood b. childhood c. Robin
    Hood d. sainthood
8. admonish   a. praise b. arrest c. await d. scold

**B. Match the definition on the left with the correct word
    on the right:**

1. through the female line   a. monitor
2. warning   b. premonition
3. sign up at school   c. maternity
4. regulate   d. metropolitan
5. gently correct   e. matrilineal
6. early suspicion   f. matriculate
7. motherliness   g. admonish
8. city   h. monitory

Words from Mythology

cereal \'sir-ē-əl\ (1) A plant that produces grain that can be eaten
as food, or the grain it produces. (2) The food made from grain.

● Rice is the main food cereal grown in Asia, whereas wheat is the
main food cereal of the West.

The Roman goddess Ceres (the Greek Demeter) was a serene goddess who did not take part in the quarrels of the other gods. She
was in charge of the food-giving plants, and the grains came to
carry her name. Cereals of the Romans included wheat, barley,
spelt, oats, and millet, but not corn (maize), which was a cereal of
the Americas.

Junoesque \ˌjü-nō-'esk\ Having mature, poised, and dignified
beauty.

● In 1876, as a centennial gift, the French sent to America a massive
statue of a robed Junoesque figure representing Liberty.

Juno was the wife of Jupiter, the chief of the Roman gods. She was
a matron, mature and well filled out. Her presence was imposing;
her authority as wife of Jupiter and her power in her own right gave

her particular dignity. But the younger Diana, goddess of the hunt, perhaps came closer to today's ideals of slim and athletic female beauty.

martial \'mär-shəl\ Having to do with war and military life.

● The stirring, martial strains of "The British Grenadiers" echoed down the snowy street just as dawn was breaking.

Mars was the Roman god of war and one of the patron gods of Rome itself. He was in charge of everything military, from warriors to weapons to provisions to marching music. Thus, when *martial law* is proclaimed, a country's armed forces take over the functions of the police. *Martial arts* are skills of combat and self-defense also practiced as sport. And a *court-martial* is a military court or trial.

Promethean \prə-'mē-thē-ən\ New or creative in a daring way.

● At his best, Steven Spielberg has sometimes shown Promethean originality in the special effects of his movies.

Prometheus was a Titan, a generation older than Zeus. When Zeus overthrew his own father Cronus and seized power, Prometheus fought on the side of the gods and against his fellow Titans. But when Zeus later wanted to destroy the race of humans, Prometheus saved them by stealing fire for them from the gods. He also taught them how to write, farm, build houses, read the stars and weather, cure themselves when sick, and tame animals—in short, all the arts and skills that make humans unique. So inventive was he that anything that bears the stamp of creativity and originality can still be called Promethean. But for his disobedience Zeus had him chained to a rocky cliff, where for many long centuries an eagle daily tore at his liver. Thus, any suffering on a grand scale can also be called Promethean.

Sisyphean \si-sə-'fē-ən\ Endless and difficult.

● High-school dropouts usually find getting a good job to be a Sisyphean task.

Reputedly the cleverest man on earth, Sisyphus tricked the gods into bringing him back to life after he died. For this they punished him by sending him back to the underworld, where he must eternally roll a huge rock up a long, steep hill, only to watch it roll back to where he started. Something Sisyphean demands the same kind of unending, thankless, and ultimately unsuccessful efforts.

titanic \tī-'ta-nik\ Having great size, strength, or power; colossal.

• The titanic floods of 1993 destroyed whole towns on the Mississippi River.

The ocean liner *Titanic* was named for its unmatched size and strength and its assumed unsinkability. But a truly titanic iceberg ripped a fatal hole in the great ship on its maiden voyage in 1912, and more than 1,500 people perished in the icy waters off Newfoundland. In Greek mythology, the original Titans also came to a bad end. They belonged to the generation of giant creators that produced the younger, stronger, cleverer gods, who soon overpowered and replaced them (see *Promethean* above).

Triton \'trī-tən\ (1) A being with a human upper body and the lower body of a fish; a merman. (2) Any of various large mollusks with a heavy, conical shell.

• In one corner of the painting, a robust Triton emerges from the sea with his conch to announce the coming of the radiant queen.

Triton was originally the son of the sea god Poseidon/Neptune. A guardian of the fish and other creatures of the sea, he is usually shown as hearty, muscular, and cheerful. Like his father, he often carries a trident (a three-pronged fork) and sometimes rides in a chariot drawn by seahorses. Blowing on his conch shell, he creates the roar of the ocean. As a decorative image, Tritons are simply the male version of mermaids. The handsome seashells that bear his name are the very conchs on which he blows. Triton has also given his name to the planet Neptune's largest moon.

vulcanize \'vəl-kə-ˌnīz\ To treat crude or synthetic rubber or plastic so that it becomes elastic and strong and resists decay.

• The native islanders had even discovered how to vulcanize the rubber from the local trees in a primitive way.

The Roman god Vulcan (the Greek Hephaestus) was in charge of fire and the skills that use fire, especially blacksmithing. When Charles Goodyear accidentally discovered how to vulcanize rubber in 1839, he revolutionized the rubber industry. He called his process *vulcanization* because it used fire to heat the rubber (before the addition of sulfur and other ingredients). His discovery influenced the course of the Civil War, when balloons made of this new, stronger rubber carried Union spies over the Confederate armies.

Quiz

Fill in each blank with the correct letter:

a.	Promethean	e.	Sisyphean
b.	titanic	f.	vulcanize
c.	Triton	g.	cereal
d.	Junoesque	h.	martial

1. Doing the laundry and the ironing always seemed ____ in their endlessness and drudgery.
2. The bout between Muhammed Ali and George Foreman matched one ____ champion against another.
3. The aging jazz singer acquired a certain ____ quality in her mature years.
4. On each arm of the great candelabra was carved a ____ blowing on his conch.
5. Corn, unknown in ancient Europe, has become a staple ____ of the modern world.
6. When Goodyear discovered how to ____ rubber, he made Henry Ford's Model T possible.
7. Edison's mind may have been the most ____ since Leonardo da Vinci's.
8. The ____ arts of the Far East have become popular in the West as means of self-defense.

Review Quizzes

A. Indicate whether the following pairs of words have the same or different meanings:

1. aquamarine / navy blue   same ___ / different ___
2. subterranean / underground   same ___ / different ___

3.	eulogy / poetry	same ___ / different ___
4.	disputatious / passive	same ___ / different ___
5.	empathy / sentimentality	same ___ / different ___
6.	Junoesque / matriarchal	same ___ / different ___
7.	Promethean / creative	same ___ / different ___
8.	penance / regret	same ___ / different ___
9.	matriculate / graduate	same ___ / different ___
10.	monitory / warning	same ___ / different ___
11.	titanic / powerful	same ___ / different ___
12.	vulcanize / organize	same ___ / different ___
13.	monitor / guard	same ___ / different ___
14.	impunity / freedom from harm	same ___ / different ___
15.	pathology / anger	same ___ / different ___
16.	metropolitan / coastal	same ___ / different ___
17.	marina / dock	same ___ / different ___
18.	putative / natural	same ___ / different ___
19.	terrarium / tank	same ___ / different ___
20.	monologue / chorus	same ___ / different ___

B. Choose the word that does not belong:

1. Sisyphean a. difficult b. unending c. demanding
   d. rolling
2. maternity a. femininity b. parenthood
   c. motherliness d. motherhood
3. mariner a. sailor b. seaman c. crew member d. archer
4. cereal a. corn b. eggplant c. rice d. barley
5. reputed a. known b. reported c. believed d. thought
6. admonish a. warn b. scold c. ask d. correct
7. premonition a. sense b. proof c. omen
   d. forewarning
8. neologism a. new theory b. new word c. new usage
   d. new phrase
9. maritime a. coastal b. nautical c. oceangoing
   d. temperate
10. apathetic a. concerned b. unconcerned c. uncaring
    d. indifferent

**C. Match the definition on the right to the correct word
on the left:**

1. punitive   a. fancy garden
2. martial   b. through the mother's line

3.	parterre	c.	relating to punishment
4.	sociopath	d.	antisocial person
5.	penal	e.	related to war
6.	matrilineal	f.	disciplinary
7.	terrestrial	g.	family history
8.	genealogy	h.	earthly

Unit 11

CANT, from the Latin verbs *canere* and *cantare*, meaning "sing," produces several words that come directly from Latin, and others that come by way of French and add an *h* to the root: for example, *chant* and *chantey*.

---

cantata \kən-'tä-tə\ A musical composition, particularly a religious work from the 17th or 18th century, for one or more voices accompanied by instruments.

● During the Baroque era, composers like Telemann composed sacred cantatas by the hundreds.

A cantata is sung, unlike a sonata, which is played on instruments only. Johann Sebastian Bach wrote the music for over 200 religious cantatas; he chose verses to set from hymns and new religious poems. His cantatas consisted of several different sections for different voices—solos, duets, and choruses. Some of his nonreligious cantatas have been performed like mini-operas.

incantation \ˌin-ˌkan-'tā-shən\ (1) A use of spells or verbal charms spoken or sung as part of a ritual of magic. (2) A formula of words used in, or as if in, such a ritual.

● He repeated the words like an incantation: "The only way! The only way! The only way!"

Magic and ritual have always been associated with chanting and music. *Incantation* comes directly from the Latin word *incantare*, "enchant," which itself has *cantare* as a root. Incantations are often in strange languages; "Abracadabra" is a not-so-serious version of an incantation.

cantor \\'kan-tər\ An official of a Jewish synagogue who sings or chants the music of the services and leads the congregation in prayer.

• The congregation waited for the cantor to begin the prayers before joining in.

The cantor is, after the rabbi, the most important figure in a Jewish worship service. The cantor not only must possess an excellent singing voice but also must know by heart long passages of Hebrew. Basically, *cantor* simply means "singer." The comedian and singer Edward Israel Iskowitz renamed himself Eddie Cantor for his chosen profession and became enormously popular on stage, screen, radio, and television for over 40 years.

descant \\'des-,kant\ An additional melody sung above the principal melody.

• The soprano added a soaring descant to the final chorus that held the listeners spellbound.

The prefix *des-*, "two" or "apart," indicates that the descant is a "second song" apart from the main melody. In popular songs a descant will often be sung at the very end to produce a thrilling climax.

LUD/LUS comes from the Latin verb *ludere*, "to play," and *ludum*, "play" or "game." An *interlude* thus is something "between games" (*inter-* meaning "between"). A *delusion* or an *illusion* plays tricks on a person.

---

allude \ə-'lüd\ To refer broadly or indirectly.

• She liked to allude constantly to her glamorous past without ever filling in the details.

Literature is full of *allusions* in which the author refers to other, earlier works. In his epic religious poem *Paradise Lost*, John Milton alludes constantly to Greek and Latin literature, but also to events of his own time such as the discoveries and new countries of the Americas. Modern authors continue to use allusions in their work, and there is a constant flow of new material available to which they can allude. Music and art are almost as full of allusions as literature is.

collusion \kə-'lü-zhən\ A secret agreement or conspiracy for an illegal or deceptive purpose.

● Cuban cigars have continued to be smoked in this country in spite of the embargo against them because of collusion between Cuban cigar makers and American smugglers.

Collusion and the verb *collude* contain the prefix *col-* (from *con-*), meaning "with"; thus, they contain the meaning "play along with." A common form of collusion involves businesses within the same industry. Rather than competing fairly, businesses will sometimes collude to keep prices artificially high. This type of *collusive* behavior has been found in businesses from oil companies to private universities to major-league baseball, whose owners were fined millions of dollars for collusion in the 1980s.

ludicrous \'lü-də-krəs\ Laughable because of clear absurdity, falseness, or foolishness.

● At the rodeo, the ludicrous antics of the clown distract the angry bull and entertain the crowd.

In Hans Christian Andersen's tale "The Ugly Duckling," the ducks find their bumbling, gawky baby's attempts to act like a duck ludicrous. When he grows into a swan, more graceful and elegant than they could ever hope to be, it is surprising that he himself doesn't find the waddling ducks ludicrous. Be careful when using the word: a comment like "What a ludicrous idea!" can be rather insulting.

prelude \'prāl-ˌyüd\ A performance, action, event, or piece of music that precedes and prepares for the more important thing that follows.

● The sound of a symphony orchestra tuning up is the *prelude* to a night of music.

A prelude (*pre-* meaning "before") goes before the main event, just as an *interlude* goes between sections of it. Dark clouds rolling in overhead can be the prelude to a storm. Graduation ceremonies are often called commencement ("beginning") because they are considered a prelude to a new life.

Quizzes

A. Choose the closest definition:

1. descant   a. climb downward   b. added melody
   c. supposed inability   d. writing table
2. allude   a. play   b. detract   c. avoid   d. refer
3. incantation   a. ritual chant   b. ceremony   c. solemn
   march   d. recorded song
4. prelude   a. aftermath   b. conclusion   c. introduction
   d. admission
5. cantata   a. snack bar   b. pasta dish   c. sung
   composition   d. farewell gesture
6. ludicrous   a. tough   b. laughable   c. simple   d. ugly
7. cantor   a. singer   b. refusal   c. traitor   d. gallop
8. collusion   a. accidental crash   b. illegal cooperation
   c. new material   d. magic spell

B. Indicate whether the following pairs of words have the same or different meanings:

1. ludicrous / deceptive   same ___ / different ___
2. incantation / sacred dance   same ___ / different ___
3. prelude / introduction   same ___ / different ___
4. descant / enchant   same ___ / different ___
5. allude / begin   same ___ / different ___
6. cantata / sonata   same ___ / different ___
7. cantor / conductor   same ___ / different ___
8. collusion / smuggling   same ___ / different ___

PHAN/PHEN, from the Greek verbs that mean "to appear or seem" or "to present to the mind," has to do with the way things seem or appear rather than the way they really are. From these roots come words such as *fanciful* and *fantasy*, in which the imagination plays an important part.

phantasm \\'fan-,ta-zəm\\ An illusion or a ghost produced by imagination or creative invention.

● When night fell, his imagination filled the old, dark house with phantasms.

In Edgar Allan Poe's poem "The Raven," a weary scholar who has fallen asleep at midnight while reading strange old books talks with a phantasm, a ghastly raven that has come to tell him that he will "nevermore" meet his dead love in a Christian afterlife, since there is none. In the words of the old saying, "The sleep of reason produces monsters"—that is, phantasms.

phantasmagoria \fan-,taz-mə-'gȯr-ē-ə\ (1) A shifting succession of things seen or imagined. (2) A collection or combination of weird or imaginary things.

● Salvador Dalí's paintings offer a bizarre phantasmagoria of odd images.

To Western eyes an Arab souk, or market, can seem like a phantasmagoria of exotic items, but a Western supermarket can look equally *phantasmagorical* to a foreigner. A film or a novel can be *phantasmagoric*. The shifting content of a dream may seem like a phantasmagoria. To Sigmund Freud, these bizarre events and images had a deeper meaning: for Freud the key to a person's psychology lay in his or her *fantasies*.

phenomenon \fi-'nä-mə-,nän\ (1) A fact or event observed or known with the senses. (2) A rare, unusual, or important fact or event.

● To Noah and the others on his ark, the appearance of a rainbow was a joyous phenomenon.

Phenomena are "things" (though not generally "objects"), and sometimes "strange or unusual things." Something *phenomenal* is extraordinary, and *phenomenally* means "extremely" or "extraordinarily." Psychic phenomena, weather phenomena, social phenomena can all be either facts or events. A phenomenon is a single thing; the plural form is *phenomena*. Take care not to mix them up.

diaphanous \dī-'a-fə-nəs\ (1) Transparent. (2) Insubstantial or vague.

● The ballerinas of Tchaikovsky's *Swan Lake* wore diaphanous costumes that seemed to float.

Light mist is diaphanous, since things may be seen at least faintly through it. Gauzy fabric is diaphanous; another word for it is "sheer." A diaphanous princess might be a fantasy vision that is hardly real at all. And a diaphanous notion would be one without much real substance behind it.

VER comes from the Latin word for "truth." A *verdict* in a trial is "the truth spoken." But a just verdict may depend on the *veracity*, or "truthfulness," of the witnesses.

---

aver \ə-'vər\ To state positively as true; declare.

● The defendant averred that she was nowhere near the scene of the crime on the night in question.

You may aver anything that you're sure of. Since the word contains the "truth" root, it basically means "confirm as true." In legal situations it means to state or allege positively as a fact; thus, Perry Mason's clients aver that they are innocent, while the district attorney avers the opposite.

verify \'ver-ə-ˌfī\ (1) To prove to be true or correct. (2) To check or test the accuracy of.

● It is the bank teller's job to verify the signature on a check.

During talks between the United States and the former Soviet Union on nuclear weapons reduction, one big problem was how to verify that weapons had been eliminated. Since neither side wanted the other to know its secrets, *verification* of the facts became a difficult issue. Because of the distrust on both sides, many thought that the real numbers would never be *verifiable*.

verisimilitude \ˌver-ə-sə-'mi-lə-ˌtüd\ (1) The appearance of being true or probable. (2) The depiction of realism in art or literature.

● By the beginning of the 20th century, the leading European painters were losing interest in verisimilitude and beginning to experiment with abstraction.

From its roots, *verisimilitude* means basically "like the truth." Most fiction writers and filmmakers aim at some kind of verisimilitude to give their stories an air of reality. This doesn't mean they need to show something actually true, or even very common— just simply possible and believable. A mass of good details in a play, novel, painting, or film may add verisimilitude. A spy novel without some verisimilitude won't interest many readers, but a fantastical novel may not even attempt to seem true to life.

verity \'ver-ə-tē\ A true fact or statement.

• Ben Franklin's statement that "in this world nothing can be said to be certain, except death and taxes" is held as a verity by many.

The phrase "eternal verity" is often used to mean an enduring truth or bit of wisdom. Some eternal verities are found in proverbs, such as "Haste makes waste." The statement in the Declaration of Independence that "all men are created equal" is now held by many Americans to be an eternal verity—but few earlier governments had ever been based on such a truth.

Quizzes

A. Fill in each blank with the correct letter:

a.	phenomenon	e.	diaphanous
b.	aver	f.	verity
c.	phantasmagoria	g.	phantasm
d.	verify	h.	verisimilitude

1. They had never before seen a natural _____ like the boiling lake.

2. A week after his mother's death, he saw her _____ beckoning to him from the dock at dusk.

3. The prosecutor expected the witness to _____ that the suspect was guilty.

4. Realists in art and literature work to achieve _____ as they sense it.

5. Each candle was surrounded by the _____ fluttering wings of moths.

6. The Mardi Gras parade was a _____ of bizarre images too numerous to even take in.

7. She was never able to _____ anything he had told her.

8. Sometimes what has always seemed a _____ suddenly is shown to be false.

B. Complete the analogy:

1. believe : doubt :: aver : _____
   a. state b. mean c. deny d. subtract
2. scent : smell :: phenomenon : _____
   a. odor b. sight c. event d. sensation
3. illusion : fantasy :: verisimilitude : _____
   a. appearance b. realism c. style d. truth
4. faint : dim :: diaphanous : _____
   a. filmy b. huge c. old-fashioned d. sensational
5. loyalty : treason :: verity : _____
   a. dishonor b. hatred c. honesty d. falsehood
6. ogre : monster :: phantasm : _____
   a. surprise b. raven c. ghost d. fanfare
7. praise : ridicule :: verify : _____
   a. testify b. contradict c. establish d. foretell
8. fantasy : illusion :: phantasmagoria : _____
   a. collection b. kaleidoscope c. sideshow d. visions

TURB comes from the Latin verb *turbare*, "to throw into confusion or upset," and the noun *turba*, "crowd" or "confusion." A *disturbance*, for example, confuses and upsets normal order or routine.

---

perturb \pər-'tərb\ To upset, confuse, or disarrange.

● News of the new peace accord was enough to perturb some radical opponents of any settlements.

If the root -*turb* means basically "upset," then *perturb* means "thoroughly upset." A person in a *perturbed* state of mind is more than merely bothered. On the other hand, someone *imperturbable* remains calm through the most trying experiences.

turbine \'tər-ˌbīn\ A rotary engine with blades made to turn and generate power by a current of water, steam, or air under pressure.

● The power plant used huge turbines powered by water going over the dam to generate electricity.

The oldest and simplest form of turbine is the waterwheel, which is made to rotate by water falling across its blades and into buckets suspended from them. Hero of Alexandria invented the first steam-driven turbine in the 1st century A.D.; but a commercially practical steam turbine was not developed until 1884. Steam-driven turbines are now the main elements of electric power stations. Jet engines are gas turbines. A *turbojet* engine uses a turbine to compress the incoming air that feeds the engine before being ejected to push the plane forward; a *turboprop* engine uses its exhaust to drive a turbine that spins a propeller.

turbulent \'tər-byù-lənt\ (1) Stirred up, agitated. (2) Stirring up unrest, violence, or disturbance.

• The huge ocean liner *Queen Elizabeth II* has never been much troubled by turbulent or stormy seas.

Often the captain of an airplane will warn passengers to fasten their seatbelts because of upper-air *turbulence,* which can make for a bumpy ride. El Niño, a seasonal current of warm water in the Pacific Ocean, may create turbulence in the winds across the United States, affecting patterns of rainfall and temperature as well. The late 1960s are remembered as turbulent years of social revolution in America and Europe. Some people lead turbulent lives, and some are constantly in the grip of turbulent emotions.

turbid \'tər-bid\ (1) Thick or murky, especially with churned-up sediment. (2) Unclear, confused, muddled.

• The crowd's mood was restless and turbid; any spark could have turned it into a mob.

The Colorado River in spring, swollen by melting snow from the high mountains, races through the Grand Canyon, turbid and churning. A chemical solution may be described as turbid rather than clear. And your emotions may be turbid as well, especially where love is involved: What did he mean by that glance? Why did she say it like that?

VOLU/VOLV comes from the Latin verb *volvere,* meaning "to roll, wind, turn around, or twist around." From this source come words like *volume,* which was originally the name of a scroll or roll of papyrus, and *revolve,* which simply means "turn in circles."

devolution \‚de-və-'lü-shən\ (1) The transfer of rights, powers, property, or responsibility to others, especially from the central to local government. (2) Evolution toward an earlier or lower state.

● In the 1980s there was a devolution of responsibility for education from the federal government to state and local governments.

Devolution implies moving backward. Once powers have been centralized in a unified government, giving any powers back to smaller governmental units can seem to be reversing a natural development. But we may also speak of moral devolution, such as occurred in Germany in the 1930s, when a country with an extraordinarily high culture became a brutal, aggressive, murderous dictatorship. The verb form is *devolve*. Thus, a job that your boss doesn't want to do may devolve upon you.

evolution \‚e-və-'lü-shən\ A process of change from a lower, simpler, or worse state to one that is higher, more complex, or better.

● Thomas Jefferson and the other Founding Fathers believed that political evolution reached its highest form in democracy.

Part of the humor of *The Flintstones* is that it contradicts what is known about evolution, since humans actually *evolved* long after dinosaurs were extinct. *Evolution* can also be used more broadly to refer to technology, society, and other human creations. For example, though many people don't believe that human beings truly become better with the passing centuries, many will argue that our societies tend to evolve, producing more goods and providing more protection for more people.

voluble \'väl-yu̇-bəl\ Speaking readily and rapidly; talkative.

● He proved to be a voluble informer who would tell stories of bookies, smugglers, and hit men to the detectives for hours.

A voluble person has words "rolling" off his or her tongue. In O. Henry's famous story "The Ransom of Red Chief" the kidnappers nab a boy who is so unbearably voluble that they can hardly wait to turn him loose again.

convoluted \'kän-və-‚lü-təd\ (1) Having a pattern of curved windings. (2) Involved, intricate.

• After 15 minutes, Mr. Collins's strange story had become so convoluted that none of us could follow it.

Convolution originally meant a complex winding pattern such as those on the brain. So a convoluted argument or a convoluted explanation is one that winds this way and that. An official form may have to wind its way through a convoluted process and be stamped by eight people before being approved. Convoluted language makes many people suspicious; as a great philosopher once said, "Anything that can be said can be said clearly."

Quizzes

A. Choose the closest definition:

1. convoluted   a. spinning b. babbling c. grinding
      d. winding
2. turbine   a. whirlpool b. engine c. headdress d. carousel
3. evolution   a. process of development b. process of
      democracy c. process of election d. process of
      elimination
4. perturb   a. reset b. inset c. preset d. upset
5. voluble   a. whirling b. unpleasant c. talkative
      d. garbled
6. turbulent   a. churning b. turning c. yearning d. burning
7. turbid   a. flat b. calm c. confused d. slow
8. devolution   a. handing down b. handing in c. turning
      up d. turning around

**B. Match the word on the left to the correct definition
     on the right:**

1.	voluble	a.	murky
2.	turbine	b.	fluent
3.	evolution	c.	seething
4.	turbid	d.	complicated
5.	devolution	e.	turning engine
6.	perturb	f.	degeneration
7.	convoluted	g.	disturb
8.	turbulent	h.	progress

FAC/FEC/FIC comes from the Latin verb *facere*, meaning "to make or do." Thus, a *benefactor* is someone who does good. To *manufacture* is to make, usually in a *factory*.

---

confection \kən-'fek-shən\ (1) A sweet food or fancy dish prepared from a variety of ingredients. (2) A piece of fine craftsmanship.

● The children's eyes grew wide with delight at the sight of the confections in the baker's window.

A confection is *confected* from several different ingredients or elements. Among the tastiest confections are the marzipan (almond-paste) creations molded and painted to look like fruit. The word can also be used to refer to any finely worked piece of craftsmanship. So the lacy box containing chocolate confections can be called a confection itself.

facile \'fa-səl\ (1) Easily accomplished. (2) Shallow, superficial.

● The principal made a facile argument for the school's policy, but no one was convinced.

A facile writer seems to write too quickly and easily, and a careful reader discovers that the writer hasn't really said very much. A facile suggestion doesn't deal with the issue in any depth, and a facile solution may be only temporarily effective.

olfactory \ol-'fak-tə-rē\ Having to do with the sense of smell.

● The olfactory sense of some dogs is so powerful that they can smell a human under 20 feet of snow.

Olfactory includes part of the Latin verb *olere*, meaning "to smell." The tasters of great wines depend more on their olfactory sense than they do on their taste buds. The olfactory nerve, which produces the sense of smell, is closely connected to the sense of taste. Since the *gustatory* (taste) nerves can only distinguish four different tastes (salt, sweet, sour, and bitter), the rest of our taste perception is actually olfactory.

proficient \prə-'fi-shənt\ Skilled in an art, occupation, or branch of knowledge.

• She's proficient at every aspect of the job; all she lacks is imagination.

Proficiency is achieved through hard work and maybe talent as well. You may be proficient at math or proficient in three languages, or you may be a proficient swimmer. A proficient pianist plays the piano with skill. But proficiency isn't genius, and even calling someone proficient may imply that the person isn't brilliantly gifted.

UT/US comes from the Latin verb *uti,* "to use, make use of, employ," and the related adjective *utilis,* "useful, fit." It is *used* in such words as *abuse,* "improper use," and *reuse,* "to use again."

---

usufruct \\'yü-zə-ˌfrəkt\\ (1) The right to use or enjoy something. (2) The legal right of using or enjoying the products or profits of something that belongs to someone else.

• When they sold the land, they retained the right by usufruct to pick the apples in the orchards they had planted.

Usufruct is a concept that has come down from ancient times. The original term in Latin was *usus et fructus,* meaning "use and enjoyment." It is an interesting concept: since the original owner can devolve the responsibility of upkeep and taxes onto someone else while keeping usufruct, he or she may get the best of the deal. Usufruct rights end at a certain point, often when the user dies, and do not permit changing or damaging the property. As Thomas Jefferson said (and many environmentalists have echoed), "The earth belongs in usufruct to the living." And as the Roman philosopher Lucretius said, life itself is given to us only in usufruct.

usury \\'yü-zhə-rē\\ The lending of money with a fee charged for its use, especially lending for an unusually high fee.

• He responded that demanding 25 percent interest on the loan was usury.

Shylock, in Shakespeare's *The Merchant of Venice,* is accused of usury, since he has bargained to take a pound of Antonio's flesh in place of the money Antonio owes him. Since this would result in Antonio's death, it seems like an excessive and *unusual* penalty for the failure to repay a debt. To the borrower, usury seems *abusive*; to the lender, it is a fair fee for use of the money. No wonder Polonius told Laertes in *Hamlet*, "Neither a borrower nor a lender be''; the borrower becomes careless about spending and ends up at the *usurer's* mercy, and the lender often becomes resented or even hated and may lose his or her money.

utilitarian \yü-,ti-lə-'tar-ē-ən\ (1) Aiming at usefulness rather than beauty. (2) Useful for a specific purpose or end.

• Their view of life was strictly utilitarian; for them there was no room for art, pleasure, or relaxed conversation.

The Shakers, a religious group that dedicated itself to work and its work to God, had a utilitarian outlook on the design of furniture and household objects. Their finished pieces—whether tables, chairs, brooms, or baskets—are beautifully simple and very well fitted to their use. But *utilitarian* often means somewhat homely. Utilitarian architecture, such as many government housing projects, may be quite ugly, for example. If we say something has utilitarian value, however, we simply mean it is useful in some way.

utility \yü-'ti-lə-tē\ (1) Usefulness. (2) A government-regulated business providing a public service; the service it provides.

• The book was an invention of such extraordinary utility that in 2,000 years no one has improved on it.

A dog bred for utility is one intended for a particular use such as hunting or herding. It may be called a *utility* dog, just as a Jeep may be called a utility vehicle. The local electric company is one kind of company often called a utility, and the electric, gas, and water service in your home are called utilities as well.

Quizzes

A. Fill in each blank with the correct letter:

a.	usufruct	e.	facile
b.	utilitarian	f.	confection
c.	utility	g.	olfactory
d.	usury	h.	proficient

1. They kept the right to use their neighbor's dock by ＿＿.

2. The interest rate for the loan offered by the bank amounted to sheer ＿＿.

3. She was quick-witted but often her reasoning was ＿＿ and not deeply thoughtful.

4. She chose an inexpensive, ＿＿ model with no radio and no power windows.

5. Mozart was ＿＿ at the piano by the age of 5.

6. The ＿＿ of his 1940s typewriter was such that he never felt the need for a word processor.

7. The gown in the window was a gorgeous ＿＿ by the designer Ariane.

8. Commuting daily through the smog-filled air, she was grateful that her ＿＿ sense was not very keen.

B. Indicate whether the following pairs of words have the same or different meanings:

1. proficient / skillful   same ＿ / different ＿
2. usufruct / sweetness   same ＿ / different ＿
3. confection / candy   same ＿ / different ＿
4. utility / tool   same ＿ / different ＿
5. olfactory / assembly   same ＿ / different ＿
6. usury / customary   same ＿ / different ＿
7. facile / slippery   same ＿ / different ＿
8. utilitarian / useful   same ＿ / different ＿

Words from Mythology and History

muse \'myüz\ A source of inspiration; a guiding spirit.

● At 8:00 each morning he sat down at his desk and summoned his muse, and she almost always responded.

The Muses were the nine Greek goddesses that presided over the arts (including *music*) and literature. Their temple was called in Latin the *Museum*. An artist or poet such as Homer, especially when about to begin work, would call on his particular Muse to inspire him. Today a muse may be one's special creative spirit, but some artists have also chosen living human beings to serve as their muses.

iridescent \ˌir-ə-'de-sənt\ Having a glowing, rainbowlike play of color that seems to change as the light shifts.

• The children shrieked with glee as they blew iridescent soap bubbles into the gentle breeze.

Iris, the Greek goddess of the rainbow, took messages from Mount Olympus to earth, and from gods to mortals or other gods, using the rainbow as her stairway. *Iridescence* is thus the glowing, shifting, colorful quality of a rainbow, also seen in an opal, a light oil slick, a butterfly wing, or the mother-of-pearl that lines an oyster shell.

mausoleum \ˌmȯ-zə-'lē-əm\ (1) A large tomb, especially one built aboveground with shelves for the dead. (2) A large, gloomy building or room.

• The family's grand mausoleum occupied a prominent spot in the cemetery, for all the good it did the silent dead within.

Mausolus was ruler of a kingdom in Asia Minor in the 4th century B.C. He beautified the capital, Halicarnassus, with all sorts of fine public buildings, but he is best known for the magnificent monument, the Mausoleum, that was built by his wife Artemisia after his death. The Mausoleum was one of the Seven Wonders of the Ancient World. Today any large tomb can be called a mausoleum, and so can any big, dark, echoing interior space.

mentor \'men-ˌtȯr\ A trusted counselor, guide, tutor, or coach.

• This pleasant old gentleman had served as friend and mentor to a series of young lawyers in the firm.

Odysseus was away from home fighting and journeying for 20 years, according to Homer. During that time, the son he left as a babe in arms grew up under the supervision of Mentor, an old and trusted friend. When the goddess Athena decided it was time to complete young Telemachus's education by sending him off to learn about his father, she visited him disguised as Mentor and they set out together. From this, anyone such as a coach or tutor who gives another (usually younger) person help and advice on how to achieve success in the larger world is called a mentor.

narcissism \\'när-si-ˌsi-zəm\ (1) Extreme self-centeredness or fascination with oneself. (2) Love or desire for one's own body.

● His girlfriend would complain about his narcissism, saying he spent more time looking in the mirror than looking at her.

Narcissus was a handsome youth in Greek mythology who inspired love in many who saw him. One was the nymph Echo, who could only repeat the last thing that anyone said. When Narcissus cruelly rejected her, she wasted away to nothing but her voice. Though he played with the affections of others, Narcissus became a victim of his own attractiveness. When he caught sight of his own reflection in a pool, he sat gazing at it in fascination, wasting away without food or drink, unable to touch or kiss the image he saw. When he finally died, the gods turned him into a flower, a narcissus, that stands with its head bent as though gazing at its own reflection. From this myth comes the name of a psychological disorder, narcissism, which is the excessive love of oneself, as well as a more common type of vanity and self-centeredness.

tantalize \\'tan-tə-ˌlīz\ To tease or torment by offering something desirable but keeping it out of reach.

● The sight of a warm fire through the window tantalized the little match girl almost unbearably.

Tantalus, according to Greek mythology, killed his son Pelops and offered him to the gods in a stew for dinner. Almost all of the gods realized what was happening and refused the meal, but Demeter took a nibble out of Pelops's shoulder. The gods reconstructed Pelops, replacing the missing shoulder with a piece of ivory, and then punished Tantalus. In Hades he stands in water up to his neck under a tree laden with fruit. Each time he stoops to drink, the water moves out of reach; each time he reaches up to pick something, the branches move beyond his grasp. He is thus eternally tantalized by the water and fruit. Today anything or anyone that tempts but is unobtainable is tantalizing.

thespian \\'thes-pē-ən\ (1) An actor. (2) Having to do with the drama; dramatic.

● In summer the towns of New England welcome troupes of thespians dedicated to presenting plays of all kinds.

Greek drama was originally entirely performed by choruses. Literary tradition says that Thespis, the Greek dramatist, was inventor of tragedy and the first to write roles for the individual actor as distinct from the chorus. Thespians fill all the roles in more modern plays. *Thespian* is also an adjective; thus, we can speak of "thespian ambitions" and "thespian traditions," for example.

zephyr \\'ze-fər\\ (1) A breeze from the west. (2) A gentle breeze.

● Columbus left Genoa sailing against the zephyrs that continually blow across the Mediterranean.

The ancient Greeks called the west wind Zephyrus and regarded him and his fellow winds as gods. A zephyr is a kind wind, bringer of clear skies and beautiful weather, though it may occasionally be more than a soft breeze.

Quiz

Fill in each blank with the correct letter:

a.	mausoleum	e.	muse
b.	thespian	f.	mentor
c.	iridescent	g.	zephyr
d.	tantalize	h.	narcissism

1. The couple felt timid and small inside the vast _____ where their lawyer asked them to come.
2. On fair days a gentle _____ would blow from morning until night.
3. The company president took the new recruit under her wing and acted as her _____ for the next several years.
4. He would often _____ her with talk of traveling to Brazil or India, but nothing ever came of it.
5. The puddle's surface was beautifully _____ in the slanting light.
6. After his last book of poetry was published, his _____ seemed to have abandoned him.
7. In everyone there is a bit of the _____ yearning for a stage.
8. By working as a model, she could satisfy her _____ while getting paid for it.

Review Quizzes

A. Choose the correct antonym and the correct synonym:

1. voluble   a. argumentative b. mumbly c. speechless
   d. talkative
2. proficient   a. lazy b. skilled c. inept d. professional
3. utilitarian   a. useless b. useful c. usual d. unusual
4. zephyr   a. stormy blast b. icy rain c. light shower
   d. gentle breeze
5. aver   a. reject b. detract c. deny d. assert
6. diaphanous   a. broken b. filmy c. muddy d. tattered
7. ludicrous   a. serious b. ordinary c. laughable
   d. amazing
8. perturb   a. soothe b. restore c. park d. upset
9. devolution   a. decay b. turn c. suggestion
   d. improvement
10. usury   a. sending b. lending c. giving d. mending
11. draconian   a. precise b. gentle c. harsh d. inaccurate
12. turbulent   a. churning b. official c. cloudy d. calm
13. tantalize   a. visit b. satisfy c. tease d. watch
14. iridescent   a. shimmering b. drab c. striped d. watery
15. mentor   a. translator b. interpreter c. guide d. student
16. phantasm   a. vision b. amazement c. actuality
    d. horror

B. Indicate whether the following pairs of terms have the same or different meanings:

1. thespian / teacher   same ___ / different ___
2. facile / nasty   same ___ / different ___
3. evolution / extinction   same ___ / different ___
4. verify / prove   same ___ / different ___
5. phenomenon / event   same ___ / different ___
6. collusion / opposition   same ___ / different ___
7. incantation / luxury   same ___ / different ___
8. turbid / muddy   same ___ / different ___
9. olfactory / smelling   same ___ / different ___
10. usufruct / right of use   same ___ / different ___

C. Fill in each blank with the correct letter:

a.	prelude	g.	confection
b.	narcissism	h.	allude
c.	descant	i.	cantor
d.	verisimilitude	j.	phantasmagoria
e.	cantata	k.	turbine
f.	verity	l.	mausoleum

1. It was accepted as a _____ in their household that the future would be better than the past.

2. They were a very attractive couple, but their _____ often annoyed other people.

3. The university chorus was going to perform a Bach _____ along with the Mozart *Requiem*.

4. The children were invited to choose one chocolate _____ apiece from the counter display.

5. He began his singing career as a _____ in Brooklyn and ended it as an international opera star.

6. She remembered Mardi Gras only as an endless _____ of swirling images.

7. One day in the cemetery the _____ door was open, and he peered in with horrified fascination.

8. She would try to _____ to the problem sometimes, but he never seemed to listen.

9. The cocktail party was only a _____ to the main event, the awards ceremony.

10. Her films showed her own reality, and she had no interest in _____.

11. The roar of the _____ was so loud they couldn't hear each other.

12. As part of their musical training, she always encouraged them to sing their own _____ over the main melody.

Unit 12

UMBR, from the Latin *umbra,* "shadow," is a shady customer. The familiar *umbrella,* with its ending meaning "little," casts a "little shadow" to keep off the sun or the rain.

adumbrate \'a-dəm-brāt\ (1) To give a sketchy outline or disclose in part. (2) To hint at or foretell.

• The Secretary of State would only adumbrate his ideas for bringing peace to Bosnia.

A synonym for *adumbrate* is *foreshadow,* which means to present a shadowy version of something before it becomes reality or is provided in full. Rats scurrying off a ship were believed to adumbrate a coming disaster at sea. A bad review by a critic may adumbrate the failure of a new film.

penumbra \pə-'nəm-brə\ (1) The partial shadow surrounding a complete shadow, as in an eclipse. (2) The fringe or surrounding area where something exists less fully.

• This area of the investigation was the penumbra where both the FBI and the CIA wanted to pursue their leads.

Every solar eclipse casts an *umbra,* the darker central area in which almost no light reaches the earth, and a penumbra, the area of partial shadow where part of the sun is still visible. *Penumbra* can thus be used to describe any "gray area" where things are not all black and white. For example, the right to privacy falls under the penumbra of the U.S. Constitution; though it is not specifically guaranteed there, the Supreme Court has held that it is implied, and thus that the government may not intrude into certain areas of a citizen's private life. Because its existence is still shadowy, however, the

Court is still determining how much of an individual's life is protected by the right to privacy.

umber \'əm-bər\ (1) A darkish brown mineral containing manganese and iron oxides used for coloring paint. (2) A color that is greenish brown to dark reddish brown.

● Van Dyke prized umber as a pigment and used it constantly in his oil paintings.

The mineral deposits of Italy provided sources of a number of natural pigments, among them umber. Since the late Renaissance, umber has been in great demand as a coloring agent. When crushed and mixed with paint it produces an olive, known as *raw umber*; when crushed and burnt it produces a darker tone, known as *burnt umber*.

umbrage \'əm-brij\ A feeling of resentment at some slight or insult, often one that is imagined rather than real.

● She often took umbrage at his treatment of her, without being able to pinpoint what was offensive about it.

An umbrage was originally a shadow, and soon also meant a shadowy suspicion. Then it came to mean displeasure as well—that is, a kind of shadow blocking the sunlight. *Umbrage* is now generally used in the phrase "take umbrage at." An overly sensitive person may take umbrage at something as small as having his or her name pronounced wrong.

VEST comes from the Latin verb *vestire*, "to clothe" or "to dress," and the related noun *vestis*, "clothing" or "garment." *Vest* is the shortest English word we have from this root, and is the name of a rather small piece of clothing.

---

divest \dī-'vest\ (1) To get rid of or free oneself of property, authority, or title. (2) To strip of clothing, ornaments, or equipment.

● In protest against apartheid, many universities in the 1980s divested themselves of all stock in South African companies.

When it turned out that the New York Marathon had been won by fraud, the "winner" was divested of her prize. When a church is officially abandoned, it is usually divested of its ornaments and furnishings. And if you decide to move or to enter a monastery, you may divest yourself of many of your possessions.

investiture \in-'ves-tə-ˌchůr\ The formal placing of someone in office.

• At an English monarch's investiture, he or she is presented with the crown, scepter, and sword, the symbols of power.

In its original meaning, *investiture* referred to clothing the new officeholder in the garments that symbolized power. The Middle Ages saw much debate over the investiture of bishops and abbots by kings and emperors. These rulers felt that high religious offices were theirs to give to whomever they chose as a reward for loyal service or as a guarantee of future support, but the popes saw these investitures as the buying and selling of church offices. The investiture struggle caused tension between popes and monarchs and even led to wars.

transvestite \tranz-'ves-ˌtīt\ A person, especially a male, who wears the clothing and adopts the mannerisms of the opposite sex.

• Gounod's opera *Romeo and Juliet* calls for a woman in the transvestite role of Romeo.

Transvestite includes the prefix *trans-*, "across," and thus means literally "cross-dresser." Today it is so acceptable for women to wear men's clothing that the word *transvestite* is generally applied only to men. In the theater, from ancient Greece to Elizabethan England, *transvestism* was common because all parts were played by men—even Juliet. Japanese Kabuki and No drama still employ transvestism of this sort.

travesty \'tra-vəs-tē\ (1) An inferior or distorted imitation. (2) A broadly comic imitation in drama, literature, or art that is usually grotesque and ridiculous.

• The senator shouted again that the new tax bill represented a travesty of tax reform.

The word *travesty* comes from the same prefix and root as *transvestite* and originally meant "to disguise." The "free elections" so often promised by military governments usually amount to a travesty of democracy—a disguise intended to fool the world. The variety show *Saturday Night Live* specializes in dramatic travesties mocking everything from political figures and issues to popular culture—"disguised" versions intended for entertainment. *Travesty* may also be a verb. Thus, Mel Brooks has travestied movies of all kinds—westerns, thrillers, and silent films, among others.

Quizzes

A. Fill in the blank with the correct letter:

a. penumbra   e. divest
b. transvestite   f. umber
c. investiture   g. umbrage
d. travesty   h. adumbrate

1. Titian employed assistants to mix the _____ and other pigments for his paintings.
2. The _____ of the prime minister was an occasion of pomp and ceremony.
3. Some people are quick to take _____ the moment they think they have been slighted.
4. Since all the judges were cronies of the dictator, the court proceedings were a _____ of justice.
5. The new director planned to _____ the museum of two of its Picassos.
6. The farther away a source of light is from the object casting a shadow, the wider will be that shadow's _____.
7. The young model became a notorious success when she was discovered to be a _____.
8. The increasing cloudiness and the damp wind seemed to _____ a stormy night.

B. Match the definition on the left to the correct word on the right:

1. resentment   a. penumbra
2. brownish color   b. travesty
3. installing in office c. transvestite
4. cross-dresser   d. adumbrate
5. imitation   e. divest
6. get rid of   f. umbrage
7. near shadow   g. investiture
8. partially disclose h. umber

THE/THEO comes from the Greek word meaning "god." *Theology* is the study of gods or religion. *Monotheism* is the worship of a single god; someone who is *polytheistic,* however, worships many gods.

apotheosis \ə-ˌpä-thē-'ō-səs\ (1) Transformation into a god. (2) The perfect example.

● After his assassination Abraham Lincoln underwent an apotheosis that transformed the controversial politician into a saintly father of democracy.

The word *apotheosis* has the prefix *apo-,* "relating to"; thus, it suggests a human who has become godlike. In Greek mythology, very few humans were *apotheosized,* but Heracles (Hercules) was one who made the grade, and there are pictures painted on ancient vases showing the big party the rest of the gods held for him when he joined them after his apotheosis. Any great classic example of something can be called its apotheosis; a collector might state, for example, that the Duesenberg Phaeton was the apotheosis of the touring car.

atheistic \ˌā-thē-'is-tik\ Denying the existence of God or divine power.

● The atheistic Madalyn Murray O'Hair successfully sought the removal of prayer from American public schools in the 1960s.

In the Roman Empire, early Christians were said to be atheistic because they denied the existence of the gods of the pantheon. The Christian church, once established, in turn condemned the unconverted Romans as *atheists* because they did not believe in the Christian God. *Atheism* is different from *agnosticism,* which claims that the existence of any higher power is unknowable.

pantheistic \ˌpan-thē-'is-tik\ (1) Seeing the power of God in all the natural forces of the universe. (2) Worshiping all gods of all creeds and cults.

● Her personal religion was almost pantheistic; she saw the holy books of Hinduism and the rituals of Caribbean folk religion as expressions of the same essential truths.

Pan means "all"; thus, *pantheistic* refers to "all gods," or alternatively to "god in all things." Originally each Roman god and goddess had a temple where sacrifices were offered and sacred objects were stored. But there came a time when too many gods demanded attention, so only a big temple in honor of the entire group would do. Thus, the great temple known as the *Pantheon* was dedicated to all the gods. (These days, *pantheon* can also refer to a group of historical superstars in any one area—the pantheon of basketball or of literature, for example.)

theocracy \thē-'ä-krə-sē\ (1) Government by officials who are regarded as divinely inspired. (2) A state governed by a theocracy.

• The ancient Aztecs lived in a theocracy in which guidance came directly from the gods through the priests.

The ancient state of Israel and its related state of Judah were *mono-theistic* (one-god) theocracies; the ancient state of the Aztecs in Mexico was a *polytheistic* (multi-god) theocracy, as was that of the ancient Sumerians. All four seem to have agreed that the power of the ruling god or gods was most forceful in high places. The Sumerians and Aztecs built enormous pyramidlike temples; the Jews sought divine guidance on mountaintops. Modern-day theocracies are rare; Iran has been the best-known recent *theocratic* government.

DE/DIV comes from two related Roman words, *deus,* "god," and *divus,* "divine." *Deism,* a philosophy that teaches natural religion, emphasizes morality, and denies that the creator god interferes with the laws of the universe, was the basic faith of many of America's Founding Fathers.

---

deity \'dē-ə-tē\ A god or goddess.

• The many-armed deity Kali, wife of Shiva, is the Hindu goddess of death.

The ancient Greek deities had special cities and places they protected in return for sacrifices and prayers and special celebrations in their honor. Athena was the deity in charge of Athens; Hera was responsible for Sparta and Argos, and Apollo for Delphi. Each deity also had responsibility for a specific function or area of life: Athena for weaving and other crafts, Hera for marriage, and Apollo for the lives of young men, music, and *divination* (foretelling the future).

deus ex machina \'dā-əs-ˌeks-'mä-ki-nə\ (1) In Greek and Roman drama, a god who enters above the stage by means of a crane and decides the play's outcome. (2) A person or thing that appears suddenly and solves an apparently unsolvable problem.

• Pinned down by enemy fire, the soldiers had nearly given up hope when a helicopter appeared like a deus ex machina.

Deus ex machina means literally "the god from the machine," referring to the crane that held the god over the stage. A character in a mystery who appears from out of nowhere with the solution near the end could be called a deus ex machina; however, dedicated mystery readers have contempt for such solutions.

divinatory \də-'vi-nə-ˌtȯr-ē\ Seeking to foresee or foretell the future, usually by interpreting signs or asking for supernatural help.

• Astrologers today claim to use divinatory methods handed down from the ancient Egyptians and Babylonians.

Throughout history, divinatory practices that seek to reveal the future have been popular. In Roman times, a *diviner* known as a "haruspex" would search the guts of sacrificed animals to foretell coming events. The flights of birds were interpreted by a type of *divination* known as "augury." Tarot cards, séances, Ouija boards, and palm readings continue to be used by people hoping to *divine* (predict) the future.

divinity \də-'vi-nə-tē\ (1) The state of being a god or goddess. (2) A god or goddess; a deity.

• Some early Christian sects, such as the Arians, questioned the actual divinity of Jesus Christ.

In the 5th century A.D., the Roman Empire was on the verge of collapse. Many Roman senators claimed that the divinities that had always protected the city had abandoned them because so many people worshiped a new divinity, the Christian God. In defense, St. Augustine wrote *The City of God,* arguing that all earthly cities must pass, and that only the one true Divinity is eternal.

Quizzes

A. Fill in each blank with the correct letter:

a. pantheistic   e. deity
b. deus ex machina   f. apotheosis
c. atheistic   g. divinatory
d. divinity   h. theocracy

1. There around the temple stood idols of all the gods of this ____ religion.

2. The psychic's ____ powers were regarded by her clients as astounding.

3. His well-known ____ beliefs meant the young politician could hope for only limited success.

4. There above the stage appeared Apollo, the ____, to solve the dilemma.

5. Being inducted into the Hall of Fame is as close as a modern ballplayer can come to ____.

6. She addressed her prayer to whatever ____ chose to listen.

7. When the young man's followers proclaimed his ____, the believing Christians were shocked.

8. The high priest in this medieval ____ was equivalent to a dictator.

B. Match the word on the left to its definition on the right:

1. deity   a. state ruled by religion
2. pantheistic   b. dramatic device
3. apotheosis   c. supreme being
4. divinity   d. nonbelieving
5. atheistic   e. godliness
6. divinatory   f. accepting all gods
7. theocracy   g. prophetic
8. deus ex machina   h. perfect example

DEMO comes from the Greek word meaning "people." A *demagogue* leads the people, usually into trouble, by lying and appealing to their prejudices.

demographic \,de-mə-'gra-fik\ Having to do with the study of human populations, especially their size, growth, density, and patterns of living.

● The government used the latest demographic figures to decide how much money to spend on education.

Demographic analysis, the statistical description of human populations, is a tool used by government agencies, political parties, and manufacturers of consumer goods. Polls conducted on every topic imaginable, from age to toothpaste preference, give the government and corporations an idea of who the public is and what it needs and wants. The government's census, which is conducted every ten years, is the largest demographic survey carried out in this country.

endemic \en-'de-mik\ (1) Found only in a given place or region. (2) Often found in a given occupation, area, or environment.

● Malaria is a disease that is endemic in tropical regions around the world.

Endemic means literally "in the population." Since the panda is found in the wild exclusively in central China and eastern Tibet, scientists say that it is "endemic to" those areas or that they are "endemic areas" for the panda. But the word can also mean simply "common" or "typical," so we can say that colds are "endemic in" nursery school and that love of Barbie dolls is "endemic among" young American girls.

pandemic \,pan-'de-mik\ Widespread and affecting a large portion of the people.

● The worldwide AIDS pandemic may eventually prove to be the most deadly such event in human history.

Pandemic is a stronger version of *epidemic*. In a pandemic outbreak, practically everyone may be affected. In 1348 a pandemic plague called the Black Death struck Western Europe and killed 25 million people. In 1918 a *pandemic* of influenza killed 20 million people around the world. Pandemic smallpox repeatedly swept through the world's populations until the 1970s, even though a vaccine had existed since 1798. When the Beatles first visited the United States in the early 1960s, they were greeted by pandemic "Beatlemania," a mild form of musical insanity.

demotic \di-'mä-tik\ Popular or common.

● Because of television, the demotic language and accents of the various regions of this country are becoming more and more similar.

Demotic describes what is done by ordinary people as a group. It often describes their speech—demotic Californian is different from demotic Texan, for example. The most demotic dress in America is probably blue jeans and sneakers, and those who wear them can be said to have demotic taste in fashion.

POPUL comes from the Latin word meaning "people," and in fact forms the basis of the word *people* itself. *Popular* means not only "liked by many people" but also "relating to the general public." *Popular culture* is thus the culture of the general public. And the *population* is the people of an area.

---

populist \'pä-pyə-list\ A believer in the rights, wisdom, or virtues of the common people.

● He decided that he would campaign as a populist in order to appeal to his working-class voters.

The word *populist* first appeared in the 1890s with the founding of the Populist Party, which stood primarily for the interests of the farmers against the big-money interests. In later years *populism* came to be associated with the white working class as well. Populism can swing from liberal to conservative. It sometimes has a religious tendency; it usually is not very interested in international affairs; it has sometimes been unfriendly to black interests; and it is often anti-intellectual. But the *populist* style always shows its concern with Americans with average incomes as opposed to the rich and powerful.

populace \'pä-pyu̇-ləs\ (1) The common people or masses. (2) Population.

● Perhaps Henry Ford's major achievement was to manufacture a car that the entire populace could afford—the Model T.

Franklin D. Roosevelt's famous radio "Fireside Chats" were designed to address the entire populace in a familiar way. He used the talks to *popularize* his economic programs and to give heart to the populace as they struggled through the Great Depression.

populous \'pä-pyù-ləs\ Numerous, densely settled, or having a large population.

• Though often ignored by Americans, Indonesia is the fourth most populous country in the world.

Modern Mexico City is the world's most populous city; its metropolitan area has about 25 million people. But even when Cortés came to the nearby Aztec city of Tenochtitlán in 1519, he found one of the largest cities in the world at that time. However, when he conquered the city in 1521 it wasn't nearly so populous, since European diseases had greatly reduced the population. (Avoid confusing *populous* and *populace*, which are pronounced exactly the same.)

vox populi \'väks-'pä-pyü-,lī\ Popular sentiment or opinion.

• Clever politicians always listen to the vox populi and adjust their opinions or language to get the voters on their side.

Vox populi is Latin for "the voice of the people." It comes from the old saying "Vox populi, vox Dei," or "The voice of the people is the voice of God"—in other words, the people are always right. In a democracy the vox populi is often regarded as almost sacred. We hear the vox populi loud and clear at every election, and by means of opinion polls we continue to hear it on every imaginable issue, from the President's personal affairs to U.S. military action overseas.

Quizzes

A. Choose the closest definition:

1. pandemic   a. isolated b. widespread c. present
        d. absent
2. populace   a. politics b. numerous c. masses
        d. popularity

3. endemic   a. common   b. absent   c. infectious
   d. occasional
4. demotic   a. devilish   b. common   c. cultural   d. useful
5. populous   a. well-liked   b. foreign   c. numerous
   d. obscure
6. demographic   a. describing politics   b. describing
   populations   c. describing policies   d. describing
   epidemics
7. populist   a. communist   b. campaigner   c. socialist
   d. believer in the people
8. vox populi   a. public policy   b. public survey   c. public
   opinion   d. public outrage

**B. Indicate whether the following pairs of words have
the same or different meanings:**

1. demotic / common   same __ / different __
2. populist / politician   same __ / different __
3. endemic / typical   same __ / different __
4. populace / popularity   same __ / different __
5. demographic / phonetic   same __ / different __
6. vox populi / mass sentiment   same __ / different __
7. pandemic / infectious   same __ / different __
8. populous / well-loved   same __ / different __

POLIS/POLIT comes from the Greek word for "city." "City-states" operated much like separate nations in ancient Greece, so all their *politics* was local, like all their public *policy*, and even all their *police*!

---

acropolis \ə-'krä-pə-ləs\ The high, fortified part of a city, especially an ancient Greek city.

• On the Athenian Acropolis, high above the rest of the city, stands the Parthenon, a temple to the goddess Athena.

Acropolis includes the root *acro-*, meaning "high." South American cities often contain a section on high ground that has been walled and built up so that the city can be defended. This fortified hill gives the defenders an automatic advantage over their attackers. In Europe, an acropolis often consisted of a walled castle inside which the population of the city and the surrounding area could retreat in case of attack. The Greeks and Romans included in their acropolises temples to the city's most important gods.

megalopolis \\me-gə-'lä-pə-ləs\ (1) A very large city. (2) A thickly populated area that includes one or more cities with the surrounding suburbs.

● With its rapid development, the southern coast of Florida around Miami quickly became a megalopolis.

A "large city" named Megalopolis was founded in ancient Greece to help defend Arcadia against Sparta. Today Megalopolis has only about 5,000 people. The megalopolis on the eastern U.S. seaboard that stretches from Boston to Washington, D.C., however, now is the home of almost 50 million people. The densely populated cities seem to flow into each other all along the coast. It is projected that this megalopolis will only grow as time goes on.

politic \'pä-lə-,tik\ (1) Cleverly tactful. (2) Wise in promoting a plan or plan of action.

● Anger is rarely a politic approach to seeking agreement, since it usually comes across as rude and self-righteous.

Once teenagers learn to drive, they quickly learn the politic way to ask for the car—that is, whatever gets the keys without upsetting the parents. It is never politic to ask for a raise when the boss is in a terrible mood. As these examples show, *politic* can be used for many such situations that have nothing to do with public *politics*.

politicize \pə-'li-tə-,sīz\ To give a political tone or character to.

● By 1968 the Vietnam War had deeply politicized most of the college campuses.

Sexual harassment was once seen as a private matter, but in recent years it has been thoroughly politicized. A number of the women who have politicized it may themselves have been politicized by it—that is, may have started to think in a *political* way because of it. Václav Havel was an *unpolitical* playwright who became politicized by events and ended up as president of the Czech Republic.

CIRCU/CIRCUM means "around" in Latin. So *circumnavigate* is "to navigate around," often describing a trip around the world, and *circumambulate* means "to walk around." A *circuit* can be a tour around an area or territory, or the complete path of an electric current.

circuitous \sər-'kyü-ə-təs\ (1) Having a circular or winding course. (2) Not forthright or direct in action.

• Some philosophers arrive at their conclusions by circuitous reasoning that most people can barely follow.

Circuitous is often the opposite of *direct*. A circuitous path is no shortcut: twisting and turning and cutting back on itself, it is the kind of route one would expect to find in the mountains. A lawyer may use circuitous arguments when defending an unsavory client. A clever businessman may use circuitous methods to raise the money for a real-estate deal. (Sometimes *circuitous* may even be a bit like *dishonest*.)

circumference \sər-'kəm-frəns\ (1) The perimeter or boundary of a circle. (2) The outer boundary or surface of a shape or object.

• To calculate the approximate circumference of a circle, multiply its diameter by 3.14.

Circumference means literally "carrying around"—that is, around the boundary of a circle or other geometric figure. Attempts have been made to measure the circumference of the earth since the time of Aristotle. Columbus believed one such calculation, and it led him to think he could reach China by sailing west more quickly than by sailing east. His measurement was wrong, calculating the Earth's circumference about a quarter too small, and many later attempts continued to produce different measurements for the earth's circumference.

circumspect \'sər-kəm-ˌspekt\ Careful to consider all circumstances and possible consequences; cautious.

• She never rushed into any decision but was instead always circumspect and thoughtful.

Since -*spect* comes from the Latin word for "look," *circumspect* basically means "looking around" yourself before you act. Being a doctor or a banker has traditionally called for a circumspect personality. In most dictatorships, authors must be circumspect in what they write, since any lack of *circumspection* could land them in prison, or worse.

circumvent \\'sər-kəm-,vent\\ (1) To make a circuit around. (2) To manage to get around, especially by clever means.

● We circumvented the traffic jam on the highway by using the back roads.

Achilles' mother, Thetis, hoped to circumvent the prophecy that Achilles would die in a war against Troy, so she disguised the boy as a woman among the women of his uncle's household. But clever Odysseus, recruiting for the Greek army, arrived disguised as a peddler, and among the jewelry pieces he displayed to the women he laid a sword. When Achilles ignored everything but the sword, he was found out and had to go to war. Though he was the best warrior on either side, Achilles could not circumvent his eventual fate, and was killed by Paris with a poison arrow to his heel.

Quizzes

A. Fill in each blank with the correct letter:

a. circumspect   e. acropolis
b. megalopolis   f. circumvent
c. circumference   g. politic
d. politicize   h. circuitous

1. She was ＿＿ enough with the chairman to get the bill through the committee.
2. Only the Tokyo-Yokohama metropolitan area rivals the ＿＿ of the East Coast.
3. The doctors were ＿＿ about the prime minister's condition that morning.
4. Her clever attempts to ＿＿ the official procedures failed miserably.
5. The entire ＿＿ of the estate was lined with tall oaks.

6. The directions they were given were inaccurate, so their
   route turned out to be a ____ one.
7. In times of danger, the entire populace retreated to
   the ____.
8. They believed that if they could ____ the peasants they
   could force the government to resign.

**B. Match the word on the left to the correct definition
on the right:**

1.	politicize	a.	high fortified area
2.	megalopolis	b.	make political
3.	circumspect	c.	avoid
4.	circumvent	d.	chain of cities
5.	politic	e.	outside
6.	acropolis	f.	cleverly tactful
7.	circumference	g.	careful
8.	circuitous	h.	roundabout

Animal Words

aquiline \'a-kwə-,līn\ (1) Relating to eagles. (2) Curving like an
eagle's beak.

● To judge from the surviving busts of noble Romans, many of the
men had strong aquiline noses.

Aquiline, from the Latin word meaning "eagle," is most often used
to describe a nose that has a broad curve and is slightly hooked,
like a beak. The word for eagle itself, *Aquila,* has been given to a
constellation in the northern hemisphere. The aquiline figure on the
U.S. seal brandishes the arrows of war and the olive branch of
peace.

asinine \'a-sə-,nīn\ Foolish, brainless.

● He's not so great when he's sober, but when he's drunk he gets
truly asinine.

The donkey or *ass* has often been accused of stubborn, willful, and
stupid behavior lacking in logic and common sense. Asinine behav-

ior exhibits similar qualities. Idiotic or rude remarks, aggressive stupidity, and general immaturity can all earn someone (usually a man) this description. If you call him this to his face, however, he might behave even worse.

bovine \\'bō-,vīn\ (1) Relating to cows and oxen. (2) Placid, dull, unemotional.

• The veterinarian specialized in bovine diseases.

Bovine comes from the Latin word for "cow." The goddess Hera, the wife of Zeus, is called "cow-eyed," and Zeus fairly melts when she turns those big bovine eyes on him. But *bovine* is normally used either technically, when discussing cows—"bovine diseases," "bovine anatomy," and so on—or to describe a human personality. However, it can be a rather unkind way to describe someone.

canine \\'kā-,nīn\ Relating to dogs or the dog family; doglike.

• Throughout the election, her husband's almost canine devotion helped her survive the tough criticism of her opponents.

Dogs are not always given credit for their independence, but they are prized for their talents and their intelligence. And canine devotion and loyalty are legendary; in the old *Lassie* and *Rin-Tin-Tin* television series, there would be at least one heroic act of devotion per show.

feline \\'fē-,līn\ (1) Relating to cats or the cat family. (2) Like a cat in being sleek, graceful, sly, treacherous, or stealthy.

• The performers moved across the high wire with feline grace and agility.

Cats have always provoked a strong reaction from humans. The Egyptians worshiped them and left thousands of feline mummies and idols as evidence. In the Middle Ages, felines were feared as agents of the devil; they were thought to creep around silently at night doing evil and caring not at all for anything except themselves. (Notice that *feline* is also a noun.) Felines from lions and tigers down to domestic cats are smooth, silent, and often sleepy; feline independence, feline treachery, and feline slyness are other traits that some have seen in these mysterious creatures.

leonine \\'lē-ə-ˌnīn\\ Relating to lions; lionlike.

• As he conducted, Leonard Bernstein would fling his leonine mane wildly about.

The Latin word for "lion" is *leon*, so the names Leon, Leo, and Leona all mean "lion" as well. A leonine head usually has magnificent hair, like a male lion's mane, and someone may give an impression of leonine power or splendor. But the leonine character in *The Wizard of Oz* is notably lacking in the courage for which members of its family are famed.

porcine \\'pȯr-ˌsīn\\ Relating to pigs or swine; piglike.

• After a lifetime of overeating, his shape was porcine; unfortunately, his manners were also.

Whether deservedly or not, pigs don't enjoy a very flattering image, and they are rarely given credit for their high intelligence. While *porcine* is not as negative a term as *swinish,* it may describe things that are fat, greedy, pushy, or generally piggish—but primarily fat. Porky Pig and Miss Piggy are not porcine in their behavior, only in their appearance—that is, pink and pudgy.

vulpine \\'vəl-ˌpīn\\ (1) Relating to foxes; foxlike. (2) Sneaky, clever, or crafty; foxy.

• One glance at the vulpine faces of the two bond traders was enough to convince him of their true character.

Foxes may have beautiful coats and tails, but they are almost impossible to keep out of the henhouse. No matter how secure the place seems to be, their vulpine craftiness will find a way in. People who display the same kind of sneaky cleverness, especially in their faces, are also called vulpine.

Quiz

Fill in each blank with the correct letter:

a.	leonine	e.	canine
b.	aquiline	f.	feline
c.	porcine	g.	vulpine
d.	asinine	h.	bovine

1. Collies and chow chows often have splendid, _____ neck ruffs.
2. The dancer performed the piece with _____ grace.
3. Proud of the _____ curve of his nose, the silent-film star presented his profile to the camera at every opportunity.
4. The slick fellow offering his services as guide had a disturbingly _____ air about him.
5. Soldiers are expected to show _____ loyalty to their unit and commander.
6. The job applicant's _____ manner suggested a lack of ambition.
7. Jeff and his crowd were in the balcony, throwing down cans and being generally _____.
8. The _____ landlord climbed the stairs slowly, gasping for breath, with the eviction notice in his hand.

Review Quizzes

A. Choose the closest definition:

1. vulpine   a. reddish   b. sly   c. trustworthy   d. furry
2. circumspect   a. boring   b. long-winded
       c. roundabout   d. cautious
3. politic   a. governmental   b. voting   c. tactful   d. clumsy
4. populous   a. numerous   b. populated   c. popular
       d. common
5. atheistic   a. without a clue   b. faithful   c. disbelieving
       d. without a doubt
6. endemic   a. local   b. neighborly   c. sensational
       d. foreign
7. circuitous   a. electrical   b. mountainous   c. indirect
       d. round
8. feline   a. sleek   b. clumsy   c. crazy   d. fancy
9. pantheistic   a. of one god   b. disbelieving
       c. nonreligious   d. accepting all gods
10. deity   a. discussion   b. decision   c. psychic   d. god
11. pandemic   a. widespread   b. infectious   c. hideous
       d. frightening
12. megalopolis   a. monster   b. dinosaur   c. huge city
       d. huge mall

13. demotic   a. reduced b. common c. upper-class
      d. demented
14. divinity   a. prophecy b. mortality c. prayer
      d. godliness
15. circumvent   a. surround b. circle c. get around
      d. discuss
16. divest   a. add on b. take off c. take in d. add up

B. Fill in each blank with the correct letter:

a. populist   f. apotheosis
b. demographic   g. bovine
c. theocracy   h. populace
d. investiture   i. politicize
e. aquiline   j. circumference

1. The _____ of the great Albert Einstein seemed to occur
   while he was still living.
2. All the _____ surveys show that the U.S. population is
   growing older.
3. Nothing ever seemed to disturb her pleasant but _____
   manner.
4. The younger ones stood around the _____ of the room
   while the older ones sat in the center.
5. The _____ of the society's new leader was a secret and
   solemn event.
6. With his _____ nose, he looked like a member of the
   ancient Roman senate.
7. By that fall they had managed to _____ the factory
   workers around the issue of medical benefits.
8. He was a _____ in his style, though he actually had a
   great deal of money.
9. The _____ of the country is mostly composed of three
   ethnic groups.
10. In a _____, the legal punishments are often those called
    for in the holy books.

**C. Match the word on the left to the correct definition
   on the right:**

1. porcine   a. half-shadow
2. divinatory   b. doglike

3. asinine	c. brownish coloring
4. penumbra	d. public opinion
5. leonine	e. cross-dresser
6. umber	f. unforeseen explanation
7. vox populi	g. uncouth
8. deus ex machina	h. plump
9. transvestite	i. like a lion
10. canine	j. prophetic

Unit 13

CORD, from the Latin word for "heart," turns up in many common English words. For example, the word *concord* (which includes the prefix *con-*, "with") means literally that one heart is *with* another heart, and thus that they are in agreement. So *discord* (with its prefix *dis-*, "apart") means "disagreement" or "conflict."

accord \ə-'kȯrd\ (1) To grant. (2) To be in harmony; agree.

● For the cast's brilliant performance of the play, the audience accorded them a standing ovation.

A new federal law may accord with—or be in *accordance* with—the guidelines that a company has already established. The rowdy behavior of the hero Beowulf accords with Norse ideals of the early Middle Ages, but would not be in accordance with the ideals of another young Danish lord of a later century, Shakespeare's Prince Hamlet.

concordance \kən-'kȯr-dəns\ An index of the important words in a book or in an author's works, with the passages in which they occur.

● A concordance to Shakespeare's plays makes it easy to find all the places he used the word *bodkin*.

A literary concordance lists all the places a given word appears in a work. *Concordance* resembles *concord*, but the "agreement" here is in the way that all the passages use the identical word. All concordances produced before the recent past had to be done by hand, and often were the work of several lifetimes. (Just imagine putting together a concordance for the Bible by hand.) Now, a computer with CD-ROM can search a book or an author's works in a flash, but concordances in book form are still valuable for many purposes.

cordial \\'kȯr-jəl\\ (1) Warm, friendly, gracious. (2) Something that warms and revives, especially a liqueur.

• After the meeting, the president extended a cordial invitation to everyone for coffee at her own house.

Anything that is cordial comes from the heart. A cordial greeting or cordial relations (for example, between two countries) are warm and honest without being passionate. A cordial or liqueur, such as crème de menthe or Drambuie, is alcoholic enough to warm the spirits and the heart.

discordant \\dis-'kȯr-dənt\\ Being at odds, conflicting, not in harmony.

• The one discordant note came from the only vegetarian present, who would not eat the main course, roast beef.

Drawing up a peace treaty may require that the parties to the treaty resolve their discordant aims. Even among allies, *discord* is not always absent. Stalin's goals after World War II did not at all *accord* with those of Russia's allies—England, America, and France; his discordant demands led to the division of Europe for almost half a century. The opinions of Supreme Court justices are frequently discordant. The discordant ethnic groups in the old Yugoslavia were controlled only by the iron hand of Marshal Tito.

CULP comes to English from the Latin word for "guilt." A *culprit* is someone who is guilty of a crime, though his or her *culpability,* or guilt, should not be assumed before it is proved.

---

culpable \\'kəl-pə-bəl\\ Deserving to be condemned or blamed.

• The company was found guilty of culpable negligence in allowing the chemical waste to leak into the groundwater.

A mother always thinks she knows which children are culpable when the cookie jar has been raided: their *culpability* is usually written all over their faces. *Culpable* is probably more commonly used in law than in everyday speech and writing.

exculpate \'ek-skəl-,pāt\ To clear from accusations of fault or guilt.

● The alleged mastermind of the plot managed to exculpate herself with an airtight alibi.

Exculpate comes to mean "to clear from guilt" through the prefix *ex-*, meaning "out of" or "away from." A suspected murderer may be exculpated by the confession of another person. The word has an extended meaning as well, referring to moral guilt or responsibility. In America a criminal is not exculpated because of a harsh childhood, but may be if found insane.

inculpate \in-'kəl-,pāt\ To accuse or incriminate; to show evidence of someone's involvement in a fault or crime.

● It was his own father who finally inculpated him, though without intending to.

Inculpate is the opposite of *exculpate*, but less often used. By inculpating someone else, an accused person may manage to exculpate himself. Through plea bargaining, the prosecution can often encourage a defendant to inculpate his friends in return for a lighter sentence.

mea culpa \,mā-ə-'kùl-pə\ An admission of personal fault or error.

● The principal said his mea culpa at the school board meeting, but not all the parents accepted it.

Mea culpa, "through my fault," comes from the prayer of confession in the Catholic Church. Said by itself today, it means "I apologize" or "It was my fault." But it is also a noun. A book may be a long mea culpa for the author's past treatment of women, or an oil company may issue a mea culpa after a tanker runs aground.

Quizzes

A. Choose the closest definition:

1. exculpate   a. convict b. prove innocent c. suspect
   d. prove absent
2. discordant   a. unpleasant b. relieved c. unlimited
   d. conflicting
3. culpable   a. disposable b. refundable c. guilty
   d. harmless
4. cordial   a. hateful b. friendly c. fiendish
   d. cool
5. inculpate   a. incorporate b. resist c. incriminate
   d. offend
6. concordance   a. index b. digit c. list
   d. disagreement
7. mea culpa   a. rejection b. apology c. admission
   d. forgiveness
8. accord   a. harmonize b. accept c. distress d. convince

**B. Match the definition on the left to the correct word
on the right:**

1. accuse   a.   accord
2. excuse   b.   concordance
3. agreement   c.   mea culpa
4. heartfelt   d.   discordant
5. grant   e.   culpable
6. blamable   f.   cordial
7. disagreeing   g.   inculpate
8. confession   h.   exculpate

DIC, from *dicere*, the Latin word meaning "to speak," says a lot. A *contradiction* (with the prefix *contra-*, "against") speaks against or denies something. A *dictionary* is a treasury of words. And *diction* is another word for speech.

---

edict \'ē-ˌdikt\ (1) An official announcement that has the force of a law. (2) An order or command.

• In 1989 an edict by the leader of Iran pronouncing a death sentence on a British novelist stunned the world.

Edicts are few and far between in a democracy, since very few important laws can be made by a president or prime minister acting alone. But when a crisis arose in the Roman Republic, the senate would appoint a dictator to rule by edict. The dictator could make decisions quickly, and his edicts could be issued faster than the senate could act. When the crisis was over, the edicts were revoked and the dictator usually retired from public life.

interdiction \ˌin-tər-'dik-shən\ (1) An edict prohibiting something. (2) The destruction of or cutting off of an enemy's line of supply.

• U.S. forces repeatedly tried to halt the North Vietnamese by interdiction of their supplies.

An interdiction comes between and forbids or takes. From 1920 to 1933 the 18th Amendment attempted to *interdict* the production and drinking of alcohol. But such an interdiction proved useless; Americans of all social classes and every degree of respectability refused to give up their beloved beverages, and all attempts to interdict the supply by the "Untouchable" Eliot Ness and other government agents could not stop the flow of illegal moonshine and bathtub gin.

jurisdiction \ˌj ̇ur-is-'dik-shən\ (1) The power or right to control or exercise authority. (2) The territory where power may be exercised.

• Unluckily for the defendants, the case fell within the jurisdiction of the federal court rather than the more tolerant state court.

Gods and goddesses often intervened in the areas under their jurisdiction. Apollo, whose jurisdiction included archery, guided the arrow that killed Achilles in the Trojan War. Poseidon, angered at the blinding of his son the Cyclops, punished Odysseus with hard wanderings over the sea, where he had final jurisdiction. Today questions of jurisdiction are generally technical legal matters— questions about which law-enforcement agency can get involved, which court will hear the case, and so on—but matters that may be all-important in the final outcome of legal cases.

malediction \ˌma-lə-ˈdik-shən\ A curse.

● In the story of Sleeping Beauty, the evil fairy hurls a malediction at the infant princess, foretelling that she will prick her finger and die.

Maledictions, "evil sayings," are used less commonly in many cultures than they used to be. The Romans had a malediction for every purpose. They inscribed these curses on lead tablets and buried them in the ground. Archaeologists have found maledictions cursing the person who stole someone's lover, the person who stole prize apples, and the person who cursed the curser. Maledictions may call for every punishment imaginable, from sickness to injury and even death.

GNI/GNO comes from a Greek and Latin verb meaning "to know" (and led to the word *know* itself). In the group of words built from this root, you may *recognize* ("know again") some and be *ignorant* of ("not know") others. An *agnostic* is someone who claims that whatever is divine cannot be known. An *ignoramus* is a person who knows absolutely nothing.

---

cognitive \ˈkäg-nə-tiv\ (1) Having to do with the process of knowing, including awareness, judgment, and understanding. (2) Based on factual knowledge that has been or can be gained by experience.

● A child is not a computer; a third-grader's cognitive abilities are highly dependent on his or her upbringing and happiness.

Cognitive skills and knowledge involve the ability to acquire factual information, often the kind of knowledge that can easily be tested. *Cognition* is thus distinguished from social, emotional, and creative development and ability.

diagnosis \ˌdī-əg-ˈnō-səs\ (1) The identification of a disease by its symptoms. (2) An investigation of and conclusion about a situation or problem.

● However, according to Marianne's diagnosis the company's problem was its managers, not its workers.

A diagnosis identifies a disease or problem through its physical evidence. One of the most useful new *diagnostic* tools is MRI, or "magnetic resonance imaging," which allows doctors to see what is going on in the soft tissue, such as muscle, cartilage, and brain, that X rays see right through. With MRI, *diagnosticians* can be far more accurate in their diagnoses. (Notice how this plural is formed.)

incognito \in-,käg-'nē-tō\ In disguise or with one's identity concealed.

● Katherine Ann Power, an activist and bank robber, lived incognito for 23 years before giving herself up in 1993.

In the famous myth of Baucis and Philemon, Zeus and Hermes visit a village incognito to test the villagers. The seemingly poor travelers are turned away from every household except that of Baucis and Philemon. This elderly couple, though very poor themselves, provide the incognito gods with a feast. When the gods finally reveal themselves, the couple is rewarded for their hospitality, and the rest of the village is destroyed for their lack of it.

prognosis \präg-'nō-səs\ (1) The chance of recovery from a given disease or condition. (2) Forecast or prophecy.

● The prognosis for a patient with chicken pox is usually excellent; the prognosis for someone with liver cancer is terrible.

Prognosis contains the prefix *pro-*, meaning "before." It is thus "knowledge beforehand," based on the normal course of events in similar situations. Economists try to *prognosticate,* or predict, what the economy will do, based on the trends they see and their knowledge of where such trends tend to lead. A prognosis of recovery and growth is obviously much better than one of recession and stagnation.

Quizzes

A. Fill in each blank with the correct letter:

a.	diagnosis	e.	interdiction
b.	malediction	f.	incognito
c.	cognitive	g.	edict
d.	jurisdiction	h.	prognosis

1. Psychology is not entirely a ____ science, since it deals with behavior as well as the mind.
2. Belief in the power of a ____ to harm has faded with the advances of science and growing rejection of superstition.
3. Movie stars often go out in public ____, in faded sweatshirts, worn-out pants, and sunglasses.
4. When their dictatorial grandfather issued an ____, everyone obeyed it.
5. The electrician made a quick ____ and fixed the heater by replacing a faulty switch.
6. The ____ for the world's climate in the next century is uncertain.
7. An ____ of their supply lines by enemy mortars on the surrounding hills meant the loyalists would have to find new routes.
8. The judge refused to consider two elements in the case, saying that they lay outside his ____.

B. Indicate whether the following pairs of words have the same or different meanings:

1. diagnosis / analysis   same ___ / different ___
2. cognitive / digestive   same ___ / different ___
3. interdiction / prohibition   same ___ / different ___
4. malediction / curse   same ___ / different ___
5. incognito / hospitable   same ___ / different ___
6. jurisdiction / power   same ___ / different ___
7. prognosis / prophecy   same ___ / different ___
8. edict / order   same ___ / different ___

APT/EPT, from *aptare*, "to fit," and *aptus*, "fit," is endlessly *adaptable*, changing itself to fit many words and purposes. You are *apt*, or "likely," to come upon them when you least expect, so *adept* are they at fitting in.

---

adaptation \a-ˌdap-'tā-shən\ Adjustment to conditions of an environment, or to a new or different use.

- Humans have undergone many adaptations since the first hominids roamed the land.

Adaptation usually makes survival or success more likely. There are moths in England that were once light gray; on the bark of a tree they were practically invisible to birds looking for food. During the Industrial Revolution in England, when factory smoke turned the trees black with grime, the light-colored moths became clearly visible and were eaten. As the years passed, the moths went through a protective adaptation and became black or dark gray like the trees, and once again invisible to the birds.

aptitude \\'ap-tə-ˌtüd\\ (1) Natural tendency, talent, or ability. (2) Ability to learn.

- She longed to learn to play piano but feared she had no aptitude for music.

Most students applying for college take both aptitude tests and achievement tests. Aptitude tests claim to measure how much you are able to learn, and achievement tests how much you have already learned. That is, a math achievement test should require that you have memorized formulas and complex operations, whereas a math aptitude test should require only that you show you can work quickly and intelligently with basic operations. Many aptitudes, both physical and mental, show up clearly in children by the age of 3 or 4.

adept \\ə-'dept\\ Expert or highly skilled.

- The dollmaker was astonishingly adept at painting the features of famous dancers on her little porcelain heads.

Charlie Chaplin was adept at far more than acting, directing, and screenwriting; he was an acrobat of professional quality, and songs he wrote became popular hits. Most of us would settle for being adept in only a couple of areas.

inept \\i-'nept\\ Foolish, incompetent, bungling.

- The government's inept handling of the whole affair led to its defeat in the next election.

Inept is the opposite of *adept*. Inspector Clouseau has been the image of *ineptitude* for a generation of moviegoers, who may have caught a glimpse of themselves in his dignified but hopeless incompetence.

ART comes from the Latin word for "skill." Until a few centuries ago, almost no one made a strong distinction between skilled craftsmanship and what we would call "art." *Art* could also mean simply "cleverness." The result is that this root appears in some words where we might not expect it.

---

artful \'ärt-fəl\ (1) Skillful. (2) Wily, crafty, sly.

• It was an artful solution: each side was pleased with the agreement, but the lawyer himself stood to make the most money off of it.

A writer may produce an artful piece of prose, one that is clearly and elegantly written. The same writer, however, could also make an artful argument, one that leaves out certain details and plays up others so as to make a stronger case. In the first instance, the writer's work is well-crafted; in the second, he or she is instead crafty. (Try not to use *artful*, however, when you really mean "artistic.")

artifact \'är-ti-ˌfakt\ A usually simple object, such as a tool or ornament, made by human workmanship or modification.

• Archaeologists have found many artifacts that help us understand how the early Anasazi people of the Southwest lived.

One of the things that makes humans unique is their ability to make and use tools. These tools and the objects made with them are artifacts, a word that literally means "made with skill." Human cultures in all eras, from the Stone Age onward, have left behind artifacts from which we can learn about their lives.

artifice \'är-tə-fəs\ (1) Clever skill. (2) A clever trick.

• By his cunning and artifice, Iago convinces Othello that Desdemona has been unfaithful.

Artifice combines the same roots as *artifact*, but usually suggests something deceptive or tricky or at least highly *artificial*. Simplicity, honesty, and genuineness are the opposites of artifice, which is related to disguise, fantasy, and complexity. Starting with the Puritans, America has traditionally prided itself on its lack of artifice, seeing a character like Huckleberry Finn as an image of the essential American. But artifice is often in the eye of the beholder, and the book *Huckleberry Finn* is itself filled with literary artifice.

artisan \'är-tə-zən\ A skilled worker or craftsperson.

● At the fair, they saw examples of the best carving, pottery, and jewelry by local artisans.

In the Middle Ages artisans organized themselves into guilds. In every city each group of artisans, such as the weavers or carpenters, had its own guild. The guilds set wages and prices for the artisans' wares, and also protected them from competing artisans who did not belong. Guilds existed in some European countries until the 19th century. In America, however, most artisans have always been fiercely independent.

Quizzes

A. Complete the analogy:

1. sensation : feeling :: aptitude : _____
   a. amount b. emotion c. talent d. article
2. mournful : sad :: artful : _____
   a. clever b. doleful c. fake d. creative
3. strong : weak :: adept : _____
   a. skilled b. easy c. inept d. unjust
4. physician : doctor :: artisan : _____
   a. plumber b. nurse c. teacher d. craftsperson
5. life : death :: adaptation : _____
   a. sensation b. excitement c. stagnation d. rejection
6. labor : strength :: artifact : _____
   a. skill b. statuette c. remains d. trick
7. clumsy : grace :: inept : _____
   a. honesty b. competence c. stupidity d. ignorance
8. confession : true :: artifice : _____
   a. skill b. honest c. false d. ridiculous

> **B. Match the definition on the left to the correct word on the right:**
>
> 1. skilled craftsman   a. artful
> 2. natural talent   b. artifice
> 3. skillfully sly   c. adaptation
> 4. expert   d. inept
> 5. slyness   e. artisan
> 6. process of change   f. aptitude
> 7. man-made object   g. adept
> 8. awkward   h. artifact

CAD/CID/CAS all comes from the same Latin verb, *cadere*, meaning "to fall, fall down, drop," or from the related noun *casus*, "fall or chance." An *accident* happens to you out of the blue. By *coincidence*, things fall together in a pattern. *Casual* dress is what you put on almost by chance. A *cascade* is a rushing down of something.

---

cadaver \kə-'da-vər\ A dead body, especially one that is to be dissected; a corpse.

● The cadaver she was given to work on was an unclaimed homeless woman and came from the Manhattan morgue.

The mystery writer P. D. James always produces a cadaver with a tale that must be unraveled by her sleuth, Adam Dalgliesh. And occasionally one of her living characters may have gaunt, *cadaverous* features, such as hollow cheeks and sunken eyes, which resemble the features of a corpse.

casualty \'ka-zhù-wəl-tē\ A person, especially a military person, or a thing that is injured, lost, or destroyed; a victim.

● When the platoon limped back to camp, they learned that Lieutenant Steiger had been a casualty of a land mine.

The casualty count in a war includes the dead, the wounded, and the seriously ill. In the American Civil War, for instance, deaths represented only about half of the total casualties—and most of the deaths resulted from infection and disease rather than from battle wounds alone. We may also use the term less literally. For example, if a woman's new husband doesn't get along with her best friend, the friendship may become a casualty of the marriage.

decadent \'de-kə-dənt\ (1) Self-indulgent. (2) Decaying or declining.

• The French Empire may have been at its most decadent just before the French Revolution.

Many of the rich people of ancient Rome lived decadent lives, full of every sort of excess imaginable, as their empire fell apart. No expense was spared to bring exotic delicacies to their tables, from African ostrich eggs to snow from the Alps—in the days before refrigeration! And Rome's emperors were often part of the problem. Commodus, the 18-year-old bodybuilder son of the emperor, was leading his troops against the barbarians on the frontier when he heard his father had died, and raced immediately back to Rome to take up a life of pleasure and *decadence*.

recidivism \ri-'si-də-ˌvi-zəm\ A tendency to fall back into earlier habits or modes of behaving, especially criminal habits.

• Recidivism among smokers who try to quit is very high.

Recidivism means literally "a falling back," and usually implies "into bad habits." Though the criminal justice system tries to reduce the rate of recidivism among criminals, most released prisoners return to a life of crime as *recidivists*.

CIS comes from the Latin verb meaning "to cut, cut down, or slay." An *incisor* is one of the big front biting teeth; beavers and woodchucks have especially large ones. A *decision* "cuts off" previous discussion and uncertainty.

---

concise \kən-'sīs\ Brief and condensed, especially in expression or statement.

• Professor Childs's exam asked for a concise, one-page summary of the causes of the American Revolution.

Most students, and many adults, think that adding unnecessary sentences with long words will make their writing more impressive. But in fact almost every reader values *concision*: concise writing is usually easier to read, better thought out, and better organized—that is, simply better writing.

excise \\'ek-ˌsīz\\ To cut out, especially surgically.

● The ancient Minoans from the island of Crete apparently excised the hearts of their human sacrifices.

Excise takes part of its meaning from the prefix *ex-*, "out." A writer may excise long passages of a novel to reduce it to a reasonable length, or merely excise sections that may give offense. A surgeon may excise a large cancerous tumor, or make a tiny *excision* to examine an organ's tissue.

incisive \\in-'sī-siv\\ Impressively direct and decisive.

● A few incisive questions were all that was needed to expose the weakness in the prosecutor's case.

To *incise* is to cut into; an incisive remark, then, "cuts into" the matter at hand. A good news analyst makes incisive comments about the story he or she is following, shedding light on the situation. A good movie critic *incisively* remarks on a film's strengths and weaknesses, helping us decide whether or not to see it.

precision \\pri-'si-zhən\\ (1) Exactness of definition or statement. (2) Accuracy of performance or measurement.

● Only slowly did he learn to speak with precision, to find the exact words for everything in place of the crude, awkward language of his friends.

The weather can never be predicted with absolute precision. Modern technology such as computer models and satellite photos help forecasters to be more *precise* than ever before, but there are so many factors involved in making the weather that any forecaster always runs the risk of being *imprecise*.

Quizzes

A. Fill in each blank with the correct letter:

a.	casualty	e.	concise
b.	decadent	f.	excise
c.	cadaver	g.	incisive
d.	precision	h.	recidivism

1. Ms. Raymond's report on her trip up the Amazon is ____ but fascinating.
2. They were a ____ crowd; rich and idle, they spent their days taking drugs and their nights hunting for pleasure in the clubs.
3. The medical students were assigned in threes to work on each ____.
4. The reporter was known for remarks that were so ____ that his interviewees were often embarrassed.
5. The first American ____ of the Revolutionary War may have been the black soldier Crispus Attucks.
6. ____ among chocolate lovers who try to limit their intake is appallingly high.
7. Before eating an apple, some people carefully ____ the brown spots.
8. What the tipsy darts players lacked in ____ they made up for in enthusiasm.

B. Choose the closest definition:

1. precision   a. accuracy   b. beauty   c. conciseness   d. dependence
2. decadent   a. rotten   b. generous   c. self-indulgent   d. ten years long
3. excise   a. tax   b. examine   c. refuse   d. cut out
4. recidivism   a. backsliding   b. backstabbing   c. backscratching   d. backslapping
5. incisive   a. damaging   b. direct   c. dirty   d. definite
6. casualty   a. serious remark   b. serious outlook   c. serious condition   d. serious injury
7. concise   a. short   b. sure   c. shifting   d. sharp
8. cadaver   a. victim   b. suspect   c. corpse   d. detective

Animal Words

apiary \'ā-pē-ˌer-ē\ A place where bees are kept for their honey.

● An apple orchard is an excellent site for an apiary, since the bees keep the apple trees productive by pollinating them.

The social life in an apiary is strange and marvelous. The queen bee, who will become the mother of an entire colony, is created by being fed "royal jelly" in her larval stage. The tens of thousands of worker bees are underdeveloped females; only a handful of the bees are male, and they do no work at all. The workers defend the hive by kamikaze means, stinging any intruder and dying as they do so.

caper \'kā-pər\ (1) A playful leap. (2) A prank or mischievous adventure.

● For their caper in the girls' bathroom, all three seniors were suspended for a week.

Caper in Latin means "a male goat." Anyone who has watched a young goat frolic in a field or clamber onto the roof of a car knows the kind of crazy fun the English word *caper* is referring to. A *capriole* is a backward kick done in midair by a trained horse. *Capricorn,* or "horned goat," is a constellation and one of the signs of the zodiac.

equestrian \i-'kwes-trē-ən\ Having to do with horseback riding.

● The equestrian acts, in which bareback riders performed daring acrobatic feats atop prancing horses, were her favorites.

The word *equestrian* comes from *equus,* Latin for "horse." War memorials often show great commanders in equestrian poses. In these sculptures the man always sits nobly upright, but the horse's stance varies. Depending on whether the rider was killed in battle or survived, was victorious or defeated, the horse stands with four, three, or two hooves on the ground. Equestrian statues have been popular through the centuries because until this century almost every commanding officer was trained in equestrian skills and combat.

lupine \'lü-ˌpīn\ Like a wolf; wolfish.

● They heard the resonant voices of a lupine chorus howling most of the night.

Lupine comes from *lupus*, the Latin word for "wolf," and the related adjective *lupinus*, "wolfish." Dogs often exhibit lupine behavior, since many of them are descended from wolves. Lupine groups have a highly organized social structure, in which leaders and followers are clearly distinguished, and dogs often show these lupine patterns when living in groups. *Lupine* is also a noun, the name of a well-known flower, which was once thought to drain, or "wolf," the soil of its nutrients.

lycanthropy \lī-'kan-thrə-pē\ The taking on of the form and behavior of a wolf by means of magic or witchcraft.

● The 1941 film *The Wolf Man* starred Lon Chaney, Jr., as a man cursed with lycanthropy.

For centuries a belief in lycanthropy has been part of the folk culture of lands where wolves exist. The word comes from the joining of two Greek roots—*lyc*, meaning "wolf," and *anthrop*, meaning "man." A victim of this enchantment is a *lycanthrope*, or werewolf. When the moon is full, the animal part of his nature takes over and he is transformed into a wolf, only much more bloodthirsty. The lycanthrope preys on humans, especially babies and buried corpses, and can even cause lycanthropy in others by biting them.

ornithologist \ˌȯr-nə-'thä-lə-jist\ A person who studies birds.

● John James Audubon, the great painter of the birds of early America, was also a writing ornithologist of great importance.

Ornithologist comes from two Greek roots, *ornith-*, meaning "bird," and *log-*, meaning "study." Roger Tory Peterson's numerous field guides have long been some of the amateur ornithologist's most useful tools.

serpentine \'sər-pən-ˌtīn\ Like a snake or serpent in shape or movement; winding.

● The Great Wall of China, the greatest construction of all time, wends its serpentine way for 1,200 miles.

A snake moves by curving and winding along the ground. Roads through the Pyrenees, the mountains that separate Spain from France, tend to be serpentine, curving back and forth upon themselves on the steep slopes. (*Serpentine* has many other meanings as well; it can describe human character or physique, for example, and it is also the name for a soft green mineral and for party streamers.)

simian \'si-mē-ən\ Having to do with monkeys or apes; monkeylike.

● In mid-afternoon the pale youth could be seen watching the simian antics in the Monkey House with strange intensity.

The Latin word for "ape" is *simia*, which itself comes from *simus*, "snub-nosed." Not only monkeys and apes can be simian. A human baby may cling to her mother in a simian way; a person may have a simian style of eating a banana; kids may display simian agility as they play on the jungle gym; and a grunt may be simian even when made by a human.

Quiz

Indicate whether the following pairs have the same or different meanings:

1. equestrian / horselike   same ___ / different ___
2. ornithologist / studier of birds   same ___ / different ___
3. lupine / apelike   same ___ / different ___
4. apiary / monkey colony   same ___ / different ___
5. lycanthropy / werewolfism   same ___ / different ___
6. caper / leap   same ___ / different ___
7. simian / clumsy   same ___ / different ___
8. serpentine / steep   same ___ / different ___

Review Quizzes

A. Fill in each blank with the correct letter:

a. artisan	k. recidivism
b. edict	l. cadaver
c. equestrian	m. inculpate

d.	artifact	n.	serpentine
e.	discordant	o.	interdiction
f.	casualty	p.	precision
g.	cognitive	q.	artifice
h.	apiary	r.	aptitude
i.	exculpate	s.	prognosis
j.	inept	t.	simian

1. The farmer tended his _____ lovingly and gathered delicious wildflower honey every year.
2. In trying to _____ herself, she only made herself look guiltier.
3. The enemy's _____ of supplies left the city helpless.
4. Though he showed astonishing mathematical _____ as a child, he spent his life as a salesman.
5. They arrived in time to see the top riders compete in the championship _____ event.
6. The doctor's _____ is guarded, but she is cautiously optimistic that recovery will be complete.
7. Fortunately, the accident caused only one minor _____.
8. We made our way slowly along the _____ course of the lazy river.
9. Each side's anger at the other has set a sadly _____ tone for the negotiations.
10. We set the clock with great _____ on the first day of every new year.
11. The thief tried hard to _____ as many of his friends in the crime as he could.
12. These beautiful handblown goblets were obviously made by a talented _____.
13. The final _____ from the presidential palace commanded every citizen to wear a baseball cap at all times.
14. The child scrambled over the wall with _____ agility.
15. As a baby, he was unusually quick to develop _____ skills.
16. She found a small clay _____ in the shape of a bear at the site of the ancient temple.
17. The local mechanics are _____ or dishonest or both, so I don't recommend them.
18. There bobbing by the wharf was a _____, the remains of a man in a white suit.

19. He used every _____ imaginable to hide his real age from the television cameras.
20. The rate of _____ for those imprisoned for felonies is alarmingly high.

B. Choose the correct synonym and the correct antonym:

1. accord   a. give one's due   b. give one's heart
   c. withhold what is earned   d. withhold approval
2. malediction   a. prayer   b. benediction   c. oath   d. curse
3. artful   a. lovely   b. sly   c. talented   d. honest
4. decadent   a. decaying   b. ten-year   c. twelfth   d. growing
5. cordial   a. amorous   b. hostile   c. terrific   d. heartfelt
6. incognito   a. indoors   b. in disguise   c. as oneself
   d. as you were
7. incisive   a. toothed   b. sharp   c. toothless   d. dull
8. concise   a. lengthy   b. wide   c. dated   d. brief
9. culpable   a. doleful   b. stentorian   c. guilty   d. innocent
10. adept   a. changed   b. skilled   c. clumsy   d. unwell

C. Choose the closest definition:

1. ornithologist   a. student of fish   b. student of words
   c. student of birds   d. student of wolves
2. mea culpa   a. through my eyes   b. through my fault
   c. through my door   d. through my work
3. lupine   a. foxy   b. horselike   c. sheepish   d. wolfish
4. adaptation   a. process of going   b. process of change
   c. process of mending   d. process of canning
5. jurisdiction   a. area of power   b. area of coverage
   c. area of damage   d. area of target
6. excise   a. take out   b. hold out   c. cut out   d. fold out
7. concordance   a. index   b. bible   c. glossary   d. contents
8. lycanthropy   a. sorcery   b. monstrosity   c. vampirism
   d. werewolfism
9. diagnosis   a. identification   b. symptoms   c. disease
   d. treatment
10. caper   a. wolf   b. goat   c. dance   d. prank

Unit 14

CRYPT/CRYPH comes from the Greek word for "hidden." To *encrypt* a message is to encode it—that is, to hide its meaning in code language. A medical term beginning with *crypto-* always means there is something hidden about the condition.

apocryphal \ə-'pä-krə-fəl\ Of doubtful genuineness or authenticity.

● Jason's story, they now realized, was completely apocryphal, though he himself may have believed it.

Both the Old and the New Testaments sometimes include books that have a doubtful status, since the leaders of the Jewish and Christian religions have determined that they aren't completely deserving of being included with the official scriptures. These documents are known as the *Apocrypha*; the root here suggests that the Apocrypha's origins are somewhat hidden and so not reliable. Today anything fake or counterfeit that is claimed to be genuine, such as the supposed diaries of Adolf Hitler in the 1980s, can be called apocryphal.

cryptic \'krip-'tik\ (1) Mysterious; puzzlingly short. (2) Acting to hide or conceal.

● Louisa threw Philip a cryptic look whose meaning he couldn't be sure of.

Until the writing on the Rosetta Stone was finally translated in the early 19th century, Egyptian hieroglyphic writing was entirely cryptic, its meaning hidden from the modern world. In the same way, a cryptic comment or remark or look is one whose meaning is unclear and perhaps even mystifying. Cryptic coloring among plants and animals acts like camouflage; some moths, although very tasty to blue jays, are *cryptically* colored to look like bugs that the jays consider inedible.

cryptography \krip-'tä-grə-fē\ (1) Secret writing. (2) The encoding and decoding of messages.

• The instructions for the missile launch are translated into code by the cryptography team.

During World War II, cryptography became an extremely complex science for both the Allied and Axis powers. The Allies managed to get their hands on the Axis machine designed to produce unbreakable codes; the Axis *cryptographers*, on the other hand, never managed to crack the Americans' ultimate code—the Navajo language. In the age of computers, cryptography has become almost unbelievably complex; it is widely used in peacetime in such areas as banking telecommunications.

crypt \'kript\ A room completely or partly underground, especially under the main floor of a church; a room or area in a large aboveground tomb.

• His old nightmare was of being locked in a crypt with corpses as his only companions.

Hidden under the main floor of a great church is often a large room, the centerpiece of which may be a tomb. Many European churches were built over the tomb of a saint or other religious figure; the great St. Peter's Church in the Vatican is an example. A large mausoleum, or aboveground tomb, may contain crypts or small chambers for individual coffins.

AB/ABS comes to us from Latin, and means "from," "away," or "off." *Abuse* is the use of something in the wrong way. To *abduct* is to "lead away from" or kidnap. *Aberrant* behavior is behavior that "wanders away from" what is usually acceptable. But there are so many words that include these roots, it would be *absurd* to try to list them all here.

abscond \ab-'skänd\ To depart in secret and hide.

● We discovered the next morning that our guest had absconded with the family silver during the night.

In J.R.R. Tolkien's novel *The Hobbit,* Bilbo Baggins absconds from Gollum's caves with the ring he has found, the ring Gollum calls "my precious"; the results of his theft and absconding are detailed in the three-volume *Lord of the Rings.* Wagner's massive four-part opera *The Ring of the Nibelung* similarly begins with a dwarf absconding with gold which he turns into a magic ring. Absconding from a problem is often only a temporary relief from it; a young couple might abscond from their parents to get married, but sooner or later they must face those parents again.

abstemious \ab-'stē-mē-əs\ Restrained, especially in the consumption of food or alcohol.

● By living an abstemious life they managed to stay very healthy and to save enough money to take a trip every few years.

Many monks of the 14th century were held to the Rule of St. Benedict, which demand an abstemious life of obedience and poverty. But not all monks could maintain such abstemious habits. Chaucer's *Canterbury Tales* contains a portrait of a monk who is anything but abstemious: for instance, although monks were supposed to follow a vegetarian diet, he is an enthusiastic hunter who loves a fat swan best. He justifies breaking the Rule by saying that it is old, and he's just keeping up with modern times.

abstraction \ab-'strak-shən\ The consideration of a thing or idea without associating it with a particular example.

● All her ideas sounded like abstractions, since in fact she had no experience of actual nursing at all.

Abstract art is art that makes little attempt to show physical objects as they are usually seen. The roots of the word mean "to pull or draw away"; therefore, an abstract design distances itself from any particular object. Theories are often abstractions, especially when they "pull back" to take a broad view and try to apply to or explain everything of a certain kind—for example, all governments, all molecules, or all rock singers.

abstruse \ab-'strüs\ Hard to understand; deep or complex.

● The professor helpfully filled the blackboard with abstruse calculations, but they only served to confuse the class more.

Very often scientific writing is filled with an abstruse special vocabulary, or jargon, which is necessary for exact and precise descriptions. Unfortunately, the language of a science like quantum physics can make an already difficult subject even more abstruse to the average person. Luckily, there are books available that untangle the *abstrusities* in this and other sciences, and explain those difficult ideas in plain, everyday terms.

Quizzes

A. Match the definition on the left to the correct word on the right:

1.	mysterious	a.	apocryphal
2.	code writing	b.	abstraction
3.	fake	c.	abscond
4.	difficult	d.	cryptic
5.	tomb	e.	abstruse
6.	theory	f.	crypt
7.	self-controlled	g.	cryptography
8.	flee	h.	abstemious

B. Fill in each blank with the correct letter:

a.	cryptic	e.	cryptography
b.	abscond	f.	abstemious
c.	abstraction	g.	apocryphal
d.	crypt	h.	abstruse

1. Many an explorer believed the _____ stories of the City of Gold and died hunting for it.

2. His answer was so short and _____ that I have no idea what he meant.

3. The great, echoing _____ of St. Stephen's Cathedral could have held hundreds of people.

4. That is merely an _____; in the real world, things work very differently.

5. The ____ vocabulary of the literature professor led many students to drop her class.
6. He led an ____ life these days and rarely thought of his former high living.
7. Their ____ hadn't been revised in years, and there were worries about the security of their data.
8. The bride is so shy that her mother fears she'll ____ from the reception.

PED comes from the Greek word for "child" this time. See also its "foot" meaning in Unit 4. The two usually aren't hard to tell apart—but don't mistake a *pediatrician* for a *podiatrist*.

---

pedagogy \'pe-də-ˌgō-jē\ The art or profession of teaching; the study of teaching.

● His own pedagogy shows great style and imagination but received little recognition.

To the Greeks, a *pedagogue* was a slave who escorted boys to school and back, taught them manners, and offered extra help with their studies after school. In time the word came to mean simply "teacher." It has an antique ring to it, so it often means a stuffy, boring teacher. *Pedagogy* doesn't have much of that ring to it. It usually means "methods of teaching," while *pedagogic* training usually includes classroom practice.

encyclopedic \in-ˌsī-klə-'pē-dik\ (1) Of or relating to an encyclopedia. (2) Covering a wide range of subjects.

● The *Jeopardy* champion displayed her encyclopedic knowledge with great success.

In Greek, *paidaea* meant "child-rearing" or "education," and *kyklios* meant "circular" or "general"; thus, an encyclopedia is a work broad enough to provide a kind of general education. The *Encyclopaedia Britannica* is a huge work that covers nearly every field of human knowledge. Some dictionaries are also encyclopedic, since they give extended information about history, technology, science, and so on. But *encyclopedic* doesn't have to refer to books: a rock-and-roll radio station may have an encyclopedic collection of popular music, for example.

pediatrician \ˌpē-dē-ə-'tri-shən\ A doctor who specializes in the diseases, development, and care of children.

• A child usually sees a pediatrician until he or she turns 15.

Pediatrics is a fairly new medical specialty; up until about a hundred years ago children were considered small adults and given the same medical treatment, only milder. Benjamin Spock was America's most famous pediatrician through the middle of this century; his book *Baby and Child Care* changed the way people looked at raising children.

pedant \'pe-dənt\ (1) A formal, unimaginative teacher. (2) A person who shows off his or her learning.

• At one time or another, every student encounters a pedant who makes even the most interesting subject tedious.

It is not always easy to tell a *pedantic* teacher from one who is simply thorough. Half of *pedantry* is in the minds of the students. A pedant need not be a teacher; anyone who displays his or her knowledge in a boring manner can qualify.

NASC/NAT/NAI comes from the Latin verb *nasci*, meaning "to be born." Words that have come directly from Latin carry the root *nasc-* or *nat-*, but those that took a detour through French bear a telltale *nai-*—words like *renaissance*, "rebirth," or *naive*, "unsophisticated."

---

cognate \'käg-ˌnāt\ (1) Related or alike by nature. (2) Related because descended from the same language.

• The Italian word *ostinato* has its English cognate in *obstinate*; both come from the Latin word *obstinatus*.

The prefix *co-*, "with," gives *cognate* the meaning "born with" and therefore "related to." This relationship applies to people as well as to words. Your relatives on your mother's side are your cognate relatives; the ones on your father's side are called *agnate*, with a basic meaning of "born to."

innate \i-'nāt\ (1) Present from birth onward; inborn. (2) Part of the essential nature of something.

● The plan has innate problems that are going to make it unworkable.

What is innate in individuals, and in the human race in general, is a constant source of disagreement. No amount of education or experience alone could produce an Isaac Newton or a W.B. Yeats, and the athletic achievements of Michael Jordan or Chris Evert Lloyd required great innate ability. But even the most *natural* geniuses or athletes must work to develop their capacities, no matter how great their *native* talent may be.

nascent \'na-sənt\ Coming or having just come into being.

● The children excitedly watched the nascent butterfly emerge from its chrysalis and begin to stretch its crumpled wings.

With the breakup of the former Soviet Union, the many nascent independent governments in Eastern Europe have had to cope with *renascent* nationalism within their borders, with every ethnic group wanting its own nation. We actually speak of nascent ideas or thoughts or social creations more often than of nascent animals.

renaissance \re-nə-'säns\ (1) Rebirth or revival. (2) The period of European history between medieval and modern times, from about the 14th to the 17th century, which saw a revival of classical culture, a flowering of the arts and literature, and the beginnings of modern science.

● Rembrandt van Rijn, the Dutch painter, was one of the greatest artists produced by the European Renaissance.

The Renaissance is known chiefly for the discoveries of its explorers, the masterpieces its artists created, and its important scientific advances. Galileo made detailed observations of sunspots and the moons of Jupiter, and Copernicus identified the Earth as a planet revolving around the sun—ideas that were considered dangerous at the time. But we may also speak of a modern-day renaissance (uncapitalized)—for example, a renaissance of folk music or of weaving. The *cognate* word *renascence* is sometimes used as an alternative form.

Quizzes

A. Indicate whether the following pairs of words have the same or different meanings:

1. nascent / preexisting   same ___ / different ___
2. encyclopedic / narrow   same ___ / different ___
3. renaissance / rebirth   same ___ / different ___
4. cognate / related   same ___ / different ___
5. pediatrician / foot doctor   same ___ / different ___
6. innate / inborn   same ___ / different ___
7. pedagogy / teaching   same ___ / different ___
8. pedant / know-it-all   same ___ / different ___

B. Match the definition on the left to the correct word on the right:

1. thorough   a. renaissance
2. beginning   b. pediatrician
3. boring teacher   c. cognate
4. related   d. encyclopedic
5. present from birth   e. nascent
6. education   f. pedant
7. revival   g. innate
8. children's doctor   h. pedagogy

FER, from the Latin verb *ferre*, means "to carry." If you *refer* to an incident in your past, you "carry back" to that time. And *transfer* means "to carry across."

---

deferential \ˌde-fə-'ren-chəl\ Showing respect or esteem.

• Wherever the chairman goes, he receives deferential treatment from his hosts.

As we all know, young people should always *defer* (that is, yield or submit) to their elders and betters, who deserve *deference* and appreciate manners that are properly deferential. Unfortunately, deference from young people isn't what it used to be. (We can also defer, or "put off," a decision until another time, but this meaning isn't found in *deferential*.)

fertile \\'fər-təl\\ (1) Bearing great quantities of fruit or imaginative ideas; productive or inventive. (2) Able to support abundant plant growth.

● Unfortunately, those with the most fertile minds often seem to have the most personal problems.

A fertile imagination and a fertile field are both very productive. The first might bring forth a whole new world, like J.R.R. Tolkien's Middle Earth; the second might bring forth enough corn for an entire town. But both have to be tended and nurtured in order to *confer* their benefits. *Fertile* and *infertile, fertility* and *infertility* often refer to the ability to bear children as well.

inference \\'in-frəns\\ (1) A conclusion arrived at from facts or statements taken as true. (2) A guess or assumption made on the basis of little or no evidence.

● Trial lawyers try to present evidence in such a way that the jury can draw from it only the inference that favors their client.

Inferences are risky. In the myth of Pyramus and Thisbe, an inference leads to disaster. When these two lovers are supposed to meet, Pyramus arrives late to find a lion and a bloodstained garment. From this he *infers* that Thisbe has been killed, and, unable to bear it, he kills himself. But Thisbe has only been hiding, and when she finds the dead Pyramus she kills herself in grief. (Shakespeare makes a humorous scene out of this story in *A Midsummer Night's Dream.* But his *Romeo and Juliet* tells the story of two lovers who die as the result of a very similar inference.)

proliferate \\prə-'li-fə-,rāt\\ To grow or increase by rapid production of new units; to multiply.

● Imitators of Ernest Hemingway began to proliferate as soon as he achieved success and popularity.

The literal meaning of *proliferate* is "to bear offspring," and all other usages begin with this. In "The Sorcerer's Apprentice" the apprentice learns how to order the first broom to multiply itself *prolifically*, but not how to command it to stop. Brooms proliferate wildly, each carrying buckets of water that soon flood the sorcerer's studio.

TRANS comes from Latin to indicate movement "through, across, or beyond" something. *Translation* carries the meaning from one language to another. A television signal is sent or *transmitted* through the air (or a cable) to your set. When making your way through a city on public *transportation,* you may have to *transfer* from one bus or subway across to another.

---

transfiguration \trans-ˌfi-gyə-'rā-shən\ A change in form or appearance; a glorifying spiritual change.

● Being in love caused a complete transfiguration of her personality.

The transfiguration of Christ from human to divine form, as his apostles watch, is related in the books of Matthew and Mark. From this Biblical origin, *transfiguration* and *transfigure* developed their general meaning, "a transformation" and "to transform." Ebenezer Scrooge undergoes a transfiguration from mean-spirited miser to loving benefactor by the end of *A Christmas Carol.* A face may be transfigured by joy, and an "ugly duckling" child may be slowly transfigured into a radiant beauty.

transfuse \trans-'fyüz\ (1) To spread into or throughout; to permeate. (2) To transfer into a vein of a person or animal.

● There was considerable excitement about the new president, who everyone expected to transfuse new life into the institution.

When blood *transfusions* were first attempted by Europeans in the early 1600s, they were met with skepticism. The established practice was to bleed patients, not transfuse them with blood. Some patients were transfused with animal blood, and so many died because of the procedure that it was outlawed in most of Europe by 1700. Not until 1900 were the major blood groups (A, B, AB, and O) recognized, making transfusions safer and more effective.

transient \'tran-chē-ənt\ (1) Not lasting long; short-lived. (2) Passing through a place and staying only briefly.

● They ran an inn in Vermont that was popular with the transient tourists who passed through the state to see the autumn foliage.

A summer job on a farm is transient work, lasting only as long as the growing season. A brief visit to a town on your way somewhere else is a transient visit. A transient mood is one that passes quickly. Doctors speak of transient episodes of dizziness or weakness, which vanish without a trace. *Transient* is also a noun, used for a person who passes through a place, staying only briefly. The hoboes and tramps of earlier years were some of our most colorful transients.

transcendent \tran-'sen-dənt\ (1) Exceeding or rising above usual limits; surpassing, supreme. (2) Beyond comprehension; beyond ordinary experience or material existence.

● Despite the chaos around her she remained calm, with a transcendent smile on her face.

In the Middle Ages the authority of the Pope was considered transcendent in Europe, above the power of kings and emperors, but in the 16th century the *transcendence* of the Papacy was challenged by Martin Luther and Henry VIII of England. A transcendent experience is one that takes you out of yourself and convinces you of a larger life or existence. In this sense, it means something close to "supernatural" or "spiritual."

Quizzes

A. Fill in each blank with the correct letter:

a. transfiguration	e. deferential
b. proliferate	f. transient
c. transfuse	g. inference
d. fertile	h. transcendent

1. Copies of American blue jeans seem to _____ in all parts of the world.
2. He lived a _____ existence, spending more nights in airport hotels than at home.
3. The private assumed her usual _____ attitude toward the lieutenant.

4. Waiting for the nurse to ____ her, she couldn't remember the accident clearly.

5. They had witnessed a complete ____, as a poor flower vendor became a lady of society.

6. The ____ Connecticut River valley is famous for its tobacco crops.

7. In search of a ____ experience, she had entered a monastery in Tibet.

8. Please don't draw the wrong ____ from what I've said about the building plans.

B. Match the word on the left to the correct definition on the right:

1. fertile	a.	supreme
2. transcendent	b.	implied conclusion
3. deferential	c.	glorification
4. transfiguration	d.	productive
5. proliferate	e.	multiply
6. transient	f.	yielding
7. inference	g.	passing
8. transfuse	h.	transfer

PON/POS, from the Latin verb *ponere*, means "put" or "place." You *expose* film by "placing it out" in the light. You *oppose* an *opponent* by "putting yourself against" him or her. You *postpone* a trip by "placing it after" its original date.

component \kəm-'pō-nənt\ A separate part of a whole; an ingredient or element.

● All the components of the agreement were in place, but the owner still hadn't given her final approval.

A component is what is "put together with" other parts to make a whole. A stereo system is made up of different components—tuner, cassette deck, CD player, phonograph, and speakers—each of which fills its own different function in the overall system. The components of a crime bill would include sections on sentencing and parole, prisons, the judicial system, and so on. But the pieces of a jigsaw puzzle may be too similar to be called components.

disposition \dis-pə-'zi-shən\ (1) Tendency, inclination. (2) Basic outlook or attitude.

● It was his classmates' disposition to argue about everything that convinced him he didn't want to be a lawyer after all.

Animals and people may have sweet or sour dispositions, or personalities. Some of them also may share the tendency, or disposition, to eat greedily, to yawn loudly, or to dash about making odd noises. But many humans have a disposition to gossip, to tell stupid jokes, and to think gloomy thoughts about the future, which your dog may not have.

repository \ri-'pä-zə-,tȯr-ē\ A place or container where something is stored.

● The 98-year old Miss Sarah turned out to be a repository of lore about the glory days of Beale Street.

A vault or safe is the most secure repository for valuable possessions such as jewelry or money. A book may be a repository of wisdom. A mine is a repository of mineral resources like raw diamonds or gold ore. In all of these lie *deposits* that have been "replaced," and there they *repose* until disturbed.

superimpose \,sü-pər-im-'pōz\ To put or place one thing over something else.

● With the transparent sheet, the teacher superimposed national boundaries on an outline of the continent of Africa.

Using "mirror shots," with semitransparent mirrors set at 45° angles to the scene, filmmakers used to superimpose shadowy images of ghosts or scenes from a character's past onto scenes from the present. In a similar way, in your own papers you may try to superimpose your own obsession with cockroaches or Wallace Beery onto every historical or economic or literary subject, to the bafflement of your professors.

TEN/TIN/TAIN, from the Latin verb *tenere* and the related word *tenax*, basically means "hold" or "hold on to." A *tenant* is the "holder" of an apartment, house, or land, but not necessarily the owner. A *lieutenant* governor may "hold the position" or "serve in lieu" of the governor when necessary.

---

abstinence \'ab-stə-nəns\ Holding oneself back voluntarily from indulging an appetite or craving.

• Burned out by too many wild nights, she moved to the country and took up a life of abstinence.

Today we usually speak of abstinence from alcohol, rich foods, or sex. But religious beliefs lead many to *abstain* from much more, and abstinence can become a way of life. Certain religious sects may demand abstinence from such things as meat, dancing, and colorful clothing.

tenacious \tə-'nā-shəs\ Stubborn or persistent in clinging to a thing.

• He was known as a tenacious reporter who would stay with a story for months, sometimes risking his health and even his life.

Success requires a tenacious spirit and a drive to achieve. Nowhere is this more apparent than in the entertainment business. Thousands of actors and actresses work *tenaciously* to have a career in the movies. But without beauty or talent, *tenacity* isn't always rewarded, and only a few become stars.

tenable \'te-nə-bəl\ Capable of being held or defended; reasonable.

• She was depressed for weeks after her professor said that her theory wasn't tenable.

Tenable means "holdable." If you hold an opinion but good evidence appears that completely contradicts it, your opinion is no longer tenable. If your own evidence is shown to be false, it ceases to be tenable evidence. So the old ideas that cancer is infectious or that leeches can cure your whooping cough and criminal insanity are now probably *untenable*.

sustenance \'səs-tə-nəns\ (1) Something that gives support or strength. (2) Food, nourishment.

● Napoleon's invading army, forced to turn back from Moscow by the terrible Russian winter, ended up eating its horses when all other sustenance ran out.

Sustenance holds us up from underneath (the prefix *sus-* being a form of *sub-*, meaning "under"). Sustenance can be either physical or emotional. So a big Sunday dinner with your family can provide you with sustenance of both kinds.

Quizzes

A. Choose the closest definition:

1.   disposition   a. temperature b. personality c. anger
         d. riddance
2.   tenacious   a. sticking b. intelligent c. loving d. helping
3.   superimpose   a. surpass b. put into c. place over
         d. amaze
4.   abstinence   a. self-help b. self-will c. self-service
         d. self-restraint
5.   repository   a. tomb b. storage container c. office
         d. library
6.   tenable   a. decent b. tough c. reasonable
         d. controllable
7.   component   a. part b. whole c. some d. all
8.   sustenance   a. substance b. apartment c. clothing
         d. nourishment

B. Indicate whether the following pairs have the same or different meanings:

1.   component / ingredient   same __ / different __
2.   sustenance / support   same __ / different __
3.   repository / return   same __ / different __
4.   abstinence / absence   same __ / different __
5.   superimpose / offend deeply   same __ / different __
6.   tenacious / sensible   same __ / different __
7.   disposition / nature   same __ / different __
8.   tenable / unlikely   same __ / different __

Number Words

MONO is Greek for "one" or "only." So a *monorail* is a railroad that has only one rail, a *monotonous* voice seems to have only one tone, and a *monopoly* puts all ownership in the hands of a single company, eliminating any competition.

---

monogamous \mə-'nä-gə-məs\ Being married to one person or having one mate at a time.

● Geese, swans, and many other birds are monogamous and mate for life.

American marriage is by law monogamous; people are permitted to have only one spouse (husband or wife) at a time. There are cultures with laws that permit marriage to more than one person at a time, or *polygamy*. Some Islamic countries permit polygamy, as do some African tribes. In this country the Mormons were *polygamous* until 1890, when they were forced to practice *monogamy* by the unsympathetic federal government.

monograph \'mä-nə-,graf\ A scholarly essay written on a single small topic and published separately.

● Her paper on the slang used by southern college students was printed as a monograph.

A monograph usually takes the form of a book, but a smallish book. The contents discuss a single area or subject. The subjects of monographs tend to be specialized—for example, *A Statistical Study of the Graphic System of Present-Day American English.*

monolithic \,mä-nə-'li-thik\ (1) Appearing to be a huge, featureless, often rigid whole. (2) Made up of material with no joints or seams.

● The sheer monolithic rock face of El Capitan looks impossible to climb, but its cracks and seams are enough for experienced rock climbers.

Monolithic combines *mono-* with *lith,* "stone," and *monolith* in its original sense means a huge stone like those at Stonehenge. Just as the face of a cliff can be monolithic, so can any huge or imposing institution. The former U.S.S.R. seemed monolithic and indestructible to the West, but the monolith crumbled with the breakup of the Soviet Union into independent republics. To a lone individual, a huge corporation or a government bureaucracy may seem equally monolithic.

monotheism \'mä-nō-thē-ˌi-zəm\ The worship of a single god.

⊚ Christian monotheism finally triumphed in the Roman Empire in A.D. 392, when worship of all the pagan gods and goddesses was forbidden.

The monotheism of the ancient Hebrews had to combat the *polytheism* (worship of many gods) of the surrounding peoples from the earliest times. As the Bible relates, several times in their history the Hebrews turned away from their *monotheistic* religion and accepted foreign gods, such as those imported by King Solomon. Their own God would then punish them, and the people of Israel would return to monotheism.

UNI comes from the Latin word for "one." A *uniform* is a single design worn by everyone. A *united* group has one single opinion or forms a single *unit*. A *unitard* is a one-piece combination leotard and tights, very good for skating, skiing, dancing—or riding a one-wheeled *unicycle*.

---

unicameral \ˌyü-ni-'ka-mə-rəl\ Having only one lawmaking chamber.

● China has a unicameral system of government; a single group of legislators meets to make its laws.

Unicameral means "one-chambered," and the term is generally used only to describe a governing body. Our federal legislature, like those of most democracies, is *bicameral,* with two legislative (lawmaking) bodies—the Senate and the House of Representatives. Except for Nebraska, all the state legislatures are also bicameral. But nearly every city is governed by a unicameral council.

unilateral \ˌyü-ni-'la-tə-rəl\ (1) Done by one person or party; one-sided. (2) Affecting one side of the body.

• The Japanese Constitution of 1947 includes a unilateral rejection of warfare as an option for their country.

The United States announced a unilateral nuclear-arms reduction in the early 1990s. Such a reduction never occurred in the previous decades, when only *bilateral* ("two-sided") negotiations—that is, negotiations with the Soviet Union—ever resulted in reductions. *Multilateral* agreements, such as those reached at the great Earth Summit in Rio de Janeiro in 1992, may involve most of the world's nations.

unison \'yü-nə-sən\ (1) Perfect agreement. (2) Sameness of musical pitch.

• Unable to read music well enough to harmonize, the village choir sang only in unison.

This word usually appears in the phrase "in unison," which means "together, at the same time" or "at the same musical pitch." Music of the early Middle Ages was written to be sung in unison, which can sound strange to modern ears used to hearing rich rhythms and harmonies. An excited crowd responding to a speaker may shout in unison, and a group of demonstrators may chant in unison.

unitarian \ˌyü-nə-'ter-ē-ən\ Relating or belonging to a religious group that believes that God exists only in one person and stresses individual freedom of belief.

• With his unitarian tendencies, he wasn't likely to get into fights over religious beliefs.

Unitarianism, originally a sect of Christianity believing in a single or *unitary* God, grew up in 18th-century England and developed in America in the early 19th century. By rejecting the idea of the three-part Trinity—God as father, son, and holy ghost—they denied that Christ was divine and thus cannot truly be considered Christian. In this century it joined with the *Universalist* Church, a movement founded on a belief in *universal* salvation—that is, the saving of every soul from damnation after death. Both have always been liberal and fairly small; today they count about half a million members.

Quiz

Fill in each blank with the correct letter:

a. monotheism   e. unitarian
b. unilateral   f. monograph
c. monolithic   g. unicameral
d. unison   h. monogamous

1. The President is allowed to make some _____ decisions without asking Congress's permission.
2. The relationship was unbalanced: she was perfectly _____, while he had two other women in his life.
3. In rejecting a _____ legislature, America seemed to follow Britain's lead.
4. The steep mountain face looked _____ and forbidding.
5. As a strict Catholic, she found _____ beliefs unacceptable.
6. Most religious groups in this country practice one or another form of _____.
7. She ordered a brief _____ on the subject of the origin of the thoroughbred.
8. The children recited the Halloween poems in _____.

Review Quizzes

A. Choose the correct synonym for the following:

1. fertile   a. green b. productive c. barren d. bare
2. unilateral   a. one-sided b. sideways c. complete d. multiple
3. abstinence   a. self-love b. self-restraint c. self-criticism d. self-indulgence
4. innate   a. natural b. acquired c. genuine d. official
5. repository   a. bedroom b. storeroom c. bank window d. dispensary
6. cryptography   a. gravestone writing b. physics writing c. code writing d. mathematical writing
7. sustenance   a. subtraction b. nourishment c. poison d. addition
8. deferential   a. respectful b. shy c. outgoing d. arrogant

9. monotheism   a. nature worship   b. worship of one god   c. worship of pleasure   d. sun worship
10. abscond   a. steal   b. discover   c. retire   d. flee
11. transcendent   a. supreme   b. beautiful   c. heroic d. intelligent
12. inference   a. conclusion   b. claim   c. concept   d. refusal
13. transient   a. flowing   b. passing   c. intense   d. speeding
14. pedagogy   a. study   b. teaching   c. research   d. child abuse
15. nascent   a. dying   b. lasting   c. eating   d. beginning
16. unison   a. solitude   b. harmony   c. collection d. agreement
17. proliferate   a. survive   b. prosper   c. multiply   d. die off
18. crypt   a. code   b. granite   c. tomb   d. church
19. superimpose   a. increase   b. lay over   c. improve d. excel
20. monogamous   a. with one spouse   b. without a spouse   c. with several spouses   d. with someone else's spouse

B. Fill in each blank with the correct letter:

a. renaissance
b. pediatrician
c. monograph
d. unitarian
e. transfiguration
f. abstraction
g. tenacious
h. disposition
i. transfuse
j. abstruse

1. In the 1990s there has been a _____ of interest in goddess worship.
2. Tuesday the baby sees the _____ for its immunizations and checkups.
3. His _____ had gotten so bad that he found himself snapping angrily at his friends.
4. The anemia was serious enough that they had to _____ him with two pints of blood.
5. The notion of a savior was foreign to his _____ beliefs.
6. The _____ promised by their leader failed to occur on the predicted day.
7. The speech contained one _____ after another, but never a specific example.

8. She would occasionally publish a short _____ on the results of her recent research.

9. The sick child's _____ grip on life was their only hope now.

10. The researcher's writing was _____ but it was worth the effort to read it.

C. Indicate whether the following pairs of words have the same or different meanings:

1. component / part   same ___ / different ___
2. pedant / pupil   same ___ / different ___
3. cryptic / tomblike   same ___ / different ___
4. monolithic / tedious   same ___ / different ___
5. abstemious / self-controlled   same ___ / different ___
6. cognate / related   same ___ / different ___
7. apocryphal / sacred   same ___ / different ___
8. tenable / reasonable   same ___ / different ___
9. unicameral / one-chambered   same ___ / different ___
10. abstruse / deep   same ___ / different ___

Unit 15

TERM/TERMIN comes from the Latin verb *terminare*, "to limit, bound, or set limits to," or the related noun *terminus*, a "limit or boundary." In English, those boundaries or limits tend to be final: to *terminate* a sentence or a meeting or a ballgame means to end it, and a *term* goes on for a given amount of time and then ends.

indeterminate \in-di-'tər-mə-nət\ Not precisely determined; vague.

• The law allowed for indeterminate sentences for certain unusual classes of offenders.

A mutt is usually the product of indeterminate breeding, since at least the father's identity is generally a mystery. An art object of indeterminate origins is normally less valued than one with a maker's name on it. If negotiations are left in an indeterminate state, nothing has been decided.

interminable \in-'tər-mə-nə-bəl\ Having or seeming to have no end; tiresomely drawn out.

• Their appeals to their audiences for money are so interminable that there's barely time for the sermons.

Nothing is literally endless except maybe the universe and time itself. So *interminable* as we use it is always an exaggeration. On an unlucky day you might sit through an interminable lecture, an interminable meeting, and an interminable film—all in less than 24 hours.

terminal \\'tər-mə-nəl\\ (1) Forming or relating to an end or limit. (2) Fatal.

● She knows these are the late stages of a terminal illness, and has already drawn up a will.

A terminal illness ends in death; with terminal boredom you are "bored to death." For some, a high-school diploma is their terminal degree; others finish college before *terminating* their education. A bus *terminal* should be the endpoint of a bus line; a computer terminal was originally the endpoint of a line connecting to a central computer. A terminal ornament may mark the end of a building, and terminal punctuation ends this sentence.

terminology \\,tər-mə-'nä-lə-jē\\ The words with specialized or precise meanings used in a field or subject.

● Civil engineers use a technical terminology that is like a foreign language to an outsider.

Terms—that is, specialized words or expressions—tend to have precise boundaries of meaning. Each field has its own terminology, or "jargon," which helps those who work in the field communicate with each other quickly and accurately. But the expert's workaday language is often the layperson's *terminological* hell.

VINC/VICT comes from the Latin verb *vincere,* which means "to conquer" or "to overcome." The *victor* defeats an enemy, whether on a battlefield or a football field. To *convince* someone that you're right is a *victory* of another kind.

---

evince \\i-'vins\\ To be outward evidence of; show or reveal.

● As a witness she evinced honesty and dignity, and the jury was favorably impressed.

A man may evince interest in a woman by casting glances, making small talk, and generally hanging around, or by even more obvious tactics. A novelist's writing may evince concern for refugees or the elderly. A country may evince a desire for closer relations by arranging a ping-pong competition, as China did with the United States in 1971.

invincible \in-'vin-sə-bəl\ Incapable of being conquered or overcome.

• The supposedly invincible Spanish Armada was defeated by a fleet of small English ships in 1588.

Antaeus, a giant and son of Poseidon, was invincible so long as he remained in contact with the ground. But his *invincibility* crumbled when he challenged Hercules to wrestle and Hercules held the giant over his head, thereby defeating his "invincible" foe.

provincial \prə-'vin-chəl\ (1) Having to do with a province. (2) Lacking polish, culture, and broad experience.

• They were both by now sick of Chicago and would gladly have exchanged the fast life for more provincial pleasures.

A *province* is an administrative section of a larger state or country. The word comes from Roman times. The Romans gained territory by conquest, and a conquered area might become a province. (There is still some question about how the word was actually formed.) The areas usually set up a local or provincial government. Life in these provinces was not as fancy as life at Rome, just as life in the rural, provincial parts of any country is not as polished or refined as life in its cities.

victimize \'vik-tə-ˌmīz\ To make a victim of; trick, deceive, or injure.

• Like most tourists there, we were victimized by the local merchants and guides.

A *victim* is the person who is victimized. Robin Hood and his band of merry men victimized the rich in order to give to the poor—but the rich noblemen and churchmen had gotten that way by victimizing the poor in the first place. Physical and emotional *victimization* by one's parents when young is a complaint heard often today from "adult children."

Quizzes

A. Choose the closest definition:

1. evince   a. reveal   b. throw out   c. eject   d. overcome
2. interminable   a. remarkable   b. unthinkable
       c. reliable   d. eternal

3. terminology   a. instruction b. design c. vocabulary
   d. technology
4. provincial   a. professional b. global c. local d. national
5. invincible   a. unsuitable b. impossible
   c. inflammable d. unconquerable
6. terminal   a. fatal b. technical c. verbal d. similar
7. indeterminate   a. lengthy b. uncertain c. unending
   d. likely
8. victimize   a. conquer b. applaud c. deceive d. invite

B. Fill in each blank with the correct letter:

a. invincible   e. indeterminate
b. terminology   f. evince
c. victimize   g. terminal
d. interminable   h. provincial

1. Her manners were a bit rough and _____, but charming.
2. All day long, reports came in of people the con man had
   tried to _____.
3. We waited anxiously for the mare to _____ signs of
   giving birth.
4. The students generally find the _____ of psychology
   fairly easy to learn and use.
5. He was a man of _____ age, and mysterious in other
   ways as well.
6. Don't you ever have those great days when you feel
   absolutely _____?
7. He gave _____ lectures, and I usually dozed off in the
   middle.
8. Last week we assumed his condition was _____; today no
   one is making predictions.

SPHER comes from the Greek word for "ball," and it appears
in words for things that have something round about them. A ball
is itself a *sphere*. The *stratosphere* and the *ionosphere* are parts of
the *atmosphere* that encircles the earth.

---

stratosphere \\'stra-tə-ˌsfir\\ (1) The part of the earth's atmosphere
that extends from about seven to about 31 miles above the surface.

(2) A very high or the highest region.

● In the celebrity stratosphere she now occupied, a fee of two million dollars a film was a reasonable rate.

The stratosphere (*strato-* simply means "layer" or "level") lies above the earth's weather and mostly changes very little. About 20 miles above the earth's surface it contains the ozone layer, which shields us from the sun's ultraviolet radiation except where it has been harmed by manmade chemicals. The levels of the *atmosphere* are marked particularly by their temperatures; the *stratospheric* temperature hovers around 32°—very moderate considering that temperatures in the *troposphere* below may descend to about -70° and in the *ionosphere* above may rise to 1000°.

biosphere \'bī-ə-ˌsfir\ (1) The part of the world in which life can exist. (2) Living things and their environment.

● The moon has no biosphere, so an artificial one would have to be constructed for any long-term stay.

The *lithosphere* is the solid surface of the earth (*lith-* means "rock"); the *hydrosphere* is the earth's water (*hydro-* means "water"), including the clouds and water vapor in the air; the *atmosphere* is the earth's air (*atmos-* means "vapor"). The term *biosphere* can include all of these and the 10 million species of living things they contain. The biosphere recycles its air, water, organisms, and minerals constantly to maintain an amazingly balanced state; human beings should probably do their best to imitate it. Though the word has a new sound to it, it was first used a hundred years ago.

hemisphere \'he-mə-ˌsfir\ Half a sphere, especially half the global sphere as divided by the equator or a meridian.

● Sailors who cross the equator from the northern to the southern hemisphere for the first time are given a special initiation.

Hemisphere includes the prefix *hemi-*, meaning "half." The northern and southern hemispheres are divided by the equator. The eastern and western hemispheres aren't divided so exactly; usually the eastern hemisphere includes all of Europe, Africa, and Australia and almost all of Asia, and the western hemisphere contains North and South America and a great deal of ocean.

spherical \\'sfir-ə-kəl\\ Relating to a sphere; shaped like a sphere or one of its segments.

● The girls agreed that the spacecraft had been perfectly spherical and deep blue, and that its alien passengers had resembled large cockroaches.

Something spherical is like a *sphere* in being round, or more or less round, in three dimensions. Apples and oranges are both spherical, though never perfectly round. A *spheroid* has a roughly spherical shape; an asteroid is often a spheroid, fairly round but lumpy.

VERT/VERS, from the Latin verb *vertere*, means "to turn" or "to turn around." An *advertisement* turns your attention to a product or service. *Vertigo* is the dizziness that results from turning too rapidly or that makes you feel as if everything else is turning.

---

divert \\dī-'vərt\\ (1) To turn from one purpose or course to another. (2) To give pleasure to by distracting from burdens or distress.

● The farmers successfully diverted some of the river water to irrigate their crops during the drought.

The Roman circus was used to provide *diversion* for its citizens— and sometimes to divert their attention from the government's failings as well. The diversion was often in the form of a fight—men pitted against lions, bears, or each other—and the audience was sure to see blood and death. A *diverting* evening in the 1990s might instead include watching several murders on a movie screen.

perverse \\pər-'vərs\\ (1) Corrupt; improper; incorrect. (2) Stubbornly or obstinately wrong.

● The unsuspected murderer had apparently felt a perverse desire to chat with the police.

The 12th-century citizens of Paris thought keeping a cat or taking a bath without clothes on were perverse—that is, satanic or ungodly. But this is an older meaning; today *perverse* usually means somehow "contradictory" or "opposed to good sense." Someone who loves great art but collects cheap figurines may admit to having perverse tastes. To desire a stable life but still go out on drinking binges could be called acting *perversely* or even self-destructively. Don't confuse *perverse* with *perverted,* which today tends to mean "having strange sexual tastes." And likewise avoid confusing their noun forms, *perversity* and *perversion.*

avert \ə-'vərt\ (1) To turn away or aside (especially one's eyes). (2) To avoid or ward off; prevent.

● General Camacho's announcement of lower food prices averted an immediate worker's revolt.

Sensitive people avert their eyes from gory accidents and scenes of disaster. But we also speak of averting the disaster itself. Negotiators may avert, or avoid, a strike by all-night talks, and leaders may work to avert a war in the same way. In the Cuban missile crisis of 1962 it seemed that worldwide nuclear catastrophe was narrowly (or barely) averted. *Aversion* means "dislike or disgust"—that is, your feeling about something you don't want to look at.

versatile \'vər-sə-təl\ (1) Turning easily from one skill to another. (2) Having many uses.

● The versatile Gene Kelly acted, sang, and directed—and dazzled America with his dancing.

The horse was the most versatile and valuable asset of the armies of Attila the Hun. A Hun could stay in the saddle for weeks at a time, opening a vein in the horse's neck to suck the blood for food. The Huns made a kind of liquor from mare's milk. Extra horses were stampeded in battle to create *diversions.* Relying on this *versatility,* Attila and the Huns conquered much of eastern and central Europe in the 5th century.

Quizzes

A. Complete the analogy:

1. pint : quart :: hemisphere : _____
   a. ocean b. continent c. sphere d. globe
2. reasonable : sensible :: perverse : _____
   a. mistaken b. stupid c. contrary d. unlikely
3. forest : trees :: stratosphere : _____
   a. gases b. clouds c. planets d. altitude
4. accept : agree :: divert : _____
   a. distress b. amuse c. differ d. disturb

5. escape : flee :: avert : _____
   a. prevent b. throw c. entertain d. alarm
6. cube-shaped : square :: spherical : _____
   a. global b. oval c. curved d. circle
7. flexible : stretchable :: versatile : _____
   a. well-rounded b. similar c. skilled d. trained
8. atmosphere : stratosphere :: biosphere : _____
   a. recycling b. hydrosphere c. energy d. earth

B. Match the word on the left to the correct definition on the right:

1.	avert	a.	with many uses
2.	spherical	b.	upper atmosphere
3.	divert	c.	wrongheaded
4.	hemisphere	d.	avoid
5.	versatile	e.	half-sphere
6.	biosphere	f.	entertain
7.	stratosphere	g.	globelike
8.	perverse	h.	life zone

MORPH comes from the Greek word for "shape." *Morph* is itself an English word with a brand-new meaning; by morphing, filmmakers can now alter photographic images or shapes digitally, making them move or transform themselves in astonishing ways.

amorphous \ə-'mȯr-fəs\ Without a definite shape or form; shapeless.

● The sculptor took an amorphous lump of clay and molded it swiftly into a rough human shape.

A new word may appear to name a previously amorphous group of people, as the word *yuppie* did in 1983. An amorphous but terrifying thing may loom in a nightmare. In all the Greek myths of the creation the world begins in an amorphous state, just as at the beginning of the Bible "the earth was without form, and void."

anthropomorphic \ˌan-thrə-pə-'mȯr-fik\ (1) Having or described as having human form or traits. (2) Seeing human traits in nonhuman things.

● The old, diseased tree had always been like a companion to her, though she knew her anthropomorphic feelings about it were sentimental.

Anthropomorphic means a couple of different things. In its first sense, an anthropomorphic cup would be a cup in the shape of a human, and an anthropomorphic god would be one that looked and acted like a human. All the Greek and Roman gods are anthropomorphic, for example, even though Socrates and even earlier Greeks believed that their fellow Greeks had created their gods in their own image rather than the other way around. In its second sense, the animal characters in *Aesop's Fables* are anthropomorphic since they all have human feelings and motivations though they don't look like humans. When the fox calls the grapes sour simply because they are out of reach, it is a very human response. At least 3,000 years after Aesop, *anthropomorphism* is still alive and well, in the books of Beatrix Potter, George Orwell's *Animal Farm*, and hundreds of animated cartoons and comic strips.

metamorphosis \ˌme-tə-ˈmȯr-fə-səs\ (1) A physical change, especially one supernaturally caused. (2) A developmental change in an animal that occurs after birth or hatching.

● Day by day we watched the gradual metamorphosis of the tadpoles into frogs.

Many myths end in a metamorphosis. As Apollo is chasing the nymph Daphne, she calls on her river-god father for help and he turns her into a laurel tree to save her. Out of anger and jealousy, the goddess Athena turns the marvelous weaver Arachne into a spider that will spin only beautiful webs. But rocks may also *metamorphose*, or undergo metamorphosis; coal under great pressure over a long period of time will become diamonds. And the transformation of caterpillars into butterflies is the most famous of natural metamorphoses.

morphology \mȯr-ˈfä-lə-jē\ (1) The study of the structure and form of plants and animals. (2) The study of word formation.

● Her biology term paper discussed the morphology of three kinds of seaweed.

Morphology contains the root *log-*, "study." *Morphologists* study plants and animals and use the information to classify species. In language, morphology considers where words come from and why they look as they do.

FORM is the Latin root meaning "shape" or "form." Marching in *formation* is marching in ordered patterns. A *formula* is a standard form for expressing information, such as a recipe or a rule written in mathematical symbols.

---

conform \kən-'fòrm\ (1) To be similar or identical; to be in agreement or harmony. (2) To follow ordinary standards or customs.

● Ignoring all pressure to conform, she would stride with her goats through the fields at sunset, her hair wild and her long skirts billowing.

Employees must usually conform with company procedures. A certain philosophy may be said to conform with American values. A Maine Coon cat or a Dandie Dinmont terrier must conform to its breed requirements in order to be registered for breeding purposes. A *nonconformist* ignores society's standards or deliberately violates them, and laughs at the whole idea of *conformity*. (Note that "conform to" and "conform with" are both correct, though "conform to" is more common.)

formality \fòr-'ma-lə-tē\ (1) An established custom or way of behaving that is required or standard. (2) The following of formal or conventional rules.

● The bride and groom wanted a small, intimate wedding without all the usual formalities.

Formal behavior follows the proper *forms* or customs, and *informal* behavior ignores them. The formality of a dinner party is indicated by such formalities as invitations, required dress, and full table settings. Legal formalities may turn out to be all-important even if they seem minor. America requires fewer formalities than many other countries (in Germany you may know people for years before using their first names, for example), but even in relaxed situations Americans may be observing invisible formalities.

formative \'fȯr-mə-tiv\ (1) Giving or able to give form or shape; constructive. (2) Having to do with important growth or development.

● She lived in Venezuela during her formative years and grew up speaking both Spanish and English.

Whatever gives shape to something else may be called formative; thus, for example, the Grand Canyon was a product of the formative power of water. But it usually applies to nonphysical shaping. An ambitious plan goes through a formative stage of development. America's formative years included experimentation with various forms of government. And the automobile was a huge formative influence on the design of many of our cities.

format \'fȯr-,mat\ (1) The shape, size, and general makeup of something. (2) A general plan, arrangement, or choice of material.

● The new thesaurus would be published in three formats: as a large paperback, as a hardcover book, and as a CD-ROM.

TV news shows seem to change their formats, or general form, as often as their anchorpeople. The situation comedy is even called a format. The format of a book or newspaper page is its design or layout.

Quizzes

A. Indicate whether the following pairs of words have the same or different meanings:

1. formative / form-giving   same __ / different __
2. morphology / shapeliness   same __ / different __
3. conform / agree   same __ / different __
4. anthropomorphic / man-shaped   same __ / different __
5. format / arrangement   same __ / different __
6. amorphous / shapeless   same __ / different __
7. formality / convention   same __ / different __
8. metamorphosis / hibernation   same __ / different __

B. Fill in each blank with the correct letter:

a. morphology   e. conform
b. formative   f. amorphous

---

c. metamorphosis   g. formality
d. format   h. anthropomorphic

1. The newspaper's new _____ led the public to expect stories of glamour and scandal.
2. The job description seemed a bit _____, and she wondered what she would really be doing.
3. While on the base, you are expected to _____ with all official rules and regulations.
4. He sees many _____ traits in his dogs, but he thinks that one of them may be a space alien.
5. He seemed to undergo a complete _____ from child to young adult in just a few months.
6. The new couple found the _____ of the dinner a little overwhelming.
7. He had spent his life on the _____ of a single genus of dragonfly.
8. Among her _____ influences she included her favorite uncle, her ballet classes, and the Nancy Drew series.

DOC/DOCT comes from the Latin *docere,* which means "to teach." A *doctor* is a highly educated person capable of instructing others in the *doctrines,* or basic principles, of his or her field—which is not necessarily medicine.

---

doctrine \'däk-trən\ (1) Something that is taught. (2) An official principle, opinion, or belief.

• According to the 19th-century doctrine of papal infallibility, the pope's formal statements on matters of faith and morals must be regarded as the absolute truth.

The original doctrines were those of the Catholic Church, especially as taught by the so-called *doctors* (or religious scholars) of the Church. Other systems, organizations, and governments have taught their own doctrines. Traditional psychiatrists may still follow the doctrines of Sigmund Freud. Old and established legal principles are called legal doctrine. Communist doctrine was often the teachings of Lenin, which were regarded as almost sacred. In 1823 the Monroe Doctrine stated that the United States opposed European influence in the Americas, and in 1947 the Truman Doctrine held that America would support free countries against enemies outside and inside.

docile \'dä-səl\ Easily led, tamed, or taught; obedient.

● Training a dog is much easier if the animal has a docile temperament to start with.

A docile patient obeys all doctors and nurses, takes the prescribed medication, and doesn't nag anyone with questions. A docile labor force doesn't make demands or form unions. A docile population is easily led by even bad leaders. And a docile spouse does what he or she is told.

doctrinaire \,däk-trə-'nar\ Tending to apply principles or theories without regard for practical difficulties or individual circumstance.

● She avoided taking a doctrinaire approach to teaching; education theories didn't always match the reality of instructing 25 lively students.

Someone doctrinaire sticks closely to official doctrines or principles. A doctrinaire judge will give identical sentences to everyone found guilty of a particular crime. A doctrinaire feminist will treat all men as if they were identical. A doctrinaire free-market economist will call for a single solution for the economic problems in all countries, regardless of their social and cultural history.

indoctrinate \in-'däk-trə-,nāt\ (1) To teach, especially basics or fundamentals. (2) To fill someone with a particular opinion or point of view.

● The sergeants had six months to indoctrinate the new recruits with army attitudes and discipline.

Indoctrinate simply means ''brainwash'' to many people. But its meaning isn't always so negative. Every society indoctrinates its young people with the values of their culture. In the United States we tend to be indoctrinated to love freedom, to be individuals, and to work hard for success, among many other things. A religious cult may indoctrinate its members to give up their freedom and individuality and to work hard only for its leader's goals. *Indoctrination* in these opposite values leads many to regard cults as dangerous.

TUT/TUI, from the Latin verb *tueri*, originally meant "to look at," but the English meaning of the root gradually came to be "to guide, guard, or teach." A *tutor* guides a student (or *tutee*) through a subject, saving the most careful tutoring for the most difficult areas.

intuition \‚in-tù-'wi-shən\ (1) The power of knowing something immediately without mental effort; quick insight. (2) Something known in this way.

● She scoffed at the notion of "women's intuition," special powers of insight and understanding that only women are supposed to have.

Intuition is very close in meaning to *instinct*. The moment someone enters a room you may feel you know *intuitively* or instinctively everything about him or her. Highly rational people may try to ignore their intuition and insist on being able to explain everything they think. Artists and creative thinkers, on the other hand, tend to rely on their intuitive sense of things. Intuition can be closely related to their imagination, which seems to come from somewhere just as mysterious.

tuition \tù-'wi-shən\ (1) The act of teaching; instruction. (2) The cost of or payment for instruction.

● As Kara happily flipped through her college catalogs, her parents looked on in dismay, mentally calculating the total tuition costs.

The sense of *tuition* meaning "teaching" or "instruction" is mostly used in Britain today. In America *tuition* almost always means the costs charged by a school, college, or university. In the mid-1990s it was possible to receive an education through college for less than $20,000; but it was also possible to spend about $200,000 in tuition and fees for a boarding-school and college education.

tutelage \'tü-tə-lij\ Instruction or guidance of an individual; guardianship.

● Under the old man's expert tutelage, they learned how to carve and paint realistic decoys.

Tutelage usually implies specialized and individual guidance. Alexander the Great was under the tutelage of the philosopher Aristotle between the ages of 13 and 16, and his *tutor* inspired him with a love of philosophy, medicine, and science. At 16 he commanded his first army, and by his death 16 years later he had founded the greatest empire ever seen. But it's not so easy to trace the effects of the brilliant tutelage he had received in his youth.

tutorial \tü-'tȯr-ē-əl\ (1) A class for one student or a small group of students. (2) An instructional program that gives information about a specific subject.

● Students tend to learn more in a tutorial than they do in a large class.

Tutorials with live tutors are useful for both advanced students and struggling ones. Most computer programs include electronic tutorials to help the user get used to the program, leading him or her through the different operations to show what the program can do. But a difficult program might still require a real-life tutor to be fully understood.

Quizzes

A. Choose the closest definition:

1. docile   a. tame   b. learned   c. taught   d. beloved
2. tuition   a. requirement   b. instruction   c. resolution   d. housing
3. indoctrinate   a. medicate thoroughly   b. research thoroughly   c. instruct thoroughly   d. consider thoroughly
4. tutelage   a. responsibility   b. protection   c. instruction   d. safeguard
5. doctrine   a. solution   b. principle   c. religion   d. report
6. tutorial   a. small class   b. large class   c. night class   d. canceled class
7. doctrinaire   a. by the way   b. by the by   c. by the rule   d. by the glass
8. intuition   a. ignorance   b. quick understanding   c. payment   d. consideration

---

B. **Match the word on the left to the correct definition on the right:**

1. indoctrinate
2. tutelage
3. doctrine
4. tutorial
5. doctrinaire
6. intuition
7. docile
8. tuition

a. instruction costs
b. easily led
c. fill with a point of view
d. insight
e. guardianship
f. teaching
g. individual instruction
h. rigidly principled

Number Words

DI/DUO, the Greek and Latin prefixes meaning "two," show up in both technical and nontechnical terms. A *duel* is a battle between two people. A *duet* is music for a *duo,* or a pair of musicians. If you have *dual* citizenship, you belong to two countries at once. Most birds are *dimorphic,* with feathers of one color for males and another color for females.

---

dichotomy \dī-'kä-tə-mē\ (1) A division into two often contradictory groups. (2) Something with qualities that seem to contradict each other.

● With her first job she discovered the dichotomy between the theories she'd been taught and the realities of professional life.

In the modern United States there is a dichotomy between life in a big city and life in the country, big-city life being fast-paced and often dangerous, and country life being slow-moving and usually safe. But the dichotomy is nothing new: the Roman poet Horace was complaining about it in the 1st century B.C. Among other eternal dichotomies, there is the dichotomy between wealth and poverty, between the policies of the leading political parties, between a government's words and its actions—and between what would be most fun to do right this minute and what would be the mature and sensible and intelligent alternative.

diplomatic \‚di-plə-'ma-tik\ (1) Relating to negotiations between nations. (2) Tactful.

● In his dealings with my cranky old Aunt Louisa, Alex was always diplomatic, and she was very fond of him.

The path from *di-*, "two," to *diplomatic* is a winding one. A Greek *diploma* was an official document folded in two and sealed, or a passport. So *diplomacy* came to mean the international carrying and exchanging of such documents for the purpose of negotiation. *Diplomats* are famous for their tact and sensitivity (and sometimes their insincerity), so it's natural that *diplomatic* should apply to social behavior as smooth and sensitive as an ambassador's.

duplex \'dü-‚pleks\ (1) Having two principal elements; double. (2) Allowing electronic communication in two directions at the same time.

● Their splendid duplex apartment had a panoramic view of Paradise Park.

Duplex can describe a confusing variety of things, depending on the technical field. Most of us use it as a noun: a *duplex* generally is either a two-family house or a two-story apartment. In computer science and telecommunications, duplex (or *full-duplex*) communication can go in both directions at once, while *half-duplex* communication can go only one way at a time. In other areas, translate *duplex* as "double" and see if the sentence makes sense.

duplicity \dù-'pli-sə-tē\ Deception by pretending to feel and act one way while acting in another.

● By the time Jackie's duplicity in the whole matter had come to light, she had moved leaving no forwarding address.

The Greek god Zeus often resorted to duplicity to get what he wanted, and most of the time what he wanted was some woman. His duplicity usually involved a disguise: he appeared to Leda as a swan, and to Europa as a bull. Sometimes he had to be *duplicitous* to get around his wife Hera. After he had had his way with Io and was about to get caught, he turned her into a cow to avoid Hera's wrath.

BI/BIN also means "two" or "double." A *bicycle* has two wheels; *binoculars* consist of two little telescopes; *bigamy* is marriage to two people at once. A road through the middle of a neighborhood *bisects* it into two pieces.

bipartisan \ˌbī-ˈpär-tə-zən\ Involving members of two political parties.

● The President named a bipartisan commission of four Republicans and three Democrats to look into the issue.

Since the United States has a two-party system of government, legislation often must have some bipartisan support in order to pass into law. Bipartisan committees review legislation, compromising on some points and removing or adding others in order to make the bill more agreeable to both parties and make bipartisan support more likely.

binary \ˈbī-nə-rē\ (1) Consisting of two things or parts; double. (2) Involving a choice between two alternatives.

● The Milky Way contains numerous binary stars, each consisting of two stars orbiting each other.

Binary has many uses, most of them in technical terms. Most computers, for example, are based on the binary number system, in which only two digits, 0 and 1, are used. (0 stands for a low-voltage impulse and 1 stands for a high-voltage impulse.) All their information is kept in this form. The word "HELLO," for example, looks like this: 1001000 1000101 1001100 1001100 1001111.

biennial \ˌbī-ˈe-nē-əl\ (1) Occurring every two years. (2) Continuing or lasting over two years.

● The great biennial show of new art usually either puzzled or angered the critics.

Biennial conventions, celebrations, competitions, and sports events come every two years. *Biennials* are plants that live two years, bearing flowers and fruit only in the second year. In contrast, *semiannual* means "twice a year." But no one can agree whether *biweekly* means "twice a week" or "every two weeks," and whether *bimonthly* means "twice a month" or "every two months.'' Maybe we should stop using both of them until we can decide.

bipolar \,bī-'pō-lər\ Having two opposed forces or views; having two poles or opposed points of attraction.

● Our bipolar earth spins on an axis that extends between the North and the South Pole.

Magnets are always bipolar: one pole attracts and the other repels or drives away. The Cold War arms race was bipolar, since it mainly involved the opposing powers of the United States and Russia. Evolutionism and creationism are bipolar views on the history of life, the two major opposing beliefs on the subject in America. And manic-depressive illness, in which the person swings between the two extremes of high excitation and deep depression, is now often called *bipolar disorder*.

Quiz

Fill in each blank with the correct letter:

a. bipolar   e. diplomatic
b. duplex   f. binary
c. biennial   g. dichotomy
d. duplicity   h. bipartisan

1. The new law was written in a thoroughly _____ way, and so passed through Congress easily.
2. In response to his angry questions she gave _____ but vague answers.
3. Powerful drugs like lithium are often prescribed for _____ depression.
4. A liar's _____ usually catches up with him sooner or later.
5. The _____ number system is at the heart of the modern technological revolution.
6. His father found there was a painful _____ between the tidy instructions and the messy assembly.
7. They shared the modest _____ with another family of four.
8. Every two years we get to hear Mildred McDermot sing "Moonlight in Vermont" at the _____ town picnic.

Review Quizzes

A. Fill in each blank with the correct letter:

a. anthropomorphic
b. doctrine
c. tuition
d. interminable
e. duplex
f. binary
g. formative
h. biennial
i. doctrinaire
j. spherical
k. provincial
l. versatile
m. conform
n. intuition
o. indeterminate
p. bipartisan
q. metamorphosis
r. diplomatic
s. tutelage
t. hemisphere

1. This marble was limestone before it underwent ___.
2. The computer works by making choices between ___ opposites.
3. The main piano competition is ___, but there are smaller ones on the off-years.
4. The number of places open is still ___, but probably about 20 or 30.
5. Your equipment doesn't ___ to our specifications, so we regret that we can't place an order.
6. My attitudes may be ___ but my ambitions are global.
7. I had an ___ wait in the doctor's office and didn't get home until 6:00.
8. The young woman's ___ told her this was a friendship she would treasure forever.
9. Hoping for a ___ career, she took three languages in college.
10. With her talent for singing, dancing, and playing piano, she was a ___ performer.
11. The governor named a ___ committee to keep the issue as nonpolitical as possible.
12. After this ___ payment there's only one more year before she graduates, thank God.
13. The ___ was roomy, but the other family made a great deal of noise.
14. Under the great man's ___, the young composer learned how to develop his ideas into full-fledged sonatas.

15. As a practicing Catholic, she thought frequently about the church _____ that life begins at conception.

16. Michelangelo's great painting shows an _____ God touching Adam's finger.

17. A _____ interpretation of these rules will leave no room for fun at all.

18. My trip to Australia was the first time I had left this _____.

19. I'd like you to write an essay about the person who had the greatest _____ influence on your thinking.

20. The inside of the _____ stone was a hollow lined entirely with purple cyrstals.

B. Choose the correct synonym and the correct antonym:

1. invincible   a. vulnerable b. unbreakable c. inedible d. unconquerable
2. divert   a. please b. entertain c. bore d. send
3. amorphous   a. beginning b. shapeless c. shaping d. formed
4. terminal   a. first b. final c. highest d. deathlike
5. duplicity   a. desire b. two-facedness c. honesty d. complexity
6. formality   a. convention b. black tie c. rationality d. casualness
7. evince   a. hide b. reveal c. conquer d. defy
8. dichotomy   a. operation b. negotiation c. contradiction d. agreement
9. docile   a. rebellious b. angry c. passive d. soft
10. perverse   a. brilliant b. reasonable c. amazing d. bizarre

C. Choose the closest definition:

1. format   a. design b. formality c. formation d. concept
2. biosphere   a. life cycle b. environment c. stratosphere d. evolution
3. morphology   a. study of structure b. study of woods c. study of butterflies d. study of geometry
4. avert   a. embrace b. prevent c. assert d. escape

5. bipolar   a. depressed b. monopolistic c. opposing
   d. two-handed
6. indoctrinate   a. teach b. demonstrate c. infiltrate
   d. consider
7. terminology   a. study b. specialty c. jargon d. symbols
8. victimize   a. suffer b. agonize c. harm d. complain
9. tutorial   a. penalty b. teacher c. classroom d. lesson
10. stratosphere   a. cloud level b. spherical body
    c. atmospheric layer d. ozone depletion

Answers

UNIT 1

p.4   A 1.d 2.g 3.f 4.c 5.h 6.e 7.b 8.a
       B 1.e 2.a 3.f 4.d 5.c 6.h 7.b 8.g

p.7   A 1.c 2.b 3.b 4.a 5.a 6.d 7.b 8.d
       B 1.b 2.d 3.a 4.b 5.d 6.d 7.b 8.a

p.11 A 1.S 2.D 3.D 4.D 5.D 6.D 7.S 8.D
       B 1.e 2.a 3.b 4.f 5.d 6.h 7.g 8.c

p.14 A 1.d 2.f 3.c 4.h 5.b 6.a 7.e 8.g
       B 1.f 2.a 3.g 4.b 5.c 6.h 7.d 8.e

p.17   1.d 2.b 3.a 4.c 5.b 6.d 7.a 8.c

p.18 A 1.e 2.d 3.k 4.b 5.h 6.l 7.f 8.j 9.g 10.c 11.n 12.a 13.m
          14.i
       B 1.d 2.a 3.d 4.c 5.b 6.b 7.d 8.a 9.c 10.c 11.c 12.a
       C 1.f 2.c 3.e 4.d 5.h 6.g 7.j 8.a 9.b 10.i

UNIT 2

p.23 A 1.c 2.b 3.d 4.a 5.d 6.b 7.c 8.b
       B 1.a 2.b 3.c 4.d 5.b 6.b 7.b 8.a

p.27 A 1.h 2.g 3.d 4.a 5.b 6.f 7.e 8.c
       B 1.f 2.d 3.b 4.g 5.h 6.c 7.e 8.a

p.30 A 1.d 2.c 3.a 4.b 5.d 6.c 7.b 8.a
       B 1.d 2.e 3.h 4.f 5.g 6.a 7.c 8.b

p.34   A 1.b 2.c 3.e 4.a 5.g 6.h 7.d 8.f
            B 1.h 2.d 3.a 4.f 5.e 6.b 7.g 8.c

p.37   1.a,c 2.d,b 3.b,a 4.c,b 5.c,a 6.a,b 7.c,a 8.d,a

p.38   A 1.c 2.b 3.b 4.d 5.b 6.c 7.d 8.a 9.c 10.b
            B 1.c 2.f 3.e 4.a 5.i 6.d 7.b 8.g 9.j 10.h
            C 1.f 2.h 3.c 4.i 5.d 6.e 7.j 8.b 9.g 10.a

UNIT 3

p.43   A 1.b 2.c 3.f 4.d 5.e 6.a 7.g 8.h
            B 1.c 2.f 3.e 4.h 5.a 6.d 7.b 8.g

p.47   A 1.b 2.c 3.c 4.b 5.d 6.c 7.a 8.a
            B 1.D 2.D 3.S 4.D 5.D 6.S 7.D 8.D

p.51   A 1.a 2.g 3.f 4.d 5.c 6.b 7.h 8.e
            B 1.D 2.D 3.S 4.D 5.S 6.S 7.D 8.D

p.55   A 1.b 2.b 3.a 4.d 5.b 6.d 7.b 8.a
            B 1.d 2.g 3.h 4.a 5.f 6.e 7.b 8.c

p.59   1.c 2.b 3.a 4.c 5.a 6.a 7.b 8.c

p.59   A 1.d 2.b 3.a 4.d 5.c 6.a 7.b 8.a
            B 1.m 2.j 3.c 4.l 5.f 6.i 7.e 8.g 9.d 10.k 11.b 12.n 13.h
               14.a 15.o
            C 1.S 2.D 3.S 4.D 5.D 6.S 7.S 8.D 9.D 10.S 11.D 12.D
               13.S 14.S 15.S

UNIT 4

p.65   A 1.S 2.D 3.D 4.S 5.D 6.S 7.D 8.S
            B 1.f 2.g 3.e 4.h 5.b 6.c 7.d 8.a

p.69   A 1.h 2.b 3.a 4.c 5.g 6.e 7.f 8.d
            B 1.a 2.c 3.h 4.g 5.f 6.b 7.e 8.d

p.73   A 1.c 2.b 3.e 4.f 5.g 6.h 7.a 8.d
            B 1.h 2.a 3.g 4.b 5.c 6.f 7.d 8.e

p.77 A 1.c 2.b 3.b 4.c 5.d 6.b 7.a 8.a
        B 1.b 2.c 3.c 4.d 5.b 6.a 7.a 8.d

p.81   1.b 2.c 3.f 4.a 5.d 6.e 7.h 8.g

p.81 A 1.a 2.b 3.d 4.d 5.b 6.c 7.a 8.b 9.b 10.c
        B 1.D 2.D 3.S 4.D 5.S 6.D 7.S 8.D 9.S 10.S
        C 1.b 2.d 3.d 4.a 5.a 6.c 7.c 8.b

UNIT 5

p.86 A 1.c 2.c 3.c 4.b 5.d 6.c 7.b 8.d
        B 1.D 2.D 3.S 4.S 5.S 6.D 7.S 8.D

p.89 A 1.d 2.g 3.c 4.b 5.a 6.e 7.h 8.f
        B 1.f 2.e 3.d 4.a 5.h 6.g 7.b 8.c

p.93 A 1.c 2.b 3.d 4.b 5.d 6.b 7.c 8.a
        B 1.D 2.S 3.D 4.D 5.D 6.S 7.S 8.D

p.97 A 1.a 2.g 3.c 4.e 5.f 6.d 7.h 8.b
        B 1.c 2.e 3.f 4.g 5.a 6.h 7.b 8.d

p.101   1.h 2.f 3.d 4.e 5.b 6.g 7.a 8.c

p.102 A 1.d 2.b 3.c 4.b 5.c 6.d 7.b 8.a 9.a 10.d
        B 1.g 2.i 3.a 4.o 5.b 6.n 7.m 8.k 9.c 10.e 11.f 12.d 13.h
           14.j 15.l
        C 1.S 2.D 3.S 4.S 5.D 6.D 7.D 8.S 9.D 10.D 11.S 12.D
           13.S 14.D 15.D

UNIT 6

p.107 A 1.c 2.c 3.c 4.c 5.b 6.a 7.b 8.d
        B 1.g 2.b 3.c 4.d 5.e 6.f 7.a 8.h

p.111 A 1.d 2.f 3.h 4.g 5.e 6.a 7.b 8.c
        B 1.b 2.c 3.d 4.a 5.b 6.a 7.c 8.d

p.115 A 1.S 2.D 3.S 4.S 5.D 6.D 7.D 8.S
        B 1.b 2.e 3.c 4.h 5.g 6.a 7.f 8.d

p.118 **A** 1.c 2.a 3.d 4.c 5.d 6.a 7.c 8.b
        B 1.f 2.c 3.e 4.b 5.d 6.a 7.h 8.g

p.122   1.c 2.c 3.b 4.a 5.a 6.b 7.c 8.a

p.122 **A** 1.g 2.a 3.j 4.c 5.i 6.b 7.d 8.e 9.h 10.f
        B 1.c 2.a 3.a 4.a 5.b 6.c 7.b 8.b 9.b 10.a
        C 1.e 2.j 3.a 4.i 5.f 6.h 7.c 8.b 9.d 10.g

UNIT 7

p.128 **A** 1.b 2.d 3.g 4.f 5.a 6.h 7.a 8.e
        B 1.c 2.e 3.f 4.h 5.a 6.g 7.d 8.b

p.132 **A** 1.c 2.d 3.c 4.b 5.b 6.a 7.d 8.b
        B 1.S 2.D 3.D 4.S 5.S 6.S 7.D 8.D

p.135 **A** 1.a 2.e 3.b 4.f 5.c 6.g 7.d 8.h
        B 1.d 2.c 3.c 4.a 5.b 6.b 7.d 8.a

p.139 **A** 1.S 2.D 3.D 4.S 5.D 6.D 7.D 8.D
        B 1.c 2.f 3.d 4.a 5.e 6.g 7.h 8.b

p.143   1.a 2.d 3.c 4.h 5.f 6.g 7.b 8.e

p.144 **A** 1.c,a 2.b,c 3.b,a 4.d,b 5.a,b 6.b,c 7.c,a 8.a,b 9.d,c
           10.c,a 11.c,b 12.d,a 13.a,c 14.c,b 15.c,d
        B 1.c 2.a 3.b 4.c 5.d 6.a 7.b 8.a 9.d 10.a 11.b 12.c 13.c
           14.a 15.c
        C 1.i 2.f 3.c 4.h 5.e 6.j 7.g 8.a 9.b 10.d

UNIT 8

p.150 **A** 1.c 2.a 3.b 4.a 5.c 6.d 7.b 8.c
        B 1.f 2.b 3.e 4.a 5.g 6.c 7.h 8.d

p.155 **A** 1.a 2.g 3.b 4.h 5.e 6.c 7.d 8.f
        B 1.D 2.S 3.D 4.S 5.S 6.D 7.D 8.D

p.158 **A** 1.D 2.D 3.S 4.D 5.D 6.D 7.D 8.S
        B 1.b 2.f 3.d 4.c 5.g 6.h 7.a 8.e

p.162   A   1.c 2.c 3.d 4.a 5.b 6.c 7.d 8.c
        B   1.e 2.d 3.g 4.h 5.c 6.f 7.a 8.b

p.166   1.g 2.f 3.e 4.d 5.a 6.h 7.b 8.c

p.167   A   1.a,c 2.d,b 3.a,d 4.b,a 5.c,a 6.d,b 7.d,a 8.a,b 9.d,c
           10.d,a
        B   1.D 2.D 3.S 4.D 5.S 6.S 7.S 8.D 9.D 10.D 11.D 12.D
           13.S 14.S 15.S 16.D 17.D 18.S 19.S 20.D
        C   1.h 2.g 3.i 4.b 5.a 6.f 7.d 8.j 9.c 10.e

UNIT 9

p.172   A   1.a 2.g 3.f 4.b 5.c 6.e 7.h 8.d
        B   1.a 2.b 3.c 4.d 5.a 6.b 7.d 8.c

p.176   A   1.b 2.a 3.b 4.a 5.b 6.b 7.d 8.d
        B   1.d 2.c 3.e 4.f 5.g 6.h 7.a 8.b

p.180   A   1.a 2.a 3.b 4.a 5.c 6.d 7.b 8.c
        B   1.S 2.D 3.S 4.D 5.S 6.S 7.D 8.D

p.183   A   1.h 2.c 3.g 4.d 5.e 6.b 7.f 8.a
        B   1.g 2.f 3.b 4.c 5.h 6.a 7.e 8.d

p.187   1.c 2.b 3.b 4.b 5.c 6.d 7.b 8.c

p.187   A   1.b 2.c 3.a 4.d 5.b 6.c 7.a 8.d 9.d 10.b
        B   1.d 2.g 3.a 4.b 5.j 6.e 7.c 8.i 9.h 10.f
        C   1.a 2.h 3.i 4.b 5.e 6.d 7.g 8.c 9.j 10.f

UNIT 10

p.192   A   1.S 2.D 3.D 4.D 5.D 6.D 7.D 8.S
        B   1.a 2.c 3.d 4.b 5.a 6.c 7.d 8.a

p.195   A   1.c 2.c 3.d 4.c 5.b 6.a 7.b 8.d
        B   1.f 2.h 3.g 4.e 5.d 6.a 7.c 8.b

p.199   A   1.a 2.g 3.c 4.f 5.b 6.h 7.e 8.d
        B   1.c 2.a 3.d 4.c 5.b 6.c 7.a 8.b

p.202   A   1.b 2.d 3.a 4.c 5.a 6.d 7.a 8.d
          B   1.e 2.h 3.f 4.a 5.g 6.b 7.c 8.d

p.206   1.e 2.b 3.d 4.c 5.g 6.f 7.a 8.h

p.206   A   1.D 2.S 3.D 4.D 5.D 6.S 7.S 8.D 9.D 10.S 11.S 12.D
             13.D 14.S 15.D 16.D 17.S 18.D 19.D 20.D
          B   1.d 2.a 3.d 4.b 5.a 6.c 7.b 8.a 9.d 10.a
          C   1.f 2.e 3.a 4.d 5.c 6.b 7.h 8.g

UNIT 11

p.212   A   1.b 2.d 3.a 4.c 5.c 6.b 7.a 8.b
          B   1.D 2.D 3.S 4.D 5.D 6.D 7.D 8.D

p.215   A   1.a 2.g 3.b 4.h 5.e 6.c 7.d 8.f
          B   1.c 2.c 3.b 4.a 5.d 6.c 7.b 8.b

p.219   A   1.d 2.b 3.a 4.d 5.c 6.a 7.c 8.a
          B   1.b 2.e 3.h 4.a 5.f 6.g 7.d 8.c

p.222   A   1.a 2.d 3.e 4.b 5.h 6.c 7.f 8.g
          B   1.S 2.D 3.S 4.D 5.D 6.D 7.D 8.S

p.226   1.a 2.g 3.f 4.d 5.c 6.e 7.b 8.h

p.227   A   1.c,d 2.c,b 3.a,b 4.a,d 5.c,d 6.c,b 7.a,c 8.a,d 9.d,a
             10.c,b 11.b,c 12.d,a 13.b,c 14.b,a 15.d,c 16.c,a
          B   1.D 2.D 3.D 4.S 5.S 6.D 7.D 8.S 9.S 10.S
          C   1.f 2.b 3.e 4.g 5.i 6.j 7.l 8.h 9.a 10.d 11.k 12.c

UNIT 12

p.232   A   1.f 2.c 3.g 4.d 5.e 6.a 7.b 8.h
          B   1.f 2.h 3.g 4.c 5.b 6.e 7.a 8.d

p.236   A   1.a 2.g 3.c 4.b 5.f 6.e 7.d 8.h
          B   1.c 2.f 3.h 4.e 5.d 6.g 7.a 8.b

p.239   A   1.b 2.c 3.a 4.b 5.c 6.b 7.d 8.c
          B   1.S 2.D 3.S 4.D 5.D 6.S 7.D 8.D

p.243   A   1.g 2.b 3.a 4.f 5.c 6.h 7.e 8.d
        B   1.b 2.d 3.g 4.c 5.f 6.a 7.e 8.h

p.246   1.a 2.f 3.b 4.g 5.e 6.h 7.d 8.c

p.247   A   1.b 2.d 3.c 4.a 5.c 6.a 7.c 8.a 9.d 10.d 11.a 12.c 13.b
             14.d 15.c 16.b
        B   1.f 2.b 3.g 4.j 5.d 6.e 7.i 8.a 9.h 10.c
        C   1.h 2.j 3.g 4.a 5.i 6.c 7.d 8.f 9.e 10.b

UNIT 13

p.253   A   1.b 2.d 3.c 4.b 5.c 6.a 7.b 8.a
        B   1.g 2.h 3.b 4.f 5.a 6.e 7.d 8.c

p.256   A   1.c 2.b 3.f 4.g 5.a 6.h 7.e 8.d
        B   1.S 2.D 3.S 4.S 5.D 6.S 7.S 8.S

p.260   A   1.c 2.a 3.c 4.d 5.d 6.a 7.b 8.c
        B   1.e 2.f 3.a 4.g 5.b 6.c 7.h 8.d

p.264   A   1.e 2.b 3.c 4.g 5.a 6.h 7.f 8.d
        B   1.a 2.c 3.d 4.a 5.b 6.d 7.a 8.c

p.267   1.D 2.S 3.D 4.D 5.S 6.S 7.D 8.D

p.267   A   1.h 2.i 3.o 4.r 5.c 6.s 7.f 8.n 9.e 10.p 11.m 12.a 13.b
             14.t 15.g 16.d 17.j 18.l 19.q 20.k
        B   1.b,d 2.d,b 3.b,d 4.a,d 5.d,b 6.b,c 7.b,d 8.d,a 9.c,d
             10.b,c
        C   1.c 2.b 3.d 4.b 5.a 6.c 7.a 8.d 9.a 10.d

UNIT 14

p.273   A   1.d 2.g 3.a 4.e 5.f 6.b 7.h 8.c
        B   1.g 2.a 3.d 4.c 5.h 6.f 7.e 8.b

p.277   A   1.D 2.D 3.S 4.S 5.D 6.S 7.S 8.S
        B   1.d 2.e 3.f 4.c 5.g 6.h 7.a 8.b

p.280   A   1.b 2.f 3.e 4.c 5.a 6.d 7.h 8.g
        B   1.d 2.a 3.f 4.c 5.e 6.g 7.b 8.h

p.284   A   1.b 2.a 3.c 4.d 5.b 6.c 7.a 8.d
          B   1.S 2.S 3.D 4.D 5.D 6.D 7.S 8.D

p.288   1.b 2.h 3.g 4.c 5.e 6.a 7.f 8.d

p.288   A   1.b 2.a 3.b 4.a 5.b 6.c 7.b 8.a 9.b 10.d 11.a 12.a 13.b
              14.b 15.d 16.d 17.c 18.c 19.b 20.a
          B   1.a 2.b 3.h 4.i 5.d 6.e 7.f 8.c 9.g 10.j
          C   1.S 2.D 3.D 4.D 5.S 6.S 7.D 8.S 9.S 10.S

UNIT 15

p.293   A   1.a 2.d 3.c 4.c 5.d 6.a 7.b 8.c
          B   1.h 2.c 3.f 4.b 5.e 6.a 7.d 8.g

p.297   A   1.c 2.c 3.a 4.b 5.a 6.d 7.a 8.d
          B   1.d 2.g 3.f 4.e 5.a 6.h 7.b 8.c

p.301   A   1.S 2.D 3.S 4.S 5.S 6.S 7.S 8.D
          B   1.d 2.f 3.e 4.h 5.c 6.g 7.a 8.b

p.305   A   1.a 2.b 3.c 4.c 5.b 6.a 7.c 8.b
          B   1.c 2.e 3.f 4.g 5.h 6.d 7.b 8.a

p.309   1.h 2.e 3.a 4.d 5.f 6.g 7.b 8.c

p.310   A   1.q 2.f 3.h 4.o 5.m 6.k 7.d 8.n 9.r 10.l 11.p 12.c 13.e
              14.s 15.b 16.a 17.i 18.t 19.g 20.j
          B   1.d,a 2.b,c 3.b,d 4.b,a 5.b,c 6.a,d 7.b,a 8.c,d 9.c,a
              10.d,b
          C   1.a 2.b 3.a 4.b 5.c 6.a 7.c 8.c 9.d 10.c

Index